The Church Made Strange for the Nations

Princeton Theological Monograph Series

K. C. Hanson, Charles M. Collier, D. Christopher Spinks,
and Robin Parry, Series Editors

Recent volumes in the series:

Mitzi J. Smith
*The Literary Construction of the Other in the Acts of the Apostles:
Charismatics, the Jews, and Women*

David Rhoads
Luke-Acts and Empire: Essays in Honor of Robert L. Brawley

Julie Woods
Jeremiah 48 as Christian Scripture:

Sherri Brown
Gift Upon Gift: Covenant through Word in the Gospel of John

Donald E. Gowan
The Bible on Forgiveness

Hemchand Gossai
Power and Marginality in the Abraham Narrative—Second Edition

Christopher L. Fisher
*Human Significance in Theology and the Natural Sciences:
An Ecumenical Perspective with Reference to Pannenberg,
Rahner, and Zizioulas*

Christopher W. Skinner
*John and Thomas—Gospels in Conflict?:
Johannine Characterization and the Thomas Question*

J. Harold Ellens
Probing the Frontiers of Biblical Studies

The Church Made Strange for the Nations

Essays in Ecclesiology and Political Theology

Edited by
Paul G. Doerksen *and* Karl Koop

PICKWICK *Publications* • Eugene, Oregon

THE CHURCH MADE STRANGE FOR THE NATIONS
Essays in Ecclesiology and Political Theology

Princeton Theological Monograph Series 171

Copyright © 2011 Wipf and Stock Publishers. All rights reserved. Except for brief quotations in critical publications or reviews, no part of this book may be reproduced in any manner without prior written permission from the publisher. Write: Permissions, Wipf and Stock Publishers, 199 W. 8th Ave., Suite 3, Eugene, OR 97401.

Pickwick Publications
An Imprint of Wipf and Stock Publishers
199 W. 8th Ave., Suite 3
Eugene, OR 97401

www.wipfandstock.com

ISBN 13: 978-1-60899-398-7

Cataloging-in-Publication data:

The church made strange for the nations : essays in ecclesiology and political theology / edited by Paul G. Doerksen and Karl Koop.

Princeton Theological Monograph Series 171

xii + 192 p. ; 23 cm. Includes bibliographical references.

ISBN 13: 978-1-60899-398-7

1. Political theology. 2. Ecclesiology. 3. Huebner, Harry John, 1943–. I. Doerksen, Paul G., 1960–. II. Koop, Karl, 1959–. III. Title. IV. Series.

BR115.P7 C3839 2011

Manufactured in the U.S.A.

Contents

Preface / vii

List of Contributors / xi

Harry Huebner: A Servant of the Church—*Gerald Gerbrandt* / 1

In the World but Not *of* the World: A Johannine Perspective on the Church-World Relationship—*Sheila Klassen-Wiebe* / 9

Building the City for Others: Beyond the Negation of Exile Toward a Future of Common Belonging in Israel-Palestine—*Alain Epp Weaver* / 21

John Howard Yoder's Ecclesiology: As Seen by an Appreciative Critic —*Waldemar Janzen* / 36

Living in the Light of Time: Historicism in Troeltsch and Yoder —*J. Alexander Sider* / 52

The Young Karl Barth's Critique of Anabaptism—*Arnold Neufeldt-Fast* / 66

Anabaptist-Mennonite Political Theology: Conceptualizing Universal Ethics in Post-Christendom—*A. James Reimer* / 80

Making Strange: Harry Huebner's Church–World Distinction —*P. Travis Kroeker* / 92

"To Serve the Dead": Fidelity and Resistance in *Antigone* —*Joseph Wiebe* / 100

Worship Made Strange—*Irma Fast Dueck* / 112

Strains in the Voice of the Church Made Strange—*Cheryl Pauls* / 123

He Who Brings Light to Dark Places: Christ and the Redemption of Memory—*Jane Barter Moulaison* / 139

Is a Christian University Strange Enough? Reflections on Loving and Hating the University—*Chris K. Huebner* / 152

Contents

14   Moving the Historic Wall of Estrangement: A Reflection on the Catholic-Mennonite Dialogue (1998–2003)—*Helmut Harder* / 161

15   Pentecost: Learning the Languages of Peace—*Stanley Hauerwas* / 177

Preface

IF, AS OLIVER O'DONOVAN SUGGESTS, THE CENTRAL WORK OF POLITICAL THEOLOGY IS to shed light from the Christian faith upon the challenge of thinking about how to live in late modern Western society, then many areas of thought need to be considered. Not least of these is the matter of the church's identity and place in the world. Various responses have been offered throughout Christian history. In the context of persecution, Christians in the ancient world tended to distance themselves from the social and civic mainstream, while in the medieval and early modern periods, the church and secular authorities often worked in close relationship, sharing the role of shaping society. In a post-Christendom era this latter arrangement has been heavily critiqued and largely dismantled, but there is no consensus in Christian thought as to what the alternative should be.

While the Radical Reformation tradition has never been uniform in its views, its representatives have often been drawn to the maxim that the church ought to be "in the world but not of it." Over the centuries this way of viewing the church's relationship to the world has never been explained, much less lived easily amidst life's many exigencies. And yet there is something to the church's peculiar and strange locatedness that may contribute to contemporary discussion, even as many adherents of the tradition increasingly find themselves participating within the conventional halls of political power. The present collection of essays, which attend to ecclesiology and political theology, are largely in sympathy with this perspective.

At the outset it is important to recognize that Radical Reformation thinking within the field of political theology, while opposed to the revival of Christendom, is not expressed primarily as a search for some "position" that can be discovered or constructed and then defended. Neither should Radical Reformation political theology be understood as some kind of denominational pursuit. Rather, following the work of John Howard Yoder, it is more accurate to think about the development of a free church stance or perspective. Yoder is careful to show a connection to the Radical Reformation of the sixteenth century without restricting the designation to any one theological notion or reformer, describing instead a set of shared experiences and a common stance that entail a desire to reform Christianity where it has gone wrong and to form communities based on an adult confession of faith, while refusing to be ruled by worldly authorities.

It is at this point in the discussion that the work of Harry Huebner serves as an important touchstone for the present collection of essays. Indeed, the title of this work is taken from the title of an essay in Huebner's important book, *Echoes of the Word: Theological Ethics as Rhetorical Practice*. Huebner represents well the tradition to which many of the contributors to this collection belong. One of the lines of inquiry for Huebner's work concerns the centrality of the church for political theology. The phrase "the church

Preface

made strange for the nations," which draws on the work of John Milbank, signals that the church, in affirming a politically embodied ecclesiology, is at the very heart of political theology. A church that is "set apart" may appear "strange" to the nations, and such a stance calls for the task of the church to be understood in terms of speaking its own language, re-narrating its own story, re-membering its own savior, and re-embodying its own ontology of peace and justice. As the church fulfills its calling in these ways, the nations will no doubt understand its acts of self-realization as "strange-making," which suggests that the church will be set apart because it is intelligible only in relation to its own identity.

As much as Huebner represents the tradition of which he is a part, however, others working either from within or in direct conversation with the Radical Reformation tradition raise interesting and important questions concerning many of the issues that Huebner raises and develops in his work. The essays in this volume might be seen as a display of the ongoing wrestling with political-theological questions in a variety of ways, drawing on sometimes widely disparate interlocutors—ancient and modern, biblical and "secular."

The book begins with a short biography of Harry Huebner by Gerald Gerbrandt, followed by three essays that attend to biblical themes as they intersect with contemporary political and theological challenges. In her analysis on being "in the world but not of it," Sheila Klassen-Wiebe untangles the various dimensions of meaning associated with the term *world* in the Gospel of John and attempts to articulate the implications of John's theology for the church as it seeks to be faithful in the world. Alain Epp Weaver considers the actual and potential political configurations in the land known variously as Israel and Palestine and contends that an exilic theology shaped by Jeremiah's call to seek the *shalom* of the city (Jer 29:7), while undoubtedly "strange" from the perspective of those who reduce political life to the form of the nation-state, can indeed underwrite forms of landedness that disrupt and transcend nationalist projects of establishing and maintaining demographic hegemony within a circumscribed territory. Offering something of a counterpoint to an exilic theology that might be construed too narrowly within a sectarian context, Waldemar Janzen maintains that the work of God cannot be limited to any one sociopolitical theology. Moreover, somewhat critical of John Howard Yoder's Jeremianic ecclesial model that emphasizes perfectionism and suffering, Janzen believes that Old Testament themes such as deliverance and blessing deserve greater consideration.

The next set of essays focuses on a few key aspects of twentieth-century theology. J. Alexander Sider claims that Ernst Troeltsch must be seen as a positive source for Yoder's ecclesiological thought, in the sense of a ghost haunting that theology rather than a marker pointing down a road Yoder refused to take. Arnold Neufeldt-Fast discovers in Karl Barth a changing presentation of Anabaptist beginnings, likely influenced through Barth's personal contacts with the Mennonite world and with scholars such as Yoder. Concluding this section is an essay by A. James Reimer that attempts to take seriously universal moral principles without surrendering the particularities of Christian theology. Reimer believes that Yoder's notion of "middle axioms" may provide some possibilities for dealing with postmodern societies in which competing religious and cultural communities seek to coexist.

Preface

The place and role of the church and its traditions become the focus in the next two contributions. Turning to the example of John the Baptist in Mark's gospel, Travis Kroeker questions whether Harry Huebner's understanding of the church is too externally visible, even triumphalist, and suggests that the church at its best should not point to itself—its structures, teachings, and traditions—so much as bear sacrificial witness to the passage of God in the world that is ever passing away. In his exploration of the classical Greek tragedy *Antigone*, Joseph Wiebe likewise is critical of traditions such as those within Christianity that seek control of place and surroundings. In his interpretation of Sophocles's play, Wiebe suggests that it is exactly in moving into the unknown and being open to the divine, an act that resists controlling the current state of affairs, that we might find the strange and uncomfortable place that the church is called to inhabit.

The contributions that follow explore Christian practices and the challenges of living in the world. Irma Fast Dueck wants to avoid the seduction of cultural relevance in Christian worship, suggesting that authentic worship is more about visiting another land that is strange and incomprehensible. Cheryl Pauls, who is also interested in liturgical process, considers how intensified forms of repetition characteristic of today's blend of worship music can aid the congregational voice in expressing the hope, confusion, and pain of the church. Jane Barter Moulaison reflects on what it means to "remember rightly in a violent world" by first critically engaging Miroslav Volf and then drawing on the wisdom of Augustine for a contemporary orientation. Finally, Chris Huebner explores the idea of the Christian university, which he believes we ought simultaneously to be for and against, such that the very idea of the Christian university constantly eludes our attempts to make sense of it.

The final two essays of the volume address ecumenical concerns. Helmut Harder's involvement in the five-year Roman Catholic–Mennonite discussions between 1998 and 2003 form the background for his essay, which explores the question of Christian unity. Harder maintains that the dialogue has contributed not only to interchurch reconciliation but also to a widening sense of responsibility to and for the world beyond the walls of the church. Next, Stanley Hauerwas argues that the Christian experience of Pentecost, which includes learning to speak as well as understand another's language, is a continuing resource God has given the church in order to relate to a world that constitutes difference. Our ability to communicate as particular linguistic communities means, according to Hauerwas, that we do not have to be isolated from another.

As editors, we offer these essays with the hope that they will stimulate further conversation regarding the church's identity and place in the world. We extend our thanks to Earl Davey, Vice President Academic, and the Faculty Research Committee at Canadian Mennonite University for the support received for this project, and we thank Maureen Epp for her excellent editorial work. We are grateful to the editors of Wipf and Stock for willingly accepting our project for publication. We especially extend our gratitude to the many authors of this volume, who stimulated our thinking and graciously worked with us in bringing this project to completion.

Finally, in recognition of Harry Huebner's work and influence among generations of scholars, church leaders, and students, we dedicate this book in his honor.

Contributors

Jane Barter Moulaison, Associate Professor of Theology at University of Winnipeg.

Paul Doerksen, Assistant Professor of Theology at Canadian Mennonite University.

Alain Epp Weaver, doctoral student, University of Chicago.

Irma Fast Dueck, Associate Professor of Practical Theology at Canadian Mennonite University.

Gerald Gerbrandt, President and Professor of Bible at Canadian Mennonite University.

Helmut Harder, Professor Emeritus at Canadian Mennonite University.

Stanley Hauerwas, Gilbert T. Rowe Professor of Theological Ethics at Duke Divinity School.

Chris K. Huebner, Associate Professor of Theology and Philosophy at Canadian Mennonite University.

Waldemar Janzen, Professor Emeritus at Canadian Mennonite University.

Sheila Klassen-Wiebe, Associate Professor of New Testament at Canadian Mennonite University.

Karl Koop, Professor of History and Theology at Canadian Mennonite University.

P. Travis Kroeker, Professor of Philosophical Theology and Ethics at McMaster University.

Arnold Neufeldt-Fast, Assistant Professor of Theology and Associate Academic Dean at Tyndale Seminary.

Cheryl Pauls, Associate Professor of Music at Canadian Mennonite University.

A. James Reimer, (deceased as of August 2010) was Professor of Religious Studies and Theology at University of Waterloo and Toronto School of Theology.

J. Alexander Sider, Assistant Professor of Religion at Bluffton University.

Joseph Wiebe, doctoral candidate at McMaster University.

Harry Huebner
A Servant of the Church

Gerald Gerbrandt

IN 1971, CANADIAN MENNONITE BIBLE COLLEGE (CMBC) IN WINNIPEG, MANITOBA, took a chance on a young philosopher in the midst of doctoral studies at the University of Toronto and appointed him to a part-time faculty position. Ever since that initial appointment, CMBC, and then Canadian Mennonite University (CMU), has served as his institutional home. Seldom has taking a risk paid such rich dividends—for an institution, its students, and for the church.

At CMBC/CMU, Harry Huebner became an inspiring professor and mentor, an influential scholar, a valued colleague, and a theological leader of the church. His passion for careful thinking, his love of the church, and his dedication to peace and justice challenged and encouraged countless students to take seriously the teachings of Jesus Christ and the church. Over the years, he helped pastors, church leaders, and laypersons think more consistently and more biblically about the place and calling of the church. It has been a privilege to have had him as a colleague and friend over these years.

Life and theology are inseparable for Huebner—frequently explicitly so, always in the background. His place in the family, his way of interacting with colleagues, his participation in the life of the congregation, his interaction with students: all have been part of his theology, benefiting from it and in turn coloring it.

Not surprisingly, then, family also plays an important part in Huebner's writing. The roles of son, sibling, spouse, parent, and grandparent have been central to his identity. In an insightful essay, "On Being Stuck with Our Parents: Learning to Die in Christ," Huebner offers a theological reflection on the experience of having his mother-in-law live with his family for a number of years at a time when she had essentially lost all memory.[1] His most recent book is a moving story of his own mother titled *And That's All There Is to Say: The Story of Margaret (Reimer) Huebner*, a profound work of love and respect that is both biography and theology.

Early family experiences were formative for Huebner. He was born at the family farm in the community of Neuhorst, Manitoba, the fourth of seven children. Not long after

---

1. In Huebner, *Echoes of the Word*, 167–75. Once Huebner has identified her in the essay she is simply referred to as "mother."

his birth, the family moved to a farm near the village of Crystal City. In 1966, he joined another Crystal City family when he married Agnes Hildebrand. Although he has lived in Crystal City for only short periods of time since his teenage years, that community has remained very much a part of his life.

At home and at church, Huebner was influenced by a variety of Mennonite spiritualities that together contributed to shaping his faith and identity. His mother was raised with a deep faith and personal piety in the Sommerfelder Church. His father brought from his Russian Mennonite Brethren upbringing an evangelical faith that found expression in music, especially choral music; for many years he conducted the church choir. The Huebner family's home congregation was Crystal City Mennonite Church, a worship center of the larger Whitewater Church, part of the Conference of Mennonites in Canada (now Mennonite Church Canada). In this mix of Mennonite traditions, Huebner grew up and was baptized. Sommerfelder—Mennonite Brethren—Crystal City Mennonite Church: these three quite distinct spiritualities all played a formative role and continue to play an aspect in his life.

At CMBC/CMU, his colleagues were a kind of second family for Huebner. Here as well he was the supportive friend and loyal servant. For many years the CMBC faculty met for more than two hours each week to address matters related to the college's vision, program, administrative and financial matters, and community concerns. Theological themes were in constant interplay with the institutional agenda. Huebner's commitment to this collective faculty process was explicit and thoroughgoing. He could participate in a debate with both logic and emotion, but when the debate was finished, he would support the outcome, regardless of what it was, because it had been arrived at together.

His commitment to CMBC/CMU, to its mission, and perhaps most significantly, to the communal discernment process, was reflected in the way he responded to invitations to complete tasks or fill roles. Frequently, I heard him say, "If that's what the institution calls me to do, then I will do it." This was no trite comment, but reflected a genuine conviction that when the community discerned a direction, the individual could not easily reject it. Huebner's willingness to take on the position of academic dean for CMBC and then of vice president and academic dean for CMU during a difficult time of program development was his way of remaining true to this conviction, even though this meant he would have less time for reading and research—activities he immensely enjoys.

Huebner's commitment to and support of his colleagues is reflected in his writing projects. Many of his publications have been done collaboratively or in the service of others. He participated in editing two Festschrifts: one for his CMBC colleague David Schroeder,[2] and one for John Howard Yoder.[3] He coauthored a work on ethics with David Schroeder[4] and edited a volume on Mennonite higher education.[5] More recently, as editor for CMU Press, Huebner has worked closely with his former colleague Waldemar Janzen and with his former college president Henry Poettcker in helping them publish their re-

2. Huebner, *Church as Theological Community*.
3. Hauerwas et al., *Wisdom of the Cross*.
4. Huebner and Schroeder, *Church as Parable*.
5. Huebner, *Mennonite Education in a Post-Christian World*.

spective biographies.⁶ Each of these contributions has supported the work of a colleague, even as it has collaboratively furthered the larger vision of the institution.

CMBC/CMU may have provided the base from which Huebner pursued his work, but the church has always been central to his thinking and writing. His reflections were never carried out in the abstract. Rather, he always tied his reflections to real congregations consisting of real groups of people. These too were a part of his emotional, spiritual, and intellectual home. Two specific congregations—Crystal City Mennonite Church and Charleswood Mennonite Church (Winnipeg)—together with the Conference of Mennonites in Canada/Mennonite Church Canada have been the concrete expressions of the body of Christ within which Huebner has worked. Until it became a part of CMU in 2000, CMBC was in essence also a program of the church, with limited separate identity. The college's mission, identity, and vision were all wrapped up in the larger Mennonite church body with its congregations across Canada. Faculty at CMBC were not only professors in a college, but simultaneously leaders and theological resources for that larger body. Part of their typical workload involved preaching and teaching in local congregations, teaching annual courses for ministers, and accompanying choir tours. In this context, Huebner developed his theology. He was always in dialogue with colleagues, church leaders, and laypeople, along with scholars from around the world.

The dialogue with wider scholarship is worth noting. Huebner recognized that theological reflection is always done from somewhere, and he was quite aware that he was working as a Mennonite theologian, worshipping in a Mennonite church, and teaching in a Mennonite institution.⁷ This environment in which he lived and worked profoundly influenced his identity. Yet his thinking, dialogue, and interests were never limited by the Mennonite world. His educational training clearly had something to do with this: virtually all of his formal training was in non-Mennonite institutions. Although Huebner spent a year at Elim Bible School in Altona (Manitoba) and another year as a student at CMBC, he eventually transferred to the University of Manitoba, where he completed his undergraduate degree with a major in philosophy. This was followed by an MA in philosophy. After completing two years toward a PhD in philosophy at the University of Toronto, with a focus on Immanuel Kant, he transferred to the University of St. Michael's College (University of Toronto), where he completed a PhD in systematic theology with a dissertation on Ernst Troeltsch. When speaking of scholars who have had a significant impact on his thinking, Huebner includes the Mennonite John Howard Yoder, but he also names scholars such as John Milbank, Stanley Hauerwas, Rowan Williams, Alisdair MacIntyre, Michel Foucault, and Jacques Derrida.⁸

Huebner stood firmly in the Mennonite world, especially as represented by CMBC/CMU and the Conference of Mennonites in Canada/Mennonite Church Canada, but the relationships and interests he developed went beyond that world. He has always valued and enjoyed ecumenical interaction, as reflected by his participation in Mennonite-Catholic dialogue. Through his work in the Middle East, Huebner has developed relationships with

---

6. Janzen, *Growing Up in Turbulent Times*; Poettcker, *A President's Journey*.
7. Huebner, *Echoes of the Word*, 3.
8. Ibid., 7–11.

people from various Christian denominations and from other faiths. His recent involvement in Christian-Muslim dialogue is one example of this. Huebner is committed to the church as the earthly body of Christ; he is part of that church as a Mennonite. But as the body of Christ, the church is much larger than the Mennonite family, and as the body of Christ, its mandate is to witness to the whole world.

Documenting the centrality of the church in Huebner's work is easy. The titles of his publications provide evidence of this, even as they point to a set of interrelated interests around this theme. His first major publication, in 1990, was an edited volume of essays in honor of his colleague David Schroeder, with the title *The Church as Theological Community*. That same year he contributed an essay on "Christology, Discipleship, and Ethics" to a volume titled *Jesus Christ and the Mission of the Church*. Three years later, he and Schroeder coauthored *Church as Parable: Whatever Happened to Ethics?* In 1997, he contributed "Church Discipline: Is It Still Possible?" to a study on church membership published by the Conference of Mennonites in Canada.[9] Huebner's contribution to a 1999 Festschrift for John Howard Yoder was titled "Moral Agency as Embodiment: How the Church Acts."[10] His recent volume of collected essays does not include the word *church* in the title, but a subsection is named "Church/World." Along with two of the essays identified above, this collection also includes the essay that gave name to both the symposium held in Huebner's honor at his retirement and this volume: "The Church Made Strange for the Nations."[11]

While documenting the significance of the church in Huebner's theology may be easy, speaking of that theme is a more complex matter and requires considerable nuance. Despite the church's centrality in his work, developing a comprehensive theology of the church has never been his primary interest. Huebner's concern is not to write a theoretical ecclesiology, or the definitive word on how to understand church. Rather, his repeated return to the topic generally relates to helping the church reflect on its place in the world, its being and acting in the world. In the introduction to his collection of essays, *Echoes of the Word*, Huebner suggests that the theologian's role is to help the church move from where it is to what it is called to be.[12] His interest in ethics and peace studies is consistent with addressing this goal. More important than getting the theory of church right is helping the church be and do what it should.

This may also speak to the difficulty in identifying Huebner's academic discipline. After all, as a contemporary scholar, he must have a discipline. How else can he be identified in the academic world? Consistent with his having done doctoral work in both philosophy and systematic theology, his academic title throughout his career has been professor of philosophy and theology, even though when he began teaching at CMBC his only formal study in theology had been a year at Elim Bible School and a year at CMBC.

Those who know Harry Huebner or have studied with him as a professor would quickly associate him with peace studies and ethics, in addition to philosophy and theol-

---

9. In *Naming the Sheep*.
10. In Hauerwas et al., *Wisdom of the Cross*, 189–212.
11. In Huebner, *Echoes of the Word*, 84–106.
12. Ibid., 3.

ogy. He has taught and written in all four areas, and is currently working on an introductory textbook on Christian ethics. Yet even these areas do not fully capture his disciplinary focus. One could add practical theology, for example, which may indeed be the best category for his work. It is not that he dabbles in multiple disciplines; for Huebner, these are not distinct disciplines as much as different avenues for getting at what is truly important. In his work they form an integrated approach that is difficult to place within traditional disciplinary categories. Despite—or perhaps because of—the centrality of the church in his work, his interests have always been broad and far-ranging. His passion has been to reflect on how the church can be more faithful, and he has adopted numerous approaches for that task.

As do the titles of his publications, the disciplinary areas with which he is identified draw attention to Huebner's interest in ethics and peace studies. Again, these are not independent subjects but arise naturally out of his focus on the church. In his work in these areas he is not attempting to develop an ethics for everyone based on universal principles or reason. Rather, he is attempting to discern what it means to live as people of God in our world. Thus nonviolence is not first of all a strategy, but is consistent with living in a way modeled after the way of Jesus Christ.

The two years (1981–1983) he served as associate country representative for Mennonite Central Committee in the West Bank were seminal for Huebner's reflections on peace and nonviolence. In a setting where violence and conflict had become part of everyday life, he had the responsibility of promoting nonviolent ways of working at conflict resolution. He had already taught peace studies and had been influenced by Yoder's emphases in *The Politics of Jesus*, but here he gained new insight into the nature, complexity, and power of conflict. The Middle East in particular—he twice made extended trips to Iraq—and questions of peace and violence became prominent in Huebner's teaching and writing. For a number of years he was active in the Peace Committee established by Mennonite Central Committee.

Huebner's emphasis on the church can easily lead to misunderstandings about his work. First, a concern for the church can be interpreted to mean a lack of concern for the world or the rest of society.[13] This accusation has been made against Huebner, but it does not fit. For him, interest in the church means interest in the world. Two of his three articles on the church in *Echoes of the Word* speak directly to this. As he highlights in "Moral Agency as Embodiment: How the Church Acts,"[14] the church is called to be a sign and witness to the world of what the kingdom of God is like. True, the church is not responsible for the world, nor does it bring about the kingdom of God—that is something only God can and will do. But the church is actively involved in the world, demonstrating to the world God's desire for it.

---

13. A similar misunderstanding frequently happens when an institution like CMU speaks of preparing people for the church. Preparing students for leadership roles in the congregation may be a part of this, but the more basic intention is to prepare students to participate in the mission of the church, whatever their occupation might be.

14. Huebner, "Moral Agency as Embodiment"; Huebner, *Echoes of the Word*, 61–83.

Second, although the church plays a central role in Huebner's theology, it is not held up as the norm or absolute, and certainly not as the primary actor in the world. His interest in the church does not replace an interest in God or Jesus Christ or Scripture, but rather is based directly on them. The church must be challenged constantly and encouraged to be more faithful to its calling. And that calling comes from God, with Jesus Christ the supreme revelation of the way of God for the world. The title of his recent collection of essays is instructive: *Echoes of the Word*. Although created or formed by God, the church remains a human community established to embody the word. In Huebner's words, "For Christians it is important to ask how *the* Word gets heard in our words. According to the prologue in the Gospel of John *the* Word became flesh and dwelt with the people, and throughout the New Testament people are invited to re-present what was given in Christ . . . The book is written in the faith that the Word can still be heard, perhaps no longer exactly as it was by the first listeners, but it still speaks."[15]

This emphasis has been consistent throughout Huebner's teaching and writing career. The teaching, life, death, and resurrection of Jesus Christ, and the Bible are foundational. "For in Christ we see again the expression of God's beautiful gift of creation that, although gone awry through sin, is re-imagined and re-expressed in the functioning of the body of Christ—the church."[16]

The significant role scripture plays in Huebner's theology is seldom noticed, and yet it provides further evidence that for him the physical church is not some absolute norm. Earlier I noted that it is difficult to restrict Huebner to one discipline, and named four or five with which people would fairly quickly associate him. I suspect, however, that most would not name Bible as a discipline within which he has worked. And I don't know if Huebner has ever taught a course within the so-called biblical studies area, but that is a shame. Both students and we colleagues would have benefited. We would not have heard something essentially different, but we would have noticed more clearly how Scripture has informed and shaped his thought.

The centrality of Jesus Christ and Scripture for Huebner in his reflections on the church has at least two implications. First, any hope for the future of the church is based not on confidence in human nature or the ability of humans to improve themselves. It is based on confidence in Jesus Christ. Huebner has no illusions about a perfect church, and at points, he has struggled with how the church operated and felt the need to challenge it directly. But hope lay elsewhere. In the hopelessness of the Middle East, he learned that hope is not a human strategy but an act of relinquishing of all strategy, as Christ did on the cross. "The cross is the embodiment of the love of God in the face of hopelessness, and the resurrection is God's answer to hopelessness."[17]

Second, as anyone who has studied with Huebner will attest, he has always taught with passion and conviction and fervor. He was never hesitant to share where he stood, or how he understood what it meant to be faithful. The rigor of his logic could be daunting as he presented his view or responded to a question. And yet, at the same time, he has

---

15. Huebner, *Echoes of the Word*, 1.
16. Ibid., 3.
17. Ibid., 6.

been very aware of the tentative nature of his understanding. Sin and human limitation, the particularities of time and culture all contribute to thwarting absolute positions. The process of doing theology thus must be communal. Dialogue may be vigorous, but no human holds the final word. The recognition that only Jesus Christ is the norm imposes a tentativeness upon all his teaching.

This combination of passion and conviction, together with the recognition that as humans we can never fully understand, has served him well as a professor. His rigorous logic has allowed him to present alternative positions with integrity. And yet, never hesitant to express his position, he has pushed and challenged and encouraged students to take seriously the revelation of Jesus Christ and the invitation to live as part of the body of Christ. As professor, theologian, and colleague, Harry Huebner has epitomized what it means to be a servant of the church, the body of Christ.

Bibliography

Hauerwas, Stanley, Chris K. Huebner, Harry Huebner, and Mark Thiessen Nation, editors. *The Wisdom of the Cross: Essays in Honor of John Howard Yoder*. Grand Rapids: Eerdmans, 1999.

Huebner, Harry. *And That's All There Is to Say: The Story of Margaret (Reimer) Huebner*. Winnipeg: 2007.

———. "Christology, Discipleship, and Ethics." In *Jesus Christ and the Mission of the Church*, edited by Erland Waltner, 56–73. Newton, KS: Faith and Life, 1990.

———, editor. *The Church as Theological Community: Essays in Honour of David Schroeder*. Winnipeg: CMBC Publications, 1990.

———. "Church Discipline: Is It Still Possible?" In *Naming the Sheep: Understanding Church Membership, Voices in Dialogue*. Winnipeg: Conference of Mennonites in Canada, 1997.

———. *Echoes of the Word: Theological Ethics as Rhetorical Practice*. Kitchener, ON: Pandora, 2005.

———, editor. *Mennonite Education in a Post-Christian World: Essays Presented at the Consultation on Higher Education, Winnipeg, June 1997*. Winnipeg: CMBC Publications, 1998.

———. "Moral Agency as Embodiment: How the Church Acts." In *The Wisdom of the Cross: Essays in Honor of John Howard Yoder*, edited by Stanley Hauerwas, Chris K. Huebner, Harry Huebner, and Mark Thiessen Nation, 189–212. Grand Rapids: Eerdmans, 1999.

Huebner, Harry, and David Schroeder. *Church as Parable: Whatever Happened to Ethics?* Winnipeg: CMBC Publications, 1993.

Janzen, Waldemar. *Growing Up in Turbulent Times: Memoirs of Soviet Oppression, Refugee Life in Germany, and Immigrant Adjustment to Canada*. Winnipeg: CMU Press, 2007.

Poettcker, Henry. *A President's Journey: The Memoirs of Henry Poettcker*. Winnipeg: CMU Press, 2009.

Yoder, John Howard. *The Politics of Jesus: Vicit Agnus Noster*. Grand Rapids: Eerdmans, 1972.

In the World but Not *of* the World

A Johannine Perspective on the Church-World Relationship

Sheila Klassen-Wiebe

CHRISTIANS IN ALL AGES AND DENOMINATIONS HAVE STRUGGLED WITH HOW TO LIVE IN the two realms of church and world. This struggle has manifested itself in a dualistic two-kingdom theology and in the widespread belief that Christians should be "in the world but not of the world,"[1] although how such a belief is expressed differs vastly depending on the individual, the ecclesial community, or the context.[2] What this phrase does identify is a certain tension between a Christian's identity in the church and in the world. Followers of Jesus can never be entirely at ease in their present existence because their primary allegiance, or "home," is elsewhere. In the language of 1 Peter, Christians are "aliens and exiles" on this earth (2:11).

One of the problems inherent in the notion of being not "of the world" is that individuals and faith communities disagree over what "world" means and which of its aspects one should reject. Some Christians hold the view that "the Christian life consists of an inner disposition living in the same outer world as everyone else."[3] Thus the soul must remain untouched by the world even as the body participates in the world's structures. For some Christians, to be in the world but not of it has meant physical withdrawal from society or nonconformity to certain cultural practices, which may mean dressing differently or not driving cars. It has meant building private religious schools, eschewing politics, or shunning certain vocations such as that of a police officer. For some Christians, including Anabaptists, not being of the world has meant taking literally Jesus's teachings in the Sermon on the Mount, so that going to war and swearing oaths, things the "world" does, are considered wrong. For some Christians, not being of the world means not participating in the materialism and individualism of much of Western society, but living simply and in community. All these expressions share a desire to be faithful to Jesus and

---

1. The phrase "in the world but not of the world" does not actually occur in the Gospel of John nor in the New Testament, despite its common usage. It is, however, a blending of two ideas that find their origin in the Fourth Gospel: disciples are "in the world" or are sent "into the world" (13:1; 17:11, 18), and disciples are not "of the world," or, as the NRSV translates, "do not belong to the world" (15:19; 17:14, 16).

2. Huebner, "Church Made Strange for the Nations," nicely summarizes some aspects of the debate.

3. Ibid., 102.

an awareness of the tension between the way of Jesus and the way of the world, but they disagree about how to live in that tension.

Perhaps if we are going to use the phrase "in the world but not of the world" to characterize Christian ecclesiology and ethics, we should pay more attention to its original context. The idea that Christians should be present in the world but not fully part of it comes from the Gospel of John, and specifically, from Jesus's prayer for his disciples shortly before his arrest (John 17), yet rarely does this narrative context or its social-historical background influence the church's appropriation of the phrase to describe its relation to the world. This does not mean that the phrase cannot have valid meaning apart from its original context; however, if we are going to co-opt it from the Fourth Evangelist, it is incumbent on us at least to ask how its original context might shed light on its meaning for the church today.

The thesis of this essay is twofold. First, if we take the Gospel of John seriously, for the church to be not of the world is not a repudiation of culture or society and is not even primarily an ethical imperative. It is rather a Christological affirmation and an identity claim. That is, to be not of the world is above all to believe in Jesus as the one sent from God to reveal God, to restore humanity's relationship with God, and to give abundant life. Second, despite the fact that the church is not of the world, it has a mission to the world—a mission that engages the world through witness, love, and the forgiving and retaining of sins.[4]

Before addressing what it means to be in the world but not of it, I want first of all to speak to the question of what the Fourth Gospel means by "world." The word *kosmos*, or "world," occurs no less than seventy-eight times in the Gospel of John, approximately five times more frequently than in the Synoptics. It appears most often on the lips of Jesus (fifty-nine times) but is also used by the narrator (twelve times) and other human speakers (seven times).[5] More than half of Jesus's uses of the word appear in the Farewell Discourse (John 13–17), and of those, most have a negative connotation. Clearly, the concept of the "world" plays an important role in John's story of Jesus.[6] Yet John's use of language is deceptively simple and notoriously slippery. Words and images are more evocative than denotative, while paradoxes and dualisms abound.

It may be tempting to associate "world" with physical creation; thus the admonition to be in but not of the world can result in a devaluation of the created order. To be sure, John's sharply dualistic language, contrasting the "flesh" or world "below" with the realm

---

4. This study will focus on the Gospel of John alone. To be sure, the Johannine Epistles also have much to say about the church's relationship to the world, but that is beyond the scope of this essay. In addition, although the Gospel shows evidence of a lengthy redactional history, this study is concerned with the narrative in its canonical form and with the theological perspective of the final product. For a description of possible redactional activity, see Brown, *Community of the Beloved Disciple*.

5. Five of the uses by the narrator appear in John 3:16–19, where the speaker is ambiguous. If Jesus's words continue to the end of chap. 3, as some argue, then *kosmos* is used by Jesus sixty-four times and by the narrator only seven times, four of which are in 1:9–10. When used by other speakers, *kosmos* appears in 1:29; 4:42; 6:14; 7:4; 11:27; 12:19; 14:22.

6. I will call the author of the Fourth Gospel "John" for the sake of convenience, while recognizing that there is considerable debate over the identity of the historical author and without making particular assumptions about that identity.

of God and Spirit (3:6; 8:23), might seem to legitimate such an assumption. As Robert Kysar notes, however, such a depreciation of the physical world and the consequent belief that Christians should "be only remotely in contact with the materiality of this earth" is a serious misunderstanding of the Gospel.[7] Rather, the *kosmos* is created by God (1:10b) and is therefore good. The fact that the Word became embodied and dwelt among earthly creatures (1:14) implies that the flesh cannot be inherently evil. Physical blessings such as bread and water, vines and sheep become vehicles of divine revelation. The possibility of experiencing eternal life now would also not be comprehensible if the material world were "inherently inimical to spiritual existence,"[8] nor would John's lively hope in a future resurrection of the body (5:28–29; 6:39–40). In short, according to the Fourth Gospel, the physical world is not inherently evil but is the creation of a good God and is a medium of divine revelation.

Frequently, *kosmos* is neither positive nor negative but simply neutral, the earthly realm of existence (e.g., 16:21; 17:5; 21:25). This neutral sense of "world" requires further elaboration, however, for it also participates in the dualism of the Gospel. The world as the realm of earthly existence is distinct from the realm of the divine. It is created and finite, not eternal and ultimate; that is, it owes its existence to God, whereas the Father and Son existed before the foundation of the world (17:5, 24). The Son enters the world from the Father, remains for a time in the world, and leaves this world to return to the Father.[9] Such a sharply dualistic, two-story universe is part of the ancient worldview of John's Gospel, but it is closely intertwined with the human, theological-ethical dualism of the Gospel as well. Although the fact that the world is finite and "other" than God is neither inherently bad nor good, in the context of John's gospel story, in which God sends Jesus into the world for a specific purpose, its identity quickly slides toward the negative. The world in its otherness from God is primarily the human world. Although this human world is occasionally neutral (7:4; 12:19), for the most part it is profoundly alienated from God. It is here that John's cosmic dualism overlaps with a human dualism. Robert Kysar suggests that John's cosmological language of an earthly sphere distinct from a heavenly sphere represents a human dualism; that is, a humanity independent of, alienated from, and opposed to God, distinct from a humanity dependent on and believing in God.[10]

Many of these occurrences of *kosmos* in the Gospel imply that the world needs something. God sent Jesus into the world to bridge the gap, to supply what the world lacks, since this need can be met only by a source outside the world.[11] John uses many metaphors to describe what Jesus brings to the needy world. He is bread and water because he brings life to a world that hungers and thirsts and harbors death (6:33, 51). He brings light to the

---

7. Kysar, *John the Maverick Gospel*, 61.

8. Pregeant, *Knowing Truth, Doing Good*, 213.

9. There are many references to Jesus coming or being sent into the world, or departing from the world (1:9; 3:17, 19; 6:14; 9:39; 10:36; 11:27; 12:46; 13:1; 16:28; 17:18; 18:37). The fact that Jesus was "in" the world for a time (1:10; 9:5; 16:28; 17:18; 18:37) and therefore away from his Father also implies that "the world" refers to the earthly realm as opposed to the heavenly realm and has a spatial, cosmological sense.

10. Kysar, *John the Maverick Gospel*, 62–64.

11. I am dependent here on Koester, *Word of Life*, 59–65, for this way of formulating human need and God's response.

world because it is in darkness (8:12; 9:5; 11:9). He brings truth to a world that is false. The world that Jesus enters is a world dominated by the evil ruler (12:31; 14:30; 16:11) and needs salvation.

The world needs saving because it is sinful, and sin in the Gospel of John is above all a relational concept. That is to say, sin is not primarily false doctrine or wrong practice but refusal to believe in God or the one whom God sent to save the world. Such belief is not mere intellectual assent but an active, dynamic relationship of trust, whereas unbelief is estrangement from God. "This primary sin of unfaith is expressed in the many 'sins' or wrongful actions that people commit. John does not speak of sins primarily as transgressions of a moral code, but he does assume that human actions reflect underlying commitments."[12]

We have seen thus far that *kosmos* is used in the Gospel to refer to the physical created order, the earthly realm that Jesus enters from the realm of the divine, and the human realm that is estranged from God and in need of saving. Although in the last of these usages *kosmos* has a distinctly negative connotation, in its need for God the world is still redeemable and the object of God's saving activity. God sent Jesus into the world to save the world (3:17; 12:47) because God loves the world (3:16).

The problem with the world arises in its response to God's saving initiative. Although some people do respond favorably to Jesus, the world does not. The uses of *kosmos* that have to do with the world's need for God and God's positive saving activity on behalf of the world appear almost entirely in the first half of the Gospel.[13] All the references to Jesus as the "light of the world," for example, appear in the first twelve chapters of the Gospel.[14] Although there are a few references to the world's active hostility and unbelief in the first half of the Gospel (e.g., 7:7), after chapter 12, the hostility to Jesus increases markedly as he moves toward his death and glorification on the cross.[15] This is the time for "the judgment of this world" (12:31) and the time for Jesus to depart from it (13:1). "It is only as the conflict grows, and when the world rejects Jesus, that the term becomes negative and stands for the source of opposition."[16] An examination of those texts in which the world is the subject of the action (as opposed to the object of God's activity) reveals that such action is almost entirely negative.[17] The world does "not know" Jesus or God (1:10c; 17:25); it cannot receive the Spirit (14:17); and it "hates" Jesus and consequently also Jesus's disciples (7:7; 15:18–19; 16:33; 17:14). The world that rejects the one sent from God to save it is governed by "the ruler of this world," who personifies all the cosmic powers that are hostile to God.[18] Notably, all three references to this "ruler" occur in the second half of the

---

12. Ibid., 66.

13. John 1:29; 3:16–17; 4:42; 6:33, 51; 8:12; 9:5; 11:9; 12:47.

14. Cassem, "Grammatical and Contextual Inventory," 89. The fact that the world is in darkness and therefore in need of something could be taken as a negative reference, but it is the world as the object of God's saving activity in Jesus that is in view here.

15. The observation that the most negative uses of "world" occur in the second half of the Gospel has been made by many scholars; see ibid.; Raabe, "Dynamic Tension," 145; and Burridge, *Imitating Jesus*, 333.

16. Burridge, *Imitating Jesus*, 333.

17. Cassem, "Grammatical and Contextual Inventory," 82–83.

18. O'Day, "Gospel of John," 793.

Gospel, and all three occur on the lips of Jesus in a prediction of the ruler's demise (12:31; 14:30; 16:11).[19]

Who is included in this negative characterization of the world? Since the evil one's influence is pervasive and inclusive, the world that God has come to save and that rejects Jesus encompasses both Jews and non-Jews.[20] The "ruler of this world" (Satan or the devil) is active not only among Jewish opponents (8:44) but also in one of Jesus's disciples (13:2, 27) and among the Romans—Pilate, for example—who actively oppose God's revelation in Jesus. Moreover, "the lines between the believing community and the unbelieving world are not static."[21] Some Jews come to believe in Jesus (11:45), and some who are initially disciples turn away (6:66). When the world comes to believe in Jesus, however, it ceases to be the "world" in the Johannine sense.

In summary, then, the "world" is an unequivocally negative concept in the Gospel only insofar as it refers to humanity in its blatant refusal to believe in Jesus, who was sent from God to save the world. It is this quality that ensures the world's dominance by the power of evil. It is not the world's unjust actions, violence, greed, adherence to values of the general society, or any such matter that damages its image—though to be sure, all such qualities are a result of its identity as the world. Rather, the Fourth Evangelist paints the world in the most negative terms because of its stance toward Jesus. The Johannine negative characterization of the world is thus not ontological nor even primarily ethical, but Christological. John's negative portrayal of the world grows out of the story of Jesus, and the most dire warnings against the world appear in that part of the story where the world has most clearly turned its back on Jesus.

Given this uniquely Johannine construct of the world, what then does it mean for disciples to be in the world but not of the world? "The phrase 'of the world' (*ek tou kosmou*) indicates both origin in the world and agreement with the world."[22] Neither Jesus nor his disciples are of the world in this sense, since their identity lies not in the world but in God. There is a difference between Jesus and his disciples in this respect, however. Jesus was never of the world because his origins are in God from the beginning (3:13, 31; 6:33; 16:27–28). Believers are also not of the world, but their origins are from God in a different sense. They have been given to Jesus, have been chosen from out of the world (15:19; 17:6); they are born from above (3:3, 7), whereas Jesus *is* from above.[23]

It is important to note that Jesus never instructs his disciples not to be of the world. The misinterpretation of the phrase as a command results from inattention to the wider

---

19. The ruler of this world "will be driven out," "has no power over" Jesus, and "has been condemned."

20. Although space prohibits discussion of the much-debated question of the relationship between "Jews" and *kosmos* in John, a careful examination of the Gospel suggests that "the world" is much broader than just the Jews who reject Jesus.

21. Koester, *Symbolism in the Fourth Gospel*, 255.

22. Raabe, "Dynamic Tension," 137.

23. Thompson, "What Is the Gospel of John?" 339. Keck, "Derivation as Destiny," 283–84, states that "when Jesus says he is 'not of this world' (17:14, 16) he means that on earth he maintained his unique derivation by not deriving the warrant for his life from 'this world' but instead by pleasing the One who sent him. For the disciples, however, their being 'not of this world' is a status acquired. As a result they do not share Jesus's ontic 'of-ness' but its consequences."

context. The phrase "of the world" occurs thirteen times in the Gospel and, with one exception (8:23), all in the second half. It is almost always spoken by Jesus, and it always has a negative connotation.[24] Once Jesus tells the Pharisees that they are of this world and he is not (8:23), and once Jesus tells Pilate that his kingdom is not of this world, for if it were, his followers would fight (18:36). In the remaining instances where this phrase is used (15:19; 17:6, 14, 15, 16), Jesus is referring to his disciples and making a statement about their identity, even praying for them. The point is that Jesus never commands his disciples to be in the world but not of the world; he simply asserts that that is what they indeed are.

To summarize, then, if one takes seriously the Johannine context, the phrase to be "in the world but not of the world" is not first of all an ethical imperative commanding believers to live separately from nonbelievers in terms of politics, culture, society, and so on. When Jesus prays for his disciples and prepares them for his departure, he reminds them of who they are. They will remain in the world after he leaves them—that is, they will continue to live among those who rejected and opposed Jesus—but they are not of the world—that is, their identity and origin is in God, from whom they have been born anew. They are not of the world because they believe in Jesus, who was sent from God to save the world. This identification with Jesus and their birth from above is, at its most basic, the key thing that distinguishes them from the world. This, of course, has other implications. It means that the disciples will not fight as does the world, which killed Jesus (18:36). It means that the world will hate them, not love them as its own (15:19). Above all, to be in the world but not of it means to believe in Jesus as the one sent from God to reveal God and to save a world alienated from God, while yet living faithfully among those who reject and oppose Jesus. But what exactly does it mean for believers to relate to such a world?

The Gospel of John has long been perceived as sectarian, ingrown, and exclusivist, with an ethic intent on shutting out the world and limiting love to other members of the faith community. Such an impression arises from the fact that the only explicit ethical command Jesus gives in the Gospel is that the disciples should "love one another" (13:34–35; 15:12), as well as from the seemingly negative portrayal of the world as hostile to believers. Nowhere does John's Jesus exhort his followers to love their enemies, turn the other cheek, or pray for those who abuse them (Matt. 5:38–48; Luke 6:27–36). For that matter, he also does not counsel love of neighbor or love of God, as he does in the Synoptics.

Crucial for understanding the Gospel's stance toward the world is the context out of which it emerged, namely, a situation of growing hostility between a minority Jewish-Christian group and its larger Jewish community, and the former's traumatic severance from its parent in faith. Many scholars understand the Gospel's three references to believers being put out of the synagogue to reflect the situation in which the Gospel was written rather than the time of the narrative itself (9:22; 12:42; 16:2). Despite general agreement about the contours of this historical situation, however, there is much debate as to the

---

24. In John 13:1 it is used by the narrator but the sense here is different; the narrator comments that the hour has come for Jesus to "depart from this world."

precise circumstances.²⁵ Suffice it to say that the Gospel likely arose out of a time of intra-Jewish conflict and painful separation between church and synagogue.

Given such a situation, a characterization of the Gospel's ethics as narrow, inwardly focused, and world-negating is inadequate, as many scholars have argued.²⁶ Although the Gospel includes no explicit command that believers should love the world, it does advocate an involvement with the world that is ultimately constructive, not disparaging. Most of Jesus's guidance on how his followers should engage the world comes in the Farewell Discourse (chaps. 13–17), as Jesus prepares them for faithful living after his departure. In these chapters Jesus sends his disciples out to engage the world through witness, love for one another, and forgiveness of sin.

The first thing to note is that Jesus sends his disciples into the world (17:18; 20:21). They do not remain in the world simply because they have no other option and must bide their time on earth until they can be transported to heaven. Rather, just as God sanctified and sent Jesus into the world with a particular mission and with a truth at odds with what the world offers, so also Jesus sets his disciples apart from the world and entrusts them with the truth in order that he might send them into the world as his witnesses (17:17–19).²⁷

The primary mission of the disciples as they are sent into the world is to engage in *marturia*, that is, witness or testimony (15:26–27); this is the language of the law court, which summons witnesses to determine the truth of what happened.²⁸ Disciples of Jesus are witnesses, qualified to speak truthfully about Jesus because they have been with Jesus "from the beginning" (*archē*) of his time on earth (15:27), just as Jesus is a reliable witness to the Father because he was with God in the beginning (*archē*) (1:2).

Jesus's most explicit instruction to his disciples to testify is framed by warnings about the world's hatred (15:18–25; 16:1–4): since the world hated and persecuted Jesus, it will hate and persecute his disciples. Jesus makes clear that he is telling them this before it happens so that when it does, they will not stumble but will remember his words. In the face of hostility, the disciples may be tempted to abandon their faith, withdraw, or be silent.²⁹ Yet Jesus calls them to speak the truth and voice their "convictions in contexts where the truth is not obvious" or where contrary claims are made.³⁰ In short, Jesus calls them to witness.

---

25. The use of polemical language by both Jews and Gentiles in the first century, uncertainty about the existence of a formal expulsion from the synagogue, and other such questions make historical reconstruction of the circumstances of the conflict difficult. See Carter, *John: Storyteller, Interpreter, Evangelist*, 166.

26. Pregeant, *Knowing Truth, Doing Good*, 200; Thompson, "What Is the Gospel of John?" 339; Burridge, *Imitating Jesus*, 334; Hays, *Moral Vision of the New Testament*, 139–40.

27. Koester, *Word of Life*, 149.

28. Keener, *Gospel of John*, 1022–23, discusses the forensic significance of the word in this context and in contemporary literature.

29. Raabe, "Dynamic Tension," 141: "In light of such a threat the disciples face the temptation of apostasy," that is, "to make friends with the world by adopting its outlook. Or they are tempted to back off and keep the saving truth to themselves. After all, who needs the grief? Yet Jesus calls His own to testify in the world openly and publicly—as Jesus spoke openly and publicly."

30. Koester, *Word of Life*, 157.

A prime example of truth-telling in the face of opposition is the blind man (9:1–41) who perseveres in testifying to Jesus despite the consequences of synagogue expulsion.

The disciples are not the first or only witnesses to the truth of God's revelation in Jesus, nor do they do it on their own strength. In their engagement with the world, the disciples continue the witness of John the Baptist, whose role in the Fourth Gospel is exclusively to testify about the one coming after him (1:7–8, 15, 19, 32, 34; 3:26; 5:33). The disciples are also "corroborating witnesses" with Jesus, who himself testifies to the truth against the world (3:11, 32; 7:7; 8:18; 18:37). They can witness courageously and effectively after Jesus departs because he gives them the Spirit to empower them. The Spirit testifies about Jesus after his ascension through the witness of the disciples by reminding them of what they have heard and by helping them discern the meaning of things they could not understand when Jesus was with them (14:26; 16:13–15). The Spirit will prove the world wrong about sin and righteousness and judgment (16:8–11). "By disclosing the world's true character, the Spirit gives believers the perspective they need to resist, so that they can maintain the integrity of their convictions."[31]

Despite the opposition that the disciples face in the world, their testimony will lead others to believe (17:20). This is already prefigured in the narrative by characters such as the Samaritans who believe because of the woman's testimony (4:41–42). The Gospel itself is the testimony of a disciple who knows and speaks what is true (19:35; 21:24), and hearers and readers who respond by believing in Jesus (20:31) exemplify the correct response to a disciple's testimony.

Another important way the disciples engage the world is through their love for each other, although such intracommunal love has usually been perceived as a way of shutting out the world, not engaging it. Jesus's commandment that his followers should love each other is the only explicit ethical instruction in the Gospel and seems to apply only to fellow believers, prompting the accusation that the Johannine Jesus has nothing to say about intercommunal social relations, not to mention love of enemies or the world. Although the Gospel nowhere advocates hatred of enemies, as do some of the Qumran texts, neither does the Johannine love command exclude love for enemies, even if the rhetoric of the Gospel is at times anything but loving toward those who oppose Jesus (e.g., 8:31–47).[32]

There are several ways, however, in which the believers' love for each other within the church does engage the world. First, mutual love both sustains the community and draws the world in by its witness. In this respect, the social-historical context of increasing estrangement between believing and nonbelieving Jews is significant. The former perceived themselves to be a persecuted minority, experiencing hostility and perhaps exclusion from the synagogues in which they had always been at home. In such a context, acts of risky service and concrete love within the community, even to the point of dying for one another, were not merely self-preserving efforts to shut out the world but acts of prophetic resistance.[33] Brian Blount compares the mutual love within the Johannine community to the

---

31. Ibid.

32. Rensberger, "Love for One Another," 306–7.

33. Hays, *Moral Vision of the New Testament*, 147. Similarly, Koester, *Word of Life*, 195, writes, "The command to love one another means that Christians bring to the world not only a doctrine about love but an

way in which mutual support and love functioned as a means of active resistance within the African-American slave culture and civil rights movement.[34] Such love is a means of sustenance for an oppressed community and a way to resist the hostile world around it. In addition, by virtue of its persistent love, the community also becomes a witness to the world around it and a means of drawing in the very world that resists it. Because of the believers' love for each other everyone will know that they are Jesus's disciples (13:34–35). The community of believers who love each other becomes an agent of transformation, for as the world sees the love of believers for each other and is drawn also to believe in the Christ who motivates such love, it ceases to be the "world."[35]

Second, the disciples' love for one another engages the world because it originates in God, whose love extends not only to believers but to the whole world (3:16). Their love for each other exists only because of and within God's prior love for them as it is revealed in Jesus; they love one another because they abide in Jesus's love for them (15:9–10). "We may speak of a Johannine triangle of reciprocity, in which God's love for the Son and for those who follow him is the foundation of the Son's love both of the Father and of those entrusted to him, as well as for the love that community members are called to have for God and for one another. And an understanding of this pattern puts the seeming limitation of love to community members into a somewhat different perspective."[36] God unconditionally loves the world that is alienated from and at enmity with its Creator, in order to restore the relationship between God and the world (3:16). The depth of this love is evident in the Son's willingness to love to the death, despite the world's hatred and rejection, and thereby to "draw all people to [himself]" (12:32). Jesus first commands his disciples to love each other after he has washed their feet, an action that symbolizes and anticipates Jesus's laying down his life for the world he loves. Judas, who will shortly betray him, is among those whose feet Jesus washes. In betraying him, Judas demonstrates that he does not believe in Jesus and thus ostensibly belongs to the world. And yet Jesus loves him, serves him, and lays down his life for him. If the disciples can keep Jesus's commandment to love each other as they abide in his love, and if their mutual indwelling love originates in Jesus's self-giving love for the world and within the "triangle of reciprocity," it is hard to see how this love could be confined within the community and how believers could be exempt from loving the world as God also loves it.[37]

---

alternative society, a counterculture in which the message of Jesus takes lived form. Christian community is not an end in itself. The love that is shared within it is a form of witness to those outside it, so that the world may know that the love of God is real (17:23)."

34. Blount, *Then the Whisper Put on Flesh*, 93–118.

35. Rensberger, "Love for One Another," 307–8. Blount, *Then the Whisper Put on Flesh*, 117, makes a similar observation: "In this oddly ironic way, by being visibly sectarian, it is actually reaching out to those who are lost in the world, and encouraging them to participate in the love that sustains it."

36. Pregeant, *Knowing Truth, Doing Good*, 201.

37. Pregeant agrees when he writes, "Although the focus on God's love for the Son and the various dimensions of reciprocity that flow from this basic affirmation are dominant, the undercurrents of emphasis on God's love for the world force us to ask how a loving God could in fact remain content with love confined to the triangle of reciprocity." Ibid., 214.

Not only does love within the church originate in God who loves the world, but believers are explicitly exhorted to love *as Jesus loved* (13:15, 34). The ethics of the Gospel is an ethics of imitation, consonant with its character as a biographical narrative (rather than an ethical treatise).[38] Although Jesus uses the specific word *example* (13:15) only when he is speaking about washing each other's feet, the example to be imitated extends beyond this one act to a life of self-sacrifice and service. Jesus himself exemplifies a love that reaches out to all, creating an inclusive and diverse community. Far from portraying an "introverted sect," the narrative "depicts a multi-ethnic, socially variegated and all-inclusive community as both the object and achievement of Jesus in his mission to bring the divine love into the world."[39] This community includes Samaritans, women, royal officials, Jews, "other sheep," and outcasts like the blind man. If the Johannine ethic is one of imitation, growing out of the story of Jesus, then the community's love must also reach out to everyone, drawing those who were part of the world into the community that will in turn witness to the same world through its love and unity.

We have seen that Jesus sends his disciples into the world to be his witnesses and, by their love for one another, to draw the world into the sphere of Jesus's love. A third and final aspect of the disciples' engagement with the world is the forgiveness and retention of sins (20:23). One might justifiably wonder whether this is part of their mission to the world or whether this task pertains only to the church. Two things suggest the former. First, Jesus's words about forgiving and retaining sins are spoken in the context of sending the disciples as the Father has sent him (20:21). And since the Father sent Jesus into the world to take away the world's sin (1:29), the disciples are also sent into the world—to witness, to love each other, and to deal with sin. Second, Jesus told them before he died that he would send them the Paraclete, the Spirit of truth, and that "when he comes he will convict the world about sin and righteousness and judgment" (16:8). Just before Jesus tells his disciples that their work involves the forgiving and retaining of sins, he bestows on them the Holy Spirit (20:22). The sphere of the Spirit's activity is the world, and the Spirit's work of "convicting the world of sin" must occur through the community to whom Jesus sends the Spirit and to whom he entrusts the task of forgiving and retaining sins.

Although the question of what it means for Jesus's disciples to forgive and retain sins is a complex one and cannot be explored fully here, a few things may be said. First, as stated previously, the world's chief problem is sin, and sin in the Gospel of John is "defined not by what one does but almost exclusively by one's relationship to Jesus, and more specifically, by whether one believes that God is present in Jesus."[40] Put simply, sin is estrangement from God and the refusal to believe in Jesus who comes from God to restore the world's relationship with God (9:41; 16:9). This underlying condition of sin produces sins, actions that affect relationships with God and other people. For the disciples to forgive and retain sins has to do, then, with confronting the unbelief of the world and the actions such unbelief produces. Second, the charge to forgive and retain sins is not given only to certain leaders among the disciples but to the whole group gathered with Jesus after his

---

38. This is an important aspect of Burridge's articulation of Johannine ethics in *Imitating Jesus*.
39. Ibid., 341.
40. O'Day, "Gospel of John," 664.

resurrection. Thus the forgiveness and retention of sins is not solely the responsibility of the clergy but belongs to all Christians, who are represented here by the disciples and who all receive the Spirit. Third, the verbs "to forgive" and "to retain" are used only here in the Gospel.[41] Surprisingly, the Fourth Gospel does not describe Jesus *forgiving* sin, as do the Synoptics. Yet Jesus takes away the sin of the world and was sent from the Father to save the world. By willingly laying down his life for the world, Jesus conveys the extent of God's love for the world and brings the world back into relationship with God by evoking faith.[42] Jesus's disciples carry on the saving work of Jesus when they forgive sins, that is, when they release people from the bonds that entrap them and that destroy their relationships with God and other people. They do this by communicating the extent of God's love as it was revealed in Jesus who laid down his life for the world. "To 'retain' sins in a Johannine sense involves exposing sin, identifying sin, and holding people to account for sin."[43] When the disciples confront the world and hold it accountable for its sin (and sin's consequences), they open the door for forgiveness and change to happen. The mission of Jesus's followers, then, includes confronting the world with its sin, retaining sin by holding the world accountable for it, and releasing or forgiving sin by drawing the world into the sphere of God's love as revealed in Jesus.

In conclusion, the Gospel of John does not have the final answer nor the only answer to what it means for the church to be in the world but not of the world, and Christians will continue to wrestle with how to live faithfully in a world whose primary allegiance is not to Jesus. At the same time, diligent attention to how the Gospel of John addresses that tension may inspire the church to reflect anew on its identity and mission and may dispel some misconceptions about what it means for the church to be in but not of the world. To be in the world is not a bad thing, since the world is God's creation and the recipient of God's saving love. However, the church's origin and identity do not lie in the world, because the world has fundamentally rejected and continues to reject God's overtures of love in Jesus, refusing to trust that in Jesus, God's saving purposes are fully revealed. Thus the church cannot be of the world, because it believes in Jesus. Being in but not of the world is not something for which believers must strive but simply describes what they are. The church's mission is not to separate itself from the unbelieving world, if such a thing were even possible. Rather, Jesus intentionally sends his followers, today as in John's day, into the world to engage it redemptively. Although such engagement can and does take many forms, in the Gospel of John it is most explicitly spoken of in three ways: the church is called to witness to the world by speaking truth even in the face of hostility, to love and serve its members and thereby draw others into the divine love, and to forgive and retain sins, both in the context of the faith community as well as in the world. When the church attends to this identity and mission, the church will indeed be "in the world but not of the world."

---

41. The verb *aphiemi* does appear elsewhere in the Gospel but not in the context of sin and not with the meaning of forgiving; elsewhere, it means "to leave, let go, allow."

42. I am indebted to Koester, *Word of Life*, 108–23, for this way of articulating the meaning of the atonement.

43. Ibid., 159.

Bibliography

Ashton, John. *Understanding the Fourth Gospel.* Oxford: Clarendon, 1991.
Blount, Brian K. *Then the Whisper Put on Flesh: New Testament Ethics in an African American Context.* Nashville: Abingdon, 2001.
Brown, Raymond E. *The Community of the Beloved Disciple.* New York: Paulist, 1979.
———. *The Gospel According to John (1–12).* Vol. 29a of *The Anchor Bible.* Garden City, NY: Doubleday, 1966.
Burridge, Richard A. *Imitating Jesus: An Inclusive Approach to New Testament Ethics.* Grand Rapids: Eerdmans, 2007.
Carter, Warren. *John: Storyteller, Interpreter, Evangelist.* Peabody, MA: Hendrickson, 2006.
Cassem, N. H. "A Grammatical and Contextual Inventory of the Use of kosmos in the Johannine Corpus with Some Implications for a Johannine Cosmic Theology." *New Testament Studies* 19 (1972) 81–91.
Hays, Richard B. *The Moral Vision of the New Testament: Community, Cross, New Creation.* San Francisco: HarperCollins, 1996.
Huebner, Harry J. "The Church Made Strange for the Nations." In *Echoes of the Word: Theological Ethics as Rhetorical Practice*, 84–106. Kitchener, ON: Pandora, 2005.
Keck, Leander E. "Derivation as Destiny: 'Of-ness' in Johannine Christology, Anthropology, and Soteriology." In *Exploring the Gospel of John: In Honor of D. Moody Smith*, edited by R. Alan Culpepper and C. Clifton Black, 274–88. Louisville: Westminster, 1996.
Keener, Craig S. *The Gospel of John: A Commentary.* Vol. 2. Peabody, MA: Hendrickson, 2003.
Koester, Craig R. *Symbolism in the Fourth Gospel: Meaning, Mystery, Community.* Minneapolis: Fortress, 1995.
———. *The Word of Life: A Theology of John's Gospel.* Grand Rapids: Eerdmans, 2008.
Kysar, Robert. *John the Maverick Gospel.* Rev. ed. Louisville: Westminster, 1993.
Lieu, Judith. "Anti-Judaism, the Jews, and the Worlds of the Fourth Gospel." In *The Gospel of John and Christian Theology*, edited by Richard Bauckham and Carl Mosser, 168–82. Grand Rapids: Eerdmans, 2008.
Long, Thomas. *Testimony: Talking Ourselves into Being Christian.* San Francisco: Jossey-Bass, 2004.
Marrow, Stanley B. "*Kosmos* in John." *Catholic Biblical Quarterly* 64 (2002) 90–102.
Meeks, Wayne A. "The Ethics of the Fourth Evangelist." In *Exploring the Gospel of John: In Honor of D. Moody Smith*, edited by R. Alan Culpepper and C. Clifton Black, 317–26. Louisville: Westminster, 1996.
O'Day, Gail R. "The Gospel of John: Introduction, Commentary, and Reflections." In *The New Interpreter's Bible*, vol. 9, edited by Leander E. Keck, 495–865. Nashville: Abingdon, 1995.
Pregeant, Russell. *Knowing Truth, Doing Good: Engaging New Testament Ethics.* Minneapolis: Fortress, 2008.
Raabe, Paul. "A Dynamic Tension: God and World in John." *Concordia Journal* 21 (1995) 132–47.
Rensberger, David. *Johannine Faith and Liberating Community.* Philadelphia: Westminster, 1988.
———. "Love for One Another and Love for Enemies in the Gospel of John." In *The Love of Enemy and Nonretaliation in the New Testament*, edited by Willard M. Swartley, 297–313. Louisville: Westminster, 1992.
Thompson, Marianne Meye. "What Is the Gospel of John?" *Word and World* 21 (2001) 333–42.

Building the City for Others

Beyond the Negation of Exile Toward a Future of Common Belonging in Israel-Palestine

Alain Epp Weaver

CAN A POLITICAL THEOLOGY OF EXILE, A THEOLOGY THAT JOINS THE LATE JOHN HOWARD Yoder in embracing "galut [diaspora] as vocation" and Stanley Hauerwas in insisting on the "resident alien" status of Christians amidst the empires of the world, offer a positive vision of landed existence? Or does such a theology simply remain mute, as its critics worry, on the question of how to live faithfully in the land?[1] Through consideration of the actual and potential political configurations in the particular land known variously as Israel and Palestine, I contend that an exilic theology shaped by Jeremiah's call to seek the *shalom* of the city of one's exile (Jer 29:7), while undoubtedly "strange" from the perspective of those who reduce political life to the form of the nation-state, can indeed underwrite forms of landedness that disrupt and transcend nationalist projects of establishing and maintaining demographic hegemony within a circumscribed territory.[2]

I begin by considering how one contemporary reflection on the theological significance of Zionism and the State of Israel, offered by Rowan Williams, mirrors the mainstream Zionist "negation of exile" (*shelilat ha-galut*) by identifying the State of Israel as the "condition" for the Jewish people's theo-political vocation and by implying that Jewish witness in exile is deficient. As a result, despite his desire to offer a "liberation theology" of good news for Palestinians and Israelis, Williams's project unwittingly participates in the

---

1. Yoder identified *galut*, or diaspora, as the location and style of the church's witness in his posthumously published book, *The Jewish-Christian Schism Revisited*. For Hauerwas on the "resident alien" status of the church, see Hauerwas and Willimon, *Resident Aliens*. Gerald Schlabach, Peter Ochs, and Michael Cartwright have raised the concern that Yoder's political theology does not adequately meet the challenge of living faithfully in the land. For more detailed discussion of Cartwright's and Ochs's critique, see chap. 3 of my *States of Exile*. For Schlabach's claim that Yoder did not do justice to the "Deuteronomic" calling to enter the land faithfully, see his "Deuteronomic or Constantinian."

2. My reflections on how a theology of exile can offer a strange disruption of nationalist visions of landedness are offered as a tribute to Harry Huebner's career-long effort to display the church's strange witness amidst the nations and to the inspiration he has provided many workers with Mennonite Central Committee in the Occupied Territories through his example of passionate theological engagement as an MCC peace worker in Jerusalem in the early 1980s. For one example of Huebner's theological analysis of the Palestinian-Israeli conflict, see his "The Morality of Peacemaking."

conceptual erasure of Palestinians, whose dispossession Israeli political theorist Amnon Raz-Krakotzkin has shown to be intertwined with the negation of exile.[3]

I then proceed, by displaying the affinities between Yoder's ecclesiology of exile and the Italian philosopher Giorgio Agamben's reflections on how the figure of the refugee disrupts the triad of territory, nation, and state, to argue that a political theology of exile can take account of the complex, binational reality of Israel-Palestine. Against ideologies of the nation-state seeking to secure homogeneous spaces within tightly policed borders, ideologies inextricably intertwined with policies and practices of dispossession, a theology of exile embraces the heterogeneous character of Israel-Palestine's places and thus offers a vision of common belonging in the land.

Rowan Williams, the State of Israel, and the Witness of "Israel under God"

The modern State of Israel "is the condition for Jewish people of faith and conscience to be able to exercise their calling."[4] So claimed Rowan Williams in the keynote address, delivered *in absentia* in April 2004, to the "Challenging Christian Zionism" conference in Jerusalem hosted by the Sabeel Ecumenical Liberation Theology Center, a Palestinian Christian organization.[5] Williams's speech is marked by a transparent desire to articulate a theological vision of the land in which Israelis and Palestinians might live in security. At the same time, however, the speech deserves attention for its embodiment of a broader failure of Christian theological assessments of Zionism to attend to the intimate relationship between the establishment of a Jewish homeland of a particular sort, on the one hand, and Palestinian dispossession, on the other.[6] Correcting for this theological blind spot, I claim, requires a more complex understanding of home and place and greater attention to an exilic theology of land than Williams provides.[7]

Williams's discussion of the State of Israel unfolds within a treatment of the theopolitical vocation of the people Israel (whom Williams names "Israel under God") to live as a "paradigm nation," a living testimony to God's righteousness.[8] While "Israel under

---

3. Williams, "Holy Land and Holy People," 293.

4. Ibid., 299.

5. Williams had agreed seven months prior to the conference to deliver the keynote address, but three weeks before the meeting apologized that he would be unable to attend, and had his Secretary for Ecumenism, Jonathan Gough, give the talk in his stead.

6. For a discussion of this broader context, see my analysis of recent statements emerging from Catholic-Jewish and Protestant-Jewish dialogues in chap. 7 of my *States of Exile*.

7. Williams's speech elicited sharply dissenting reactions from the conference attendees, in particular from Palestinian Christians. While Williams repudiated Christian Zionism of the premillennial dispensationalist variety, in which the establishment of a Jewish state serves as a key moment in the unfolding of an apocalyptic drama, his critics argued that his claim that the modern State of Israel is scripturally warranted, serving as a necessary condition for the Jewish people to live out its vocation as a paradigm nation, constitutes a Christian Zionism of a different sort. See the critical responses to Williams's address gathered in the conference proceedings, *Challenging Christian Zionism*: Kuttab, "An Open Letter to Archbishop Rowan Williams"; Ruether, "Christian Zionism and Main Line Western Christian Churches"; Tobin, "On Knowing One's Place"; and Lewis, "Response to Rowan Williams' Message to the Sabeel Conference."

8. The Jewish people, or "Israel under God," are called by God to live as "the *paradigm nation*, the example

God" cannot be collapsed into the modern State of Israel, Williams insists, the latter can make the witness of the former possible: "The modern political reality of Israel is not biblical Israel, but it is ideally one of the conditions for biblical Israel's message and witness to be alive in the world today—a context in which God's people manifest God's justice."[9]

The land, understood "as a condition for stable, hospitable law-governed life together," thus serves as the location for Israel under God living out its vocation.[10] Furthermore, the State of Israel should, according to Williams, exist "in the light of the biblical vision of justice."[11] Given the history of Jewish persecution in the West, culminating most horrifically in the Holocaust, the State of Israel represents an "intelligible requirement" for Israel under God's theo-political vocation of embodied witness as a paradigm nation. "The community of faithful Jewish people committed to justice and wisdom in the world today, as a community consciously living before God, has its rationale in the calling to embody justice and wisdom," Williams emphasizes. "[T]o have a homeland in which to exercise the political virtue this involves is an intelligible requirement, especially in the light of a history in which this liberty has been systematically denied for so many centuries by Western Christians. To be hospitable, you must have a home."[12] Israel under God's witness as a paradigm nation cannot flourish over time in diaspora, but instead needs the State of Israel as its "condition" and "intelligible requirement": "when the Jewish people have an identity only as dispersed minorities," Williams maintains, "the witness of a nation existing solely because of God's call to wisdom and justice is weakened, and sooner or later the nations around will begin to lose awareness of their moral accountability."[13]

This claim about the weakened witness of minority Jewish communities in diaspora sheds light on how Williams's use of terms such as *home* and *homeland*, which he deploys without defining, is captive to the form of the nation-state. What is it about the State of Israel as a Jewish homeland that, from Williams's perspective, makes it the condition for Israel under God's exercise of theo-political virtue? Williams does not explicitly answer, but implicitly the answer is clear. If the minority character of Jewish life in diaspora yields a weakened witness, then the antidote, on Williams's account, must be to secure Jewish demographic hegemony within a circumscribed territory. The State of Israel and the idea of a Jewish homeland are thus implicitly defined (*a*) in negative terms as the negation of the minority life of exile, which has proven to be unstable at best and death-dealing at worst; and (*b*) in positive terms as a polity in which a Jewish demographic majority is established and maintained.

---

held up to all nations of how a people lives in obedience to God and justice with one another." This people "exists solely because of God's loving choice; they have been called out of another nation specifically to live as a community whose task is to show God's wisdom in the world." Williams, "Holy Land and Holy People," 294.

9. Ibid., 296.
10. Ibid.
11. Ibid., 299.
12. Ibid., 296.
13. Ibid., 298.

The Negation of Exile, Palestinian Dispossession, and the Denial of Complex Space

This theological argument for the State of Israel as the condition for the witness of Israel under God unconsciously echoes a central Zionist trope, namely, the "negation of exile." As Amnon Raz-Krakotzkin has convincingly argued, the interrelated notions of the negation of the diaspora, the "return to the land" (*ha-shiva le-eretz yisrael*), and the "return to history" (*ha-shiva la-historia*) function as central concepts in the conception of history and the collective memory of the Israeli political imagination.[14] "With the concepts of the negation of exile and the return to history," Raz-Krakotzkin asserts, "the Jewish Zionist implantation in Palestine comes to be considered as the restoration of Jewish sovereignty, the return of the Jewish people to a land presented as its own (and supposedly empty), and as the success of Jewish history, the fulfillment of millenarian aspirations. The return to history is presented as the return to national and political sovereignty, which the Jews had known in biblical antiquity and in the Second Temple period."[15] Jewish life in exile, from the perspective of mainstream Zionism, is negated as abnormal or even diseased, a problematic condition to be remedied through *aliyah*, or ascent, to the land of Israel and through the "return" of the Jewish people to the history of nation-states. Exile is represented by Zionism as "a defective existence, incomplete or abnormal, a situation in which 'the spirit of the nation' could not fully express itself": the Jewish nation can only find its fulfillment in its own land and with its own state.[16]

Taken together, the "negation of exile," "return to the land," and "return to history" tropes place Zionism squarely in the context of European nationalism and romanticism. The "history" designated by the Zionist "return to history," Raz-Krakotzkin explains, is the history "of the nineteenth century, which makes the nation the exclusive, sovereign subject. The return to history signifies the return to national sovereignty and is accompanied by the rejection of the passivity attributed to the Jew of the diaspora who lives in the messianic expectation of divine intervention."[17] The discourse around the negation of exile, meanwhile, "reveals the properly theological dimension of the national conscience," with the "secularism" of "secular Zionism" uncovered as "the nationalization of the theological myth reformulated through concepts borrowed from European romanticism."[18]

Through its negative evaluation of Jewish life in exile, Zionist narrations of history mimic Christian theologies of repudiation that cast exile as divine punishment upon the Jewish people for their rejection of Jesus as the Messiah. "Christianity considers the exile of the Jews as their 'departure from history,'" Raz-Krakotzkin observes, "that is to say, their departure from the context of grace. Exile is the consequence of their sins, above all their

---

14. My discussion of the Zionist motifs of "the negation of exile" and "the return to history" has been primarily informed by Amnon Raz-Krakotzkin, *Exil et souveraineté*. All translations from the original French are mine. See also Piterberg, *Returns of Zionism*, especially chap. 3; Myers, *Re-Inventing the Jewish Past*; Ratzaby, "Polemic about the Negation of the Diaspora," and Don-Yehiya, "Negation of Galut in Religious Zionism."

15. Raz-Krakotzkin, *Exil et souveraineté*, 27.

16. Ibid.

17. Ibid., 41.

18. Ibid., 32. See also Raz-Krakotzkin, "National-Colonial Theology."

refusal of the Good News. Their exile is the proof of their condition as sinners, and only theirs—and as a consequence, it is proof of the truth of Christianity."[19] Zionist claims to "return" to history thus implicitly agree with this negative Christian evaluation of Jewish life in exile.

The Zionist appraisal of exile, Raz-Krakotzkin emphasizes, deviates sharply from Rabbinic Judaism's conceptualization of exile as a metaphysical condition marking all of earthly existence. "In traditional Judaism," he states, "exile is not solely the condition of the Jews, but characterizes the situation of the world in general."[20] By highlighting absence and the incompleteness of human existence, "the concept of exile opposes itself to any attempt to underwrite 'the history of the conquerors.'"[21] Negating exile, in contrast, goes hand in hand with justifying the history of the victors, a history that erases the past of the conquered. The negation of the exile shapes a "Zionist conscience" that rests on "effacing and repression," on the erasure not only of Jewish life in diaspora but also of Palestine's history prior to the Zionist return.[22] Mainstream Zionist imagination conceptually removes Palestinians from view, heralding the settlement of a land without a people for a people without a land, and such conceptual erasure proves a perilously short distance from actual practices and policies of the forcible dispossession of Palestinians.[23]

Raz-Krakotzkin's analysis of the negation of exile and return to history tropes in Zionist thought illuminates the intertwined shortcomings of Williams's theological argument for the State of Israel. First, Williams passes over the inextricable interconnection between mainstream Zionist visions and the establishment of the State of Israel, on the one hand, and Palestinian dispossession, on the other. To be sure, he does make brief reference to "the outrage of Deir Yassin," site of the best-known massacre of Palestinians by Israeli forces during the 1948 war.[24] Yet Williams appears not to understand that for Palestinians, the outrage represented by Deir Yassin consists not primarily in the scores of Palestinians killed but in the village's representative status for the more than five hundred Palestinian towns and villages destroyed and the more than seven hundred thousand Palestinians made homeless during what Palestinians call the *Nakba*, or catastrophe, of 1948.[25]

Even Williams's critique of Israeli policies exposes the limits of his vision. What if, Williams asks, "a point comes at which the location of Israel under God becomes bound up with policies which undermine the possibilities for others of a stable homeland, the kind of setting which alone makes political virtue possible?"[26] Such a question should naturally lead one to emphasize that the creation of a Jewish state in Palestine, under-

19. Raz-Krakotzkin, *Exil et souveraineté*, 46.
20. Ibid., 39.
21. Ibid.
22. Ibid., 32.
23. See, for example, Raz-Krakotzkin, "A Peace without Arabs."
24. Williams, "Holy Land and Holy People," 301.
25. For a catalogue of the destroyed villages, see Abu-Sitta, *Atlas of Palestine, 1948*, and Khalidi, *All That Remains*. For a comprehensive overview of historical, legal, and political issues concerning Palestinian refugees from the 1948 War, see Badil's *Survey of Palestinian Refugees and Internally Displaced Persons, 2006–2007*.
26. Williams, "Holy Land and Holy People," 296.

stood as a state with a demographic Jewish majority within specific boundaries, required the expulsion of Palestinians from their homes, yet Williams avoids the essential task of launching such a fundamental critique. Williams can grant the importance of criticizing the violence and injustice of particular Israeli policies, such as those tied to its military occupation of the West Bank, East Jerusalem, and the Gaza Strip, but his analysis does not struggle with the violence and dispossession required to establish the type of polity he contends is the condition for faithful Jewish witness.[27] If Israel under God cannot adequately live out its witness as a paradigm nation as minority communities in diaspora, and if the State of Israel thus represents the condition for the fulfillment of that witness, then a place must be created in which the Jewish people can live as a majority. During the first half of the twentieth century, mainstream Zionists of the left and the right clearly recognized that establishing and securing such demographic hegemony would require Palestinian displacement (often euphemistically termed "transfer"). As Jacqueline Rose observes, Zionism "always knew the violence of its own path."[28] Williams, in contrast, passes over this Palestinian dispossession in almost complete silence: Palestinian exile is thus effaced in Williams's theological account, just as the theological value of Jewish life in exile is implicitly negated.

The second problem with Williams's description of the State of Israel as the condition of Jewish witness involves inadequately theorized conceptions of place and home. "To be hospitable, you must have a home," Williams claims, stressing the need for a "homeland" as an "intelligible requirement" for the "exercise of political virtue."[29] What he means by "home" and "homeland," Williams does not directly say. However, by attending to how Williams devalues minority life in diaspora, one can deduce the implied definitions: "home" would seem to be a place in which demographic hegemony has been secured within a bounded territory. Such a definition of home would accord well with standard nationalist conceptualizations of place that, as the geographer Doreen Massey explains, "have been attempts to fix the meaning of places, to enclose and defend them: they construct singular, fixed and static identities for places, and they interpret places and bounded enclosed spaces defined through counterposition against the Other who is outside."[30]

Such nationalist construals of place, Massey contends, fail to do justice to the complex and fluid character of place. Massey explains that "what is specific about a place, its iden-

---

27. Williams grants that Christians must not collude "with uncritical attitudes towards Israeli government policy" (ibid., 294), yet by remaining silent about the massive dispossession of 1948 essential for the founding of the State of Israel, Williams practices his own form of theological collusion.

28. Rose, *Last Resistance*, 13. For an overview of Palestinian dispossession in the course of the *Nakba*, see Pappé, *The Ethnic Cleansing of Palestine*.

29. Williams, "Holy Land and Holy People," 296.

30. Massey, *Space, Place, and Gender*, 168. For Massey, accounts of place in terms of "the security of boundaries" and of the "defensive and counterpositional definition of identity" such boundaries aim to secure are "culturally masculine" (7). It is no accident that the Israeli Zochrot Association, which seeks to "remember the *Nakba* in Hebrew" through the physical commemoration of destroyed Palestinian villages inside Israel has chosen as a name the feminine plural participle of the Hebrew verb *zachar*, "to remember," juxtaposing "masculine" character of nationalist understandings of history and place with emplaced acts of "feminine" counter-memory. See chap. 10 of my *States of Exile*, as well as Bronstein, "*Nakba* in Hebrew," 221.

tity, is always formed by the juxtaposition and co-presence there of particular sets of social interrelations, and by the effects which that juxtaposition and co-presence produce."[31] In contrast to nationalist portrayals of place as simple, static, and bounded, Massey advocates a complex and fluid "view of place" in which "localities can in a sense be present in one another, both inside and outside at the same time," an understanding of place that "stresses the construction of specificity through interrelations rather than through the imposition of boundaries and the counterposition of one identity against another."[32] The critical task, then, is to uncover the complexity and fluidity of places that nationalist imaginations seek to obscure or erase.[33] In Israel-Palestine specifically, the challenge facing a theological assessment of Zionism and the State of Israel is to embrace the binational character of Israel-Palestine's places as a promise rather than to reject it as a threat to be walled off or uprooted. This critical task takes on greater urgency given what analysts have described as the eclipse of a two-state resolution of the Palestinian-Israeli conflict.[34] In such a context, searching for binational forms of coexistence that go beyond the dreams of homogeneous space fostered by nation-state ideologies—perhaps a binational federation of Israeli and Palestinian communities—becomes imperative.[35]

Yoder, Agamben, and the Witness of Exile in the Land

Williams's theological evaluation of the State of Israel falls short by not taking up this critical task, succumbing instead to nationalist portrayals of place as tightly bounded and fixed.[36] Williams's failure on this score is regrettable, given that his theological reflections on the Palestinian-Israeli conflict otherwise have much to commend them, including his affirmation of the mystery of God's enduring covenantal relationship with the Jewish people and his concern that Israeli and Palestinian alike might live securely in the land.[37]

---

31. Massey, *Space, Place, and Gender*, 168.

32. Ibid., 7.

33. The Zochrot Association discussed in n. 30, above, embodies such critical practice in its commemorations at the sites of destroyed Palestinian villages. Through such actions they call attention to (while also creating) what Michel Foucault called heterotopias, by which he meant "something like counter-sites, a kind of effectively enacted utopia in which the real sites, all the other real sites that can be found within the culture, are simultaneously represented, contested, and inverted." See Foucault, "Of Other Spaces," 24. Through the highlighting and creating of such heterotopias, or what anthropologists Efrat Ben-Ze'ev and Ibrahim Aburaiya call "middle-ground" spaces, at the sites of destroyed Palestinian villages, the Zionist effacing of Palestinian exile is uncovered and contested. See Ben Ze'ev and Aburaiya, "'Middle-Ground' Politics and the Re-Palestinianization of Places in Israel."

34. For one example among many, see the essays in Hilal, *Where Now for Palestine?* and Makdisi, *Palestine Inside Out*.

35. Among recent arguments for some form of binational accommodation in Palestine-Israel, see Benvenisti, *Son of the Cypresses*; Tilley, *One-State Solution*; and Abunimah, *One Country*.

36. "I am not discussing here the rights and wrongs of binational or unitary solutions to the tormenting problems of the region," Williams stresses ("Holy Land and Holy People," 296). Such a refusal to discuss political formations beyond the nation-state represents an abdication of theological responsibility.

37. Williams writes that "I cannot understand any attitude that assumes the calling of the Jewish people is not still a calling to be special, by God's gift and grace" (ibid., 302). Some of Williams's critics arguably engage in a supersessionist form of argumentation. Jonathan Kuttab, for example, insists on juxtaposing the spiritual

These shortcomings of Williams's argument can be addressed, I contend, by jettisoning his problematic recapitulation of the Zionist negation of exile: as an examination of the writings of John Howard Yoder and Giorgio Agamben shows, the perspective from exile can shape a theology of landedness that disrupts the form of the nation-state.

Like Williams, Yoder sought to think beyond theological repudiations of Judaism. Like Williams, Yoder understood the people Israel as called to live the embodied witness of a paradigm nation. Like Williams, Yoder asserted that Christians must grapple with Jews about what it means to witness to God today. Yoder differed from Williams, however, in advancing a positive theological evaluation of Jewish life in exile, an analytical move that results in an assessment of Zionism and the State of Israel sharply divergent from that of Williams.

In a posthumously published collection of essays, Yoder maintained that the Jewish-Christian schism "did not have to be," claiming that the divide between Christians and Jews could start to be overcome through a recognition of a common calling to seek the *shalom* of the cities of their exile. This calling, Yoder believed, had been better preserved within the Rabbinic Judaism of the diaspora than in a Christianity that had become all too much at home in the world, captive to what Yoder termed the "Constantinian" identification with the dominant social order.[38] Exile, for Yoder, represents an ethic, theology, and spirituality of "not being in charge," of embracing "galut as vocation."[39] This missiological interpretation of exile emerges from Yoder's narration of the people Israel's history as a story of a people called by God to be radically dependent upon God alone. Israel's fundamental identity "was not defined first by a theoretical monotheism, by cult or *kaschrut*, nor by the Decalogue. It was rather defined by the claim of the tribes to 'have no king but JHWH/Adonai,'" a claim that developed from the Abrahamic and Mosaic trust in God and that stood in uneasy tension with, and at times pointed toward the rejection of, Israelite monarchy.[40] The people Israel, in Yoder's account, are called to embody this paradigmatic existence of radical reliance upon God alone in order to bear witness to God's wisdom and righteousness. The arc of the biblical narrative, from Abraham to Jesus, bears witness to this vocation. "What begins in Abraham, and crests in Jesus," Yoder insists, "is not merely a different set of ideas about the world or about morality: it is a new definition of God. A

---

with the political, Christ's universal kingdom with "the Old Testament covenant of tribal possession" it has superseded ("An Open Letter," 306). Robert Tobin, meanwhile, contrasts "Christian and Jewish conceptions of covenant and belonging" with one another, presenting one as marked by "radical inclusiveness" and the other by "tribal exclusiveness" ("On Knowing One's Place," 317). I differ from these critiques in that I join Williams in affirming God's enduring covenant with the Jewish people, while denying the linkage Williams establishes between such an affirmation and a positive theological evaluation of the modern State of Israel.

38. See Yoder, *Jewish-Christian Schism*. Yoder began distributing these essays as a Shalom Desktop Packet starting in 1996, one year before his death. For critical evaluations of Yoder's theological revision of the Jewish-Christian relationship, see the introductions, chapter responses, and afterword by editors Ochs and Cartwright in the published version of the collection; chaps. 1–3 of Weaver, *States of Exile*; and Friesen, "Yoder and the Jews."

39. For Yoder, Jeremiah's call to the exiles in Jer 29:7 was a call to embrace "galut as vocation." *The Jewish-Christian Schism*, 190. Yoder characterizes the style of theo-political witness to which Jews and Christians are both called as one of "not being in charge." Ibid., chap. 9, "On Not Being in Charge."

40. Ibid., 71.

God enters into relations with people who does not fit into the designs of human communities and their rules."[41]

What connects Abraham's radical reliance on God to the insistence in the holy war traditions that God, not the people, will fight and to Jeremiah's admonition to the uprooted people Israel to seek the peace of the city of their exile (Jer 29:7) is the calling to trust in God alone for one's protection and salvation and to embody a communal politics of "not being in charge" commensurate with that trust. Yoder explains that this trust in God "opens the door to his saving intervention. It is the opposite of making one's own political/military arrangements. Jeremiah's abandoning statehood for the future is thus not so much forsaking an earlier hope as it is returning to the original trust in JHWH."[42] Israelite kingship (or, to be anachronistic, "statehood") is, in this telling of the biblical narrative, something of an anomaly, subject to critique from within the scriptural witness that points back to Israel's reliance on God.[43] The exile in Babylon thus represents not a disruption in God's plans for his people but rather an opportunity to return to radical dependence on God. "The move to Babylon was not a two-generation parenthesis, after which the Davidic or Solomonic project was supposed to take up again where it had left off. It was rather the beginning, under a firm fresh prophetic mandate, of a new phase of the Mosaic project."[44]

Biblical exile, in Yoder's telling, thus cannot be reduced simply to divine punishment but in fact represents a new chapter in the people Israel's learning to depend on God alone, bearing witness through that reliance to God's wisdom and righteousness. This positive judgment concerning exile in turn informs Yoder's understanding of post-biblical history. While Christianity abandoned the path of radical dependence on God alone, entering into fateful compromises with empire (summed up for Yoder by the term *Constantinianism*), Rabbinic Judaism kept alive the "not in charge" way of life proclaimed by Jeremiah and fulfilled in Jesus. Thus, Yoder claims that "for over a millennium the Jews of the diaspora were the closest thing to the ethic of Jesus existing on any significant scale anywhere in Christendom."[45] Zionism, in turn, represented for Yoder a Jewish counterpart of Christian Constantinianism, a falling away from the vocation of embodying a counter-politics of radical dependence on God alone amidst empires that glory in military might. "The whole point of Hebrew identity since Abraham is a call to be doing something else amidst the world's power arenas," Yoder insists. "It is only by being something different that Jewry in fact has survived; it is only in order to be something morally different that Jewry is called to survive."[46] Zionism, with its drive for the Jewish people to be a nation like other

41. Ibid., 243.

42. Ibid., 71.

43. Yoder notes that "both in doctrine and in sociology the king is relativized. He is at best the servant of divine righteousness, not its origin," ibid., 73. For Yoder, the Israelite temptation to kingship prefigures the Christian temptation of Constantinianism. Cartwright observes that for Yoder, the "Davidic Project" of constituting "a monarchy in Jerusalem was prototypical of Christian forms of faithlessness." Cartwright, "Editors' Introduction," in Yoder, *Jewish-Christian Schism*, 20.

44. Yoder, *Jewish-Christian Schism*, 184. Also: "To be scattered is not a hiatus, after which normality will resume. From Jeremiah's time on . . . dispersion shall be the calling of the Jewish faith community" (183).

45. Ibid., 81–82.

46. Ibid., 85.

nations, threatens to compromise this calling. Yet in the midst of Zionism triumphant, a Jewish minority, represented by thinkers and groups as diverse as Martin Buber, Steven Schwarzschild, and the anti-Zionist, ultra-Orthodox *neturei karta*, have in different ways rejected "the model of nationalism, triumphalism, and the very notion that Jews should want to be like their neighbors even in external social organization."[47]

This abbreviated summary of Yoder's revision of the Jewish-Christian schism has sought to underscore the fact that attempts to move beyond theologies of replacement or supersession need not join Williams in valorizing the State of Israel as the condition for faithful Jewish witness today.[48]

However, skeptics might ask, can a political theology of exile offer a vision of life in the land? For example, is Yoder's exilic theology unable to say anything affirmative about Jewish landedness, as his critics contend?[49] Apart from critiquing specific forms of Zionism, what might a theology of exile have to say about the emplaced realities of Palestinians and Israelis? Answers to these questions can be found within Yoder's work, albeit in undeveloped form, but before turning to consider his responses, one can observe that the tropes of diaspora, exile, and the refugee have been advanced by a wide variety of critical theorists offering political visions that disrupt and transcend nationalist politics based on seeking demographic hegemony within defined territories.[50] The reflections of Italian philosopher Giorgio Agamben on the figure of the refugee and on Jerusalem are particularly suggestive of the type of landed politics with which Yoder's theology of exile would have strong affinity.[51]

Taking a short essay by Hannah Arendt as his starting point, Agamben contends that "the refugee is perhaps the only thinkable figure for the people of our time and the only category in which one may see today—at least until the process of dissolution of the nation-state and of its sovereignty has achieved its completion—the forms and limits

---

47. Ibid. "A tiny but growing number of Jews with strong roots in the theology of Jewish existence before Auschwitz," Yoder observed, "have since the beginnings of Zionism seen Israeli statehood in the same terms in which Jotham (Judg. 9) and Samuel (I Sam. 8) saw Canaanite kingship: not as an absolute evil which it should be possible to reject completely, but as an accommodation, regrettable, to the ways of the Gentiles, an innovation which will disappoint, which will not deliver on its promises." Ibid., 84–85.

48. Problems with Yoder's account certainly exist. Yoder's critics have rightly expressed concern that the way in which he develops his vision of Christians and Jews discovering a shared vocation of living the embodied witness of communities in exile threatens to obscure or even deny any positive theological value to Jewish difference. In addition to the critical introductions, chapter responses, and afterword by Cartwright and Ochs in Yoder, *Jewish-Christian Schism*, see Boyarin, "Judaism as a Free Church." Yet such problems can be addressed, I believe, without requiring a qualification of Yoder's retrieval of exile as theological counter-politics; see Boyarin, "Judaism as a Free Church," and Weaver, *States of Exile*, chaps. 1 and 3.

49. Michael Cartwright expresses this concern by claiming that Yoder has broken apart the "triad" of Torah–people–land. See Cartwright, "Afterword: 'If Abraham Is Our Father,'" in Yoder, *The Jewish-Christian Schism*, 219.

50. Representative works include Appadurai, *Modernity at Large*, esp. 21–22; Boyarin and Boyarin, *Powers of Diaspora*; and James Clifford, "Diasporas."

51. I will be examining the second chapter of Agamben's *Means without End*, titled "Beyond Human Rights," originally published in English as "We Refugees," trans. Michael Rocke in *Symposium*. I will follow Binetti and Casarino's translation of *Means without End* except in one place, for reasons discussed in n. 58, below.

of a coming political community."⁵² The refugee, according to Agamben, represents "a disquieting element in the order of the nation-state," in that "by breaking the identity between the human and the citizen and that between nativity and nationality, it brings the originary fiction of sovereignty to crisis."⁵³ The intrusion of the refugee disrupts the nationalist attempt to collapse nation and territory into one another. The refugee thus stands either as a threat or as the harbinger of a new form of political community. For Agamben, it is clearly the latter, as the refugee confronts nation-states with the necessity of finding "the courage to question the very principle of the inscription of nativity as well as the trinity of state-nation-territory that is founded on that principle" and of discovering new political forms.⁵⁴

Agamben's writings on the shape of such new political forms are for the most part elusive and cryptic.⁵⁵ His vision begins to achieve specificity, however, in his discussion of Jerusalem and Israel-Palestine. From the observation that "one of the options taken into consideration for solving the problem of Jerusalem is that it becomes—simultaneously and without any territorial partition—the capital of two different states," Agamben extrapolates what he calls "the paradoxical condition of reciprocal extraterritoriality (or, better yet, aterritoriality)" as "a model of new international relations."⁵⁶ In the case of Israel-Palestine, such a politics of reciprocal extraterritoriality would represent an exodus from captivity to political programs wedded to the form of the nation-state (be they mainstream Zionist or Palestinian nationalist), with their drive to secure demographic hegemony or even exclusivity within policed borders, programs that in Israel-Palestine have, through a series of legal and physical exclusions, reduced Palestinian existence to "bare life."⁵⁷ "Instead of two national states separated by uncertain and threatening boundaries," Agamben explains, "one could imagine two political communities dwelling in the same region and in exodus one into the other, divided from each other by a series of reciprocal extraterritorialities, in which the guiding concept would no longer be the *ius* [right] of the citizen but rather the *refugium* [refuge] of the individual."⁵⁸

Such a politics of reciprocal extraterritoriality acts to "perforate" "homogeneous national territories," turning them into spaces in which all who dwell within them stand "in

---

52. Agamben, *Means without End*, 16. Agamben refers to Arendt's essay, "We Refugees," most recently included in Hannah Arendt, *The Jewish Writings*.

53. Agamben, *Means without End*, 21.

54. Ibid., 24.

55. See, for example, Agamben, *Coming Community*.

56. Agamben, *Means without End*, 24.

57. For analyses of contemporary realities in Israel-Palestine drawing on Agamben's notion of "bare life," see Hanafi, "Spacio-cide and Bio-Politics," and Youssef, "Peace Material."

58. Agamben, "We Refugees," 118. I have used Rocke's translation of this passage, given Binetti and Casarino's mistranslation of "in esodo l'una nell'altra" as "in a condition of exodus from each other" in *Means without Ends*, 24. The prepositional phrase "nell'altra" means *into* the other, not *from* the other. Rocke's translation, in addition to being grammatically correct, preserves Agamben's point that the two communities are heading out from a past of being bound to the circumscribed politics of the nation-state into a future of being mutually implicated with each other. For the original Italian, see Agamben, *Mezzi senza fine*, 27.

a position of exodus or refuge" into each other.[59] In the case of Israel-Palestine, such perforation means the disruption of geographies of exclusivist possession, and the uncovering of a binational geography shaped by exile. Taking up Arendt's description of refugees as "the vanguard of their people," Agamben applies the phrase to the 425 Palestinians whom Israel had expelled to the hills of southern Lebanon at the time he wrote the essay. But, he explains, these refugees are a "vanguard"

> not necessarily or not merely in the sense that they might form the originary nucleus of a future national state, or in the sense that they might solve the Palestinian question in a way just as insufficient as the way in which Israel has solved the Jewish question. Rather, the no-man's-land in which they are refugees has already started from this very moment to act back onto the territory of the state of Israel by perforating it and altering it in such a way that the image of that snowy mountain has become more internal to it than any other region of Eretz Israel. Only in a world in which the spaces of states have been thus perforated and topologically deformed and in which the citizen has been able to recognize the refugee that he or she is—only in such a world is the political survival of humankind today thinkable.[60]

Agamben thus parallels Yoder's insistence that true political identity is discovered from the perspective of the exile or the refugee. Furthermore, Yoder's theology of exile results in a vision of landedness quite similar to Agamben's notion of reciprocal extraterritorialities, a similarity most evident in Yoder's discussion of the "otherness of Jerusalem." For Yoder, "the otherness of Jerusalem, as cipher for the otherness of God, points us away from possessiveness and toward the redefinition of providence so as to favor the outsider," thus enacting a negative judgment on nationalist politics that establish exclusivist correlations between nation and territory.[61] The recognition that the land belongs to God, that we are all exiles who ultimately have our dwelling in God (Ps 90:1) brings with it a critical judgment on any human claims to sovereignty. Any such appropriation of sovereignty and possession, Yoder maintains, must be evaluated according to "whom it excludes or expels." God's people do not fulfill their witness as a paradigm nation by replicating nationalist politics of exclusion and dispossession, but are instead called to embody a politics of exile in the land. "Those who enter Jerusalem's gates sing that it is 'built to be a city where people come together in unity' (Ps 122:3)," Yoder observes. Accordingly, he concludes, "Those people are qualified to work at the building of the city who build it for others."[62]

A theology that does not join Williams in negating exile but instead embraces exile as the location of the witness of God's people can thus offer a positive account of life in the land, one that transcends the nation-state politics to which Williams remains beholden. Ironically, Williams's reflections themselves offer hints of a path not taken. "If only Jerusalem could be, in the full biblical sense, a sign lifted up among the nations, not of nationalist rivalry but of common belonging!" Williams concludes his essay. While

---

59. Agamben, *Means without End*, 25.

60. Ibid., 25–26.

61. Yoder, *Jewish-Christian Schism*, 162. "Authentic reverence before divine sovereignty must accordingly mean a critical judgment upon nationhood/statehood in its modern as well as its medieval forms" (163).

62. Ibid., 164.

such a future "seems almost unimaginable," it is nevertheless our job "to imagine, day by day, and to pray and work and risk for that end and for all that goes with it."[63] If Williams had taken this conclusion seriously, he would have been able to offer a true liberation theology advocating a binational future of mutuality in Israel-Palestine, one that stressed the common belonging of Israeli and Palestinian in one land, their mutual exodus one into the other, rather than baldly insisting on the State of Israel as the condition for the Jewish people's contemporary witness as the paradigm nation. For Williams to be able to articulate such a theology, however, would require him to revisit his problematic negation of exile. Williams's own writings would assist him in doing so. As he underscores elsewhere: "Christ will always be in exile, a refugee, in a world constrained by endless struggles for advantage, where success lies always in establishing your position at the expense of another's."[64] A political theology of common belonging, be it in Israel-Palestine or elsewhere, must be attentive to the exclusions political formations create and the violence and dispossession they perpetrate, in the process of moving haltingly toward a politics in which all persons will come to recognize the exiles that they are, and so embrace the task of seeking the peace of the cities of their exile.

63. Williams, "Holy Land and Holy People," 303.
64. Williams, *Christ on Trial*, 45.

Bibliography

Abunimah, Ali. *One Country: A Bold Proposal to End the Palestinian-Israeli Impasse*. New York: Metropolitan, 2006.

Abu-Sitta, Salman. *Atlas of Palestine, 1948*. London: Palestine Land Society, 2005.

Agamben, Giorgio. *The Coming Community*. Translated by Michael Hardt. Minneapolis: University of Minnesota Press, 1993.

———. *Means without End: Notes on Politics*. Translated by Vincenzo Binetti and Cesare Casarino. Minneapolis: University of Minnesota Press, 2000.

———. *Mezzi senza fine: Note sulla politica*. Turin: Bollati Boringhieri, 1996.

———. "We Refugees." Translated by Michael Rocke. *Symposium* 49 (1995) 114–19.

Appadurai, Arjun. *Modernity at Large: Cultural Dimensions of Globalization*. Minneapolis: University of Minnesota Press, 1996.

Arendt, Hannah. "We Refugees." In *The Jewish Writings*, edited by Jerome Kohn and Ron H. Feldman, 264–74. New York: Schocken, 2007.

Badil. *Survey of Palestinian Refugees and Internally Displaced Persons, 2006–2007*. Bethlehem: Badil Resource Center for Palestinian Residency and Refugee Rights, 2007.

Benvenisti, Meron. *Son of the Cypresses: Memories, Reflections, and Regrets from a Political Life*. Berkeley: University of California Press, 2007.

Ben Ze'ev, Efrat, and Ibrahim Aburaiya. "'Middle-Ground' Politics and the Re-Palestinianization of Places in Israel." *International Journal of Middle East Studies* 36 (2004) 639–55.

Boyarin, Daniel. "Judaism as a Free Church: Footnotes to John Howard Yoder's *The Jewish-Christian Schism Revisited*." *Cross Currents* 56 (2007) 6–21.

Boyarin, Daniel, and Jonathan Boyarin. *Powers of Diaspora: Two Essays on the Relevance of Jewish Culture*. Minneapolis: University of Minnesota Press, 2002.

Bronstein, Eitan. "The *Nakba* in Hebrew: Israeli-Jewish Awareness of the Palestinian Catastrophe and Internal Refugees." In *Catastrophe Remembered: Palestine, Israel, and the Internal Refugees*, edited by Nur Masalha, 214–43. London: Zed, 2005.

Clifford, James. "Diasporas." *Cultural Anthropology* 9 (1994) 303–38.

Don-Yehiya, Eliezer. "The Negation of Galut in Religious Zionism." *Modern Judaism* 12 (1992) 129–55.

Foucault, Michel. "Of Other Spaces." *Diacritics* 16 (1986) 22–27.

Friesen, Duane. "Yoder and the Jews: Cosmopolitan Homelessness as Ecclesial Model." In *A Mind Patient and Untamed: Assessing John Howard Yoder's Contributions to Theology, Ethics, and Peacemaking*, edited by Ben C. Ollenburger and Gayle Gerber Koontz, 145–60. Telford, PA: Cascadia, 2004.

Hanafi, Sari. "Spacio-cide and Bio-Politics: The Israeli Colonial Conflict from 1947 to the Wall." In *Against the Wall: Israel's Barrier to Peace*, edited by Michael Sorkin, 158–73. New York: New Press, 2005.

Hauerwas, Stanley, and William H. Willimon. *Resident Aliens: Life in the Christian Colony*. Nashville: Abingdon, 1989.

Hilal, Jamil, editor. *Where Now for Palestine? The Demise of the Two-State Solution*. London: Zed Books, 2007.

Huebner, Harry. "The Morality of Peacemaking: Reflections on the Arab/Israeli Conflict." *Conrad Grebel Review* 4 (1986) 201–24.

Khalidi, Walid, editor. *All That Remains: The Palestinian Villages Occupied and Depopulated by Israel in 1948*. Washington, DC: Institute for Palestine Studies, 1992.

Kuttab, Jonathan. "An Open Letter to Archbishop Rowan Williams." In *Challenging Christian Zionism: Theology, Politics, and the Israel-Palestine Conflict*, edited by Naim Ateek, Cedar Duaybis, and Maurine Tobin, 304–7. London: Melisende, 2005.

Lewis, Helen. "A Response to Rowan Williams' Message to the Sabeel Conference." In *Challenging Christian Zionism: Theology, Politics, and the Israel-Palestine Conflict*, edited by Naim Ateek, Cedar Duaybis, and Maurine Tobin, 319–28. London: Melisende, 2005.

Makdisi, Saree. *Palestine Inside Out: An Everyday Occupation*. New York: Norton, 2008.

Massey, Doreen. *Space, Place, and Gender*. Minneapolis: University of Minnesota Press, 1994.

Myers, David N. *Re-Inventing the Jewish Past*. New York: Oxford University Press, 1995.

Pappé, Ilan. *The Ethnic Cleansing of Palestine*. Oxford: Oneworld, 2006.
Piterberg, Gabriel. *The Returns of Zionism: Myths, Politics, and Scholarship in Israel*. New York: Verso, 2008.
Ratzaby, Shalom. "The Polemic about the Negation of the Diaspora in the 1930s and Its Roots." *Journal of Israeli History* 16 (1995) 19–38.
Raz-Krakotzkin, Amnon. *Exil et souveraineté: Judaïsme, sionisme, et pensée binationale*. Paris: La Fabrique, 2007.
———. "A National-Colonial Theology—Religion, Orientalism, and the Construction of the Secular in Zionist Discourse." *Tel Aviver Jahrbuch für deutsche Geschichte* 30 (2002) 312–26.
———. "A Peace without Arabs: The Discourse of Peace and the Limits of Israeli Consciousness." In *After Oslo: New Realities, Old Problems*, edited by George Giacaman and Dag Jorund Lonning, 59–76. London: Pluto, 1998.
Rose, Jacqueline. *The Last Resistance*. New York: Verso, 2007.
Ruether, Rosemary Radford. "Christian Zionism and Main Line Western Christian Churches." In *Challenging Christian Zionism: Theology, Politics, and the Israel-Palestine Conflict*, edited by Naim Ateek, Cedar Duaybis, and Maurine Tobin, 146–62. London: Melisende, 2005.
Schlabach, Gerald. "Deuteronomic or Constantinian: What Is the Most Basic Problem for Christian Social Ethics?" In *The Wisdom of the Cross: Essays in Honor of John Howard Yoder*, edited by Stanley Hauerwas, Chris K. Huebner, Harry Huebner, and Mark Thiessen Nation, 449–71. Grand Rapids: Eerdmans, 1999.
Tilley, Virginia. *The One-State Solution: A Breakthrough for Peace in the Israeli-Palestinian Deadlock*. Ann Arbor: University of Michigan Press, 2005.
Tobin, Robert B. "On Knowing One's Place: A Liberationist Critique of Rowan Williams' 'Holy Land and Holy People.'" In *Challenging Christian Zionism: Theology, Politics, and the Israel-Palestine Conflict*, edited by Naim Ateek, Cedar Duaybis, and Maurine Tobin, 308–18. London: Melisende, 2005.
Weaver, Alain Epp. *States of Exile: Visions of Diaspora, Witness, and Return*. Scottdale, PA: Herald, 2008.
Williams, Rowan. *Christ on Trial: How the Gospel Unsettles Our Judgment*. Grand Rapids: Eerdmans, 2000.
———. "Holy Land and Holy People." In *Challenging Christian Zionism: Theology, Politics, and the Israel-Palestine Conflict*, edited by Naim Ateek, Cedar Duaybis, and Maurine Tobin, 293-303. London: Melisende, 2005.
Yoder, John Howard. *The Jewish-Christian Schism Revisited*. Edited by Michael G. Cartwright and Peter Ochs. Grand Rapids: Eerdmans, 2003.
Youssef, Maisaa. "Peace Material: Giorgio Agamben and the Israeli Palestinian Peace Accords." *New Formations* 62 (2007) 106–22.

John Howard Yoder's Ecclesiology
As Seen by an Appreciative Critic

Waldemar Janzen

Impressed but Uneasy

I FIRST ENCOUNTERED YODER'S THOUGHT IN MY SECOND YEAR OF SEMINARY STUDY AT the Evangelical Lutheran Seminary in Waterloo, Ontario, in the 1954–55 academic year. With some excitement, several younger Mennonite ministers introduced me to the first issue of a pamphlet series called *Concern*, which promised to be an avant-garde voice of younger Mennonite theologians. The pamphlet contained the essay "The Anabaptist Dissent: The Logic of the Place of the Disciple in Society," by a twenty-seven-year-old John Howard Yoder.[1] This article called forth in me a reaction that was both deep and ambivalent, and one that has not changed much in my over fifty years of engagement with Yoder's theology.

For both Yoder and me it was World War II and its aftereffects that set the stage for our theological thinking.[2] Born of Mennonite parents in Ukraine, I had not experienced "church" during the atheist Soviet years. As refugees in Germany, my mother and I had established temporary "church homes" in Lutheran churches. We received much hospitality, both materially and spiritually, from Protestant and Catholic Christians (and from many without a Christian commitment).[3]

With this background I read Yoder. His case for Christian pacifism was clearly argued and helpful. Although I had by now become a member of a Mennonite congregation in Canada, I was struggling intensely with the question of nonresistance. World War III loomed on the horizon, at least in the perception of many refugees from Europe. Conscription might be imminent, and I would be of conscription age. War was not theory

---

1. Yoder, "Anabaptist Dissent."

2. Earl Zimmerman writes: "The social and political issues in postwar Europe, relationships with European Mennonites, ecumenical conversations with European Protestants, and the WCC debate on the question of war, were the significant arenas within which John Howard Yoder first formulated and articulated his theological ethics." *Practicing the Politics of Jesus*, 94; see also 70–100.

3. For more details, see Janzen, *Growing Up in Turbulent Times*.

for me, but experienced reality. Eventually, it was the peace position—which I came to accept as biblically mandated—together with my family heritage, that kept me in the Mennonite fold. Thus Yoder's clarion call to peace was a help to me.

Yoder's peace position was tied, however, to an ecclesiology that I found troubling in the extreme. Almost all the vintage axioms, key words, and phrases of his theology were already present in that early essay.[4] Christian life is defined most basically in *ethical* terms.[5] *Specific* ethical guidance sufficient for life is found in the *New* Testament. The church is the *people of God*, made up of those committed to obedient *discipleship*, centrally marked by a life of love expressing itself in *nonviolence* and the readiness to suffer, in other words, to *take up the cross*. Suffering will mark the people of God, for their life according to the *ethic of Jesus* will unavoidably *clash with the principalities and powers*, that is, the unregenerated *world* with its violence. The church is a *sociological* structure among others, but one marked by a historically distinct and *new ethical reality* expressive of the *kingdom of God* that has come with the death and resurrection of Jesus and will be established fully in God's time. This sociological otherness makes the church a *sect*.[6] In the present, the Holy Spirit empowers "[t]he disciple, i.e., the Christian who sees his 'Christian-ness' as being an ethical matter,"[7] to live *in the perfection of Christ*. This, rather than mere forgiving mercy, is the meaning of grace.

Over against this sectarian, sociologically, and ethically defined Anabaptist *believers' church*, and sharply set apart from it, are the other churches that have suffered the "Constantinian shift" or "fall," the churches that have been seduced by Emperor Constantine's elevation of the church to worldly status and power. Toleration by the state is not the worst of this, however; the greater problem is the churches' assumption of their (ethical) *responsibility* for non-Christian society as axiomatic. This, according to Yoder, has obliterated the line between the violent state and the nonresistant church. The latter, he claims, can be responsible only for the ethics of its own life. God governs both church and state, but in distinct ways. Confusing this distinction has in turn led the "responsible" churches, both Catholic and Protestant, to continual ethical compromise. Since a life of following Jesus cannot be expected of general society, these churches have declared radical discipleship as impossible and therefore irrelevant. "What results is a relativism and opportunism, with no standards definable as valid for all, and with any compromise justified."[8] Through the centuries, "responsible" theologians have therefore drawn their theology and ethics from other sources: "from the Old Testament theocracy, from justification by faith, from Aristotle, or from the idea of the Kingdom of God (anywhere but from New Testament ethics)."[9] Rejection of the love ethic (a position apparently possessed

---

4. Not long before his death, Yoder referred retrospectively to this article as "my programmatic essay." Yoder, *For the Nations*, 3 n. 5.

5. Yoder, "Anabaptist Dissent," 45; all italics in the following summary are mine. This summary is not a précis, but follows instead my own arrangement of key points.

6. Yoder uses this term repeatedly, stating, however, that it should not be taken in the theological meaning of "sect." For Yoder's reflection on his later understanding and use of *sect*, see Yoder, *For the Nations*, 3–5.

7. Yoder, "Anabaptist Dissent," 49.

8. Ibid., 58.

9. Ibid., 50.

only by Anabaptists) as ultimately determinative "really leaves nothing else to build on than situation (opportunism) or sentiment (intuitionism)."[10]

The impact of Yoder's logic on me was profound and lasting. With Yoder, I sincerely wished to be a Christian, following Jesus in my daily living. I was also well aware that such a commitment could lead to suffering. But I had also come to know the church—in its Lutheran and Catholic versions—during my refugee life. How could Yoder, from the vantage point of a tiny perfectionist sect, tarnish all other Christians since Constantine as living lives guided merely by opportunism and intuitionism, rather than by the New Testament? Had all those Lutherans and Catholics who gave us food, shelter, protection, and help really acted from unreflected situation ethics and opportunism? Had they not been shaped by the Bible, the catechism, and other Christian sources taught to them by their Christian parents, teachers, and ministers? Yoder himself claimed that true Christian faith expresses itself not only in correct doctrine, but even more prominently in obedient Christian living. True enough, and I had experienced that witness by Lutherans and Catholics. I had since then also experienced the Christian love of Mennonite Central Committee workers, Mennonite relatives, and my new Mennonite home congregation in Waterloo, but their love was, in my perception, cut of no other cloth than the love extended to me by non-Mennonite Christians.

My experience in postwar Germany also made Yoder's disparaging of a Christian sense of "responsibility" for general society problematic. After Germany's total defeat and the breakdown of all its wider political and social structures, people looked to the one institution that had retained a semblance of respect and authority: the church (both Protestant and Catholic). It had not always been obedient to Christ under the dictatorships, but it had a ground to stand on—its biblical and historical faith—and from which to search for guidance for a defeated, demoralized, and suffering people. And it tried. In the church, I sensed a knowledge of the Holy One who directs history and offers grace, forgiveness, and new direction to those who seek. No matter how "Constantinian" the wider church might be from Yoder's perspective, I would not have wished it to have felt less "responsible" for the whole country than it did.[11]

I had a further problem with Yoder's article. After an externally turbulent childhood and youth, I had immigrated to Canada. We immigrants hoped for a country at peace, an orderly society, enough to eat, the means to meet our other daily needs, freedom of worship, and a future to which we could look forward; in biblical terms, the blessings of a promised land, although in my mind I never applied that term to Canada. Yoder's picture of the faithful Christian life as an inevitable collision course with the violence dominating all of the non-Christian or "Constantinian Christian" society surrounding us was not an inviting one. I knew all too well that Christian faith might lead to persecution, but to think of such suffering as the inescapable, even constitutive mark of faithful Christian living was too much like our experience in the Soviet Union. I asked myself: Is that actually the

---

10. Ibid., 64.

11. I realize now, of course, that "Constantinianism" means much more in Yoder's theology than Constantine's conversion. For a concise but very helpful interpretation of Yoder's "Constantinianism," see Huebner, "Christian Life as Gift and Patience," 28–30.

good news of God's salvation in Jesus Christ? Everything within me rebelled against such a view. Yoder mentions the resurrection once in his article, but the gloom and weight of a discipleship bound for the cross seemed to me to be the last word, an end in itself, which for me in "its general tone could hardly be called redemptive."[12] The result—and one that has remained in my mind ever since then—was an ambivalence in my attitude toward Yoder's theology.

Something I did not particularly notice when reading Yoder's article at that time was his almost exclusive recourse to the *New* Testament. He mentions the Old Testament only twice, and in both places it figures as an inappropriate source of theology and ethics resorted to by the mainline churches, leading to false theological conclusions that could have been avoided if the New Testament had been used instead. I was still unwary then of the widespread Mennonite dismissal of the Old Testament, so that these negative perspectives did not draw my attention.[13]

The following academic year, 1955–1956, saw me as a student at the Mennonite Biblical Seminary in Chicago. It was a rich year of encountering Mennonite intellectuals, including John Howard Yoder. I was also introduced to "The Anabaptist Vision"[14] by Harold S. Bender, which—as I recognized—formed the broader background and perspective for Yoder's thought but was not without problems for me.[15] I was not unwilling to learn from Yoder and Bender, but my initial ambivalence remained.[16] With time I discovered that other Mennonite scholars who, like I, are deeply respectful of Yoder also share a number of my reservations.[17]

As I pursued my own career in the field of Old Testament studies, I began to sense that greater recourse to the Old Testament might have enriched what seems to me to be, throughout Yoder's works, a rather one-sided ecclesiology. I believe that the heirs of Yoder's theology—and I am one of them—might profit from some of the Old Testament enrichments, if not correctives, that I can only begin to sketch very briefly in the second part of this essay.

---

12. Words with which Yoder describes British Puritanism in "Anabaptist Dissent," 53. Some years later, when I was already teaching at Canadian Mennonite Bible College, John Howard Yoder was our guest lecturer, and again, he conveyed to me the impression of proclaiming a discipleship defined one-sidedly by suffering; having the cross, rather than resurrection, as its end. When I tried to discuss this with him, he said, in a dismissive tone, something like this: "Oh, you want me to say happier things? I don't have to; enough others are doing that already."

13. For my later assessment of this matter, see Janzen, "Canonical Rethinking."

14. Bender, "Anabaptist Vision."

15. In particular, my Russian-Mennonite background seemed at times to be sidelined as a scarcely relevant, if not outrightly aberrant, branch of the Anabaptist-Mennonite story. A. James Reimer also associates his similarly ambivalent responses to Yoder with his own Russian–Canadian Mennonite background; see his "Theological Orthodoxy and Jewish Christianity," 432–33.

16. This may be the place to acknowledge the contribution of the honoree of this Festschrift, my longtime colleague and friend Harry Huebner, to my better understanding of Yoder's thought. I wish to thank him for the many stimulating and enriching conversations we had, both on Yoder and on many other topics.

17. A brief, kind, but open and comprehensive critique is offered by A. James Reimer in "Mennonites, Christ, and Culture." A more extensive, appreciative, but also critical review of Yoder's ecclesiology can be found in Enns, *The Peace Church*, 106–44.

THE CHURCH MADE STRANGE FOR THE NATIONS

Rethinking Aspects of Yoder's Ecclesiology

Israel and the Church: The Pilgrim People of God

John Howard Yoder builds his ecclesiology squarely on the New Testament, with only sporadic reference to the Old Testament.[18] With time I came to realize that my persistent ambivalence toward Yoder's ecclesiology is related to this "demotion" of the Old Testament in his writings.[19] I will argue below that the New Testament's understanding of the church—just like other major New Testament themes—is deeply rooted in the Old Testament, and that a more adequate recourse to the Old Testament can lead to much-needed correctives for certain imbalances in Yoder's ecclesiology.

My problem with Yoder's ecclesiology centers on the radical dualism that results from what he calls the "Constantinian shift."[20] Yoder claims throughout his work that the radical otherness of the true church, in its concrete political/social expression, from the world—the state, society, and all "power structures," as well as the "Constantinian" mainline churches that have aligned themselves to a smaller or greater extent with these—must inevitably lead to a collision course ending in suffering or martyrdom for the true church, understood as the "believers' church(es)." This suffering, or "the cross," as Yoder characteristically puts it, "is not a detour or a hurdle on the way to the kingdom, nor is it even the way to the kingdom; it is the kingdom come."[21] It is Yoder's stark characterization of this apparently ultimate goal of the road of discipleship, together with his underemphasis of the resurrection (although he assumes the latter), which makes suffering (if not always outright martyrdom) appear to be *the* validating mark of the church; a message that in "its general tone could hardly be called redemptive."[22] In the words of German Mennonite theologian Fernando Enns: "In the end, simply suffering *per se* would achieve legitimization."[23] A no less troubling consequence of this dualism is the apparent absence

---

18. This assessment is not invalidated by the fact that a fairly consistent position on Yoder's part regarding the Old Testament can be reconstructed on the basis of a few of his essays and some of his eventually published class notes. Especially relevant for this purpose are the two essays "The Original Revolution" and "If Abraham Is Our Father," in Yoder, *Original Revolution*, 13–33 and 91–110, respectively. (Yoder's interest in Rabbinic Judaism in his later years is a very different matter, although it throws much light on his eventual position on the Old Testament. This will be considered below.) A comprehensive and empathetic reconstruction of Yoder's position (in comparison to that of Oliver O'Donovan) has recently been offered by Paul Doerksen in his doctoral dissertation, "Beyond Suspicion," chap. 1, 19–95. Doerksen's fine study did not come to my attention until this essay was essentially completed, and limitations of time and space allow me only to refer to it in a few footnotes on the following pages.

19. I use *demotion* advisedly. *Neglect* would suggest an inadvertent lack of awareness on Yoder's part, which is quite unthinkable, while *rejection* would be too negative. Yoder certainly knew the Old Testament well and did use it very effectively at times.

20. Others have also perceived this as a problem and offered various proposals for addressing it. Gerald Schlabach's critique, like mine, has recourse to the Old Testament for proposing a corrective strategy. I agree with much of his argumentation, but cannot engage in dialogue with him here. See Schlabach, "Deuteronomic or Constantinian."

21. Yoder, *Politics of Jesus*, 61.

22. See above, n. 12.

23. Enns, *Peace Church*, 142.

of a positive theological valuation of the biological and social realms of life, such as the family, the land, and life-sustaining work, to name just a few.[24] What recourse can be found in turning to the roots of ecclesiology in the Old Testament for a modification of the one-sidedness in Yoder's theology, as I perceive it—a modification, however, that remains faithful to Jesus and the New Testament? Where are these roots to be found in the Old Testament?

Tracing the theme of the church from the New Testament back into the Old is as complex as tracing the trunk of a tree into its root system. The most obvious path to follow seems to lie in pursuing the Greek term *ekklesia* (church) to its Old Testament roots. The Greek occurrences of *ekklesia* in the Septuagint almost always translate the Hebrew word *qahal*.[25] In the Old Testament, *qahal* has the very general basic meaning of "assembled group of people." The nature of the gathering or assembly is determined by a modifier or the context (e.g., *qahal YHWH*, "assembly of the LORD," Deut 23:2; but also *qahal haneviim nibbeim*, "company of the prophets in a frenzy," 1 Sam 19:20). In other words, *qahal* by itself does not necessarily function as a theological term, much less as a technical designation of an ongoing faith group in any sense equivalent to *ekklesia* (church) in the New Testament and early Christianity.[26] Every other New Testament term traced to the Old Testament is even less helpful in leading us to the church's antecedent(s) in the Old Testament. Is there in the Old Testament a typologically closer equivalent to the New Testament's and early Christianity's "church"?

In his J. J. Thiessen Lectures at the Canadian Mennonite Bible College, Yale theologian George Lindbeck caught my interest when he stated that in Christianity's struggles for identity during its early centuries, only those churches survived that understood themselves in analogy to Old Testament Israel as a whole. All the others atrophied as "heresies" and died.[27] Other recent theologians have also argued for the historical continuity and typological correspondence of the church with "Israel," the people of God, over against the long-held assumption of a supersession of Israel by the church.[28]

I will sketch Lindbeck's argumentation briefly.[29] He defines the church as "the messianic pilgrim people of God *shaped by Israel's story*."[30] He tests this definition by asking two questions: First, "Is the church of which the Bible tells us primarily the people of God, or is some other designation more fundamental?" And second, "Does one get closer to its

---

24. Late in his life, and in response to frequent criticism, Yoder attempted to affirm the church's positive contribution to wider society (in addition to prophetic judgment inevitably leading to collision and persecution) in his little book *Body Politics* (1992). This, however, is but a small move toward addressing the deficiency named above.

25. See Schmidt, "εκκλησία [ekklesia]."

26. For a detailed survey of the range of connotations of *qahal*, extending from a numerically large assembly of people to specific delimitations of the composition of such an assembly, see the detailed survey of Old Testament books, segments, and literary strata by Hossfeld and Kindl in "lhq [*Qahal*]."

27. Lindbeck, "Church as Hermeneutical Community."

28. In his own way, Yoder also seeks continuity between Israel and the church; see the two articles in *The Original Revolution*, mentioned above, n. 18, and the discussion under "The 'Jeremianic Model,'" below.

29. Lindbeck, *Church in a Postliberal Age*, esp. 145–65, "The Church."

30. Ibid., 146 (my italics).

essence if one calls it, for example, the body of Christ or the community of the Spirit or the worshiping assembly or an event, an institution or a liberation movement?"[31] With these questions in mind, he tests his definition—taking it as his hypothesis—exegetically by pursuing four heuristic guidelines for reading the New Testament. Assuming Lindbeck's conclusions in advance, I will summarize them as findings.[32]

1. "Early communal Christian self-understanding was narrative-shaped." The Christian communal story was the story of real people "in all their actual and potential messiness" as well as their holiness. "An invisible church is as biblically odd as an invisible Israel."

2. "For the early Christians . . . Israel's history was their only history," to be seen, of course, "through the prism of Christ." And "the Hebrew Scriptures were the sole ecclesiological textbook" they had.

3. Not only was Israel's story the early Christians' only story; "[i]t was the whole of that story which they appropriated." The early Christians applied to themselves not only the favorable presentations of faithful remnants found in the Old Testament, but also all the accounts of Israel's wickedness and unfaithfulness. Thus Paul warns his readers not to be like the disobedient Israelites in the wilderness, considering this an actual danger for them (1 Cor 10:5–10). Peter warns that judgment will begin with the household of God, citing Old Testament references (1 Pet 4:17–18). An unfaithful church can be cut off just as an unfaithful synagogue can (Rom 11:21). More examples could be cited.

4. "From this it follows . . . that Israel and the church were one people for the early Christians . . . The Church is simply Israel in the time between the times."[33] "The inclusion of the Gentiles is represented in Ephesians as the most wondrous aspect of the work of Christ (Eph. 2:11—3:11)."

If Lindbeck's (and others') thinking along these lines is right—and I believe it is—then drawing on the Old Testament, not merely as historical background for Jesus and the New Testament but as canonical resource for interpreting Jesus's message and work, becomes imperative for Christians.[34] If that were taken seriously, then Yoder's ecclesiol-

---

31. Ibid., 148.

32. The quotations in the following four points are taken from ibid., 149–52.

33. A more nuanced yet compact analysis of the church as the "People of God' in continuity with Israel can be found in Harrington, *God's People in Christ*. See also Shaw, *Pilgrim People of God*, especially chap. 7, "Jesus and the People of God," 118–39.

34. I find this aspect missing or underdeveloped in Yoder's works. In his most explicit and nuanced treatment of canonical authority, Yoder mentions or alludes to the Old Testament a mere four times, in contrast to numerous references to the New Testament and its sub-parts. None of the four instances makes any clear statement regarding the Old Testament's authority. One could ask whether the frequent references to "Scripture" and "canon" include the Old Testament, but since all biblical examples adduced in Yoder's argumentation are drawn from the New Testament, this is at best very questionable. See Yoder, "Authority of the Canon," 265–90; for the four Old Testament references, see pp. 265, 282, 286, 288.

ogy would need to be reshaped at some significant points; but through such reshaping, it would come into its own in a way not evident to me as it stands.[35]

The "Jeremianic Model": Critique and Alternative Proposal

In his later years Yoder was increasingly drawn to Rabbinic Judaism. This also led him to devote more attention to the Old Testament, but in a manner that made it subservient to his already firmly established ecclesiology, derived from his reading of the New Testament and of the sixteenth-century Anabaptists. Instead of giving the Old Testament a voice in his interpretation of these sources, he now forced it into their service by developing his notion of a so-called Jeremianic shift, or model, on the basis of Jeremiah 29 and making that chapter the pivotal point for an idiosyncratic reconstruction of the whole Old Testament canon.[36]

The "Jeremianic shift" is spelled out most fully in Yoder's essay "'See How They Go with Their Face to the Sun.'"[37] He derives his Jeremianic model from a letter by the prophet Jeremiah, written from Jerusalem before its destruction in 587 BCE, to the Judeans already exiled to Babylon earlier. Jeremiah encourages the exiles to build houses, plant gardens, marry and have children, and generally "seek the welfare [*shalom*] of the city where I [God] have sent you into exile, and pray to the LORD on its behalf, for in its welfare you will find your welfare" (Jer 29:6–7).

Here, according to Yoder, begins "the Jeremianic phase of creating something qualitatively new in the history of religions"[38] that would last from Jeremiah's age to that of Theodore Hertzl. The main features of the new missionary faith community among the nations here supposedly initiated, and continued in the later synagogues, are these: (1) communal identity is provided by texts, with no need for temple and priesthood; (2) "worship" consists of reading and singing the texts; (3) ten households suffice to constitute a "valid local cell [a synagogue] of the world Jewish community"[39]—no priestly or hierarchical center is needed; (4) international unity of the faith community is sustained by intervisitation, intermarriage, commerce, and rabbinic consultation; and (5) the "ground floor of identity is the common life itself, the walk, *halakah* [i.e. law], and the shared remembering of the story behind it."[40]

---

35. Fernando Enns observes: "Yoder's schematized view [of a 'Constantinian' church and an idealized believers' church] is also seen in his failure to reflect theologically on the relationship between the church and Israel." Enns, *Peace Church*, 142.

36. Paul Doerksen highlights the centrality of this notion for Yoder: "The so-called Jeremianic shift might be described as the hinge upon which Yoder's theopolitical thought swings." Doerksen, "Beyond Suspicion," 58.

37. Published after Yoder's death in John Howard Yoder, *Jewish-Christian Schism*, 183–204. (First delivered as an address in 1995.) The essay's title is a line from Stefan Zweig's poem/drama *Jeremiah*; see below. See also the other essays in *Jewish-Christian Schism*.

38. Yoder, *Jewish-Christian Schism*, 186.

39. Ibid., 187.

40. Ibid.

Yoder introduces the Jeremianic model obliquely, by reviewing it in the form given to it by the German-Jewish author Stephan Zweig in his poem/drama *Jeremiah*. One might think at first that Yoder finds in Zweig's visionary art a happy literary rendering, selected from the Bible, that offers a suitable image of his own ideal of a Christian/Anabaptist faith community. The matter becomes problematic, however, when Yoder proceeds from art to exegesis by adducing heavy interpretive methodology to assert the claim that Jeremiah's letter is indeed the divinely authorized prophetic directive to bring about no less than a paradigm shift (my term here) in the form and direction of the people of God in the Old Testament and beyond.

To do so, Yoder employs a mix of historical-critical and canonical moves to reinterpret the Old Testament canon. David and Jeremiah become pivotal in his reconstruction. Interpreting the Deuteronomistic texts (especially Samuel-Kings) by privileging the "antimonarchical" passages (e.g., 1 Sam 8), Yoder judges the Davidic dynasty in Judah as well as the shorter monarchical rule in Israel to be a centuries-long story of apostasy. "God finally gave up on both of them," claims Yoder.[41] The demise of monarchy opened the way, according to Yoder, for the Jeremianic course correction toward Rabbinic Judaism centered in the synagogue, as characterized above. This Judaism became very adaptable worldwide to all kinds of situations, peacefully and skillfully "seeking the welfare of the city" for many centuries in multiple positive ways that are often not sufficiently recognized. Yoder almost turns effusive in praise of it.

The Jeremianic shift was not a start *de novo*, however, claims Yoder. The confusion of tongues and dispersion of nations in the Tower of Babel story (Gen 11) should not—as is generally done—be seen as judgment, but rather as grace. By scattering the tower builders, God returns them to a divinely intended life of dispersion. "Babel in the myth of Genesis places the multiplicity of cultures under the sign of the divine will."[42] Thus the Jeremianic model is, for Yoder, a return to God's primeval creation design.[43] Various other stories

---

41. Ibid., 188. One cannot but think of this view of the "Davidic project" as a retrospective reading of the Davidic story through the glasses of Yoder's "Constantinian fall" of the church. In seeing such a "fall" with the introduction of monarchy in Israel, and especially with David, supported largely by a reading of the Deuteronomistic History with a strong antimonarchical bias, Yoder adopts the perspective of Millard C. Lind, who posits a covenant-based pre-monarchical Israel, which waged "holy war" in utter trust of God, led by prophets and achieving victory divinely through miracles, in contrast to a later, monarchical Israel ruled by the Davidic dynasty and trusting in human military power. The prophets, however, continued to challenge these developments for centuries. See Lind, *Yahweh Is a Warrior*. A basic problem here, taken over by Yoder, is the narrowing of the analysis of monarchy to a dualism. In contrast to this, Gerald Gerbrandt, in a study demonstrating the basically pro-monarchical stance of the Deuteronomistic History, points out that the proper question is not "King or no king?" but rather, "What kind of kingship the Deuteronomist saw as ideal for Israel, or what role he expected the king to fulfill within Israel." Gerbrandt, *Kingship According to the Deuteronomistic History*, 189. Gerbrandt's research shows that not only is kingship desirable and necessary, according to the Deuteronomistic History, but that the ideal king acts as the administrator of covenant and of justice (pp. 189–94).

42. Yoder, *Jewish-Christian Schism*, 189. Yoder is correct insofar as the story does imply a protective grace, although its punitive meaning must also be acknowledged, especially on the basis of its place in a sequence of texts in Gen 1–11 that combines judgment and grace. The full grace dimension of the tower story does not lie in the dispersing, but follows in the call to Abraham issued in Gen 12.

43. The likelihood that the tower story was shaped during the exile draws it even closer to the Jeremianic perspective, according to Yoder.

scattered through the Old Testament are also paradigmatic for Israel's call to a mission as strangers among the nations, seeking the welfare of their host societies: the stories of Joseph, Daniel and friends, Esther and Mordecai. Dispersion, homelessness, and exile as mission are treated by Yoder as the faith community's almost mythically recurring model for all time, while any notions of "landedness" (not his term), permanence, or home represent control through the exertion of power and violence, that is, evidence of the Davidic/Constantinian fall.[44]

But what about the return from exile proclaimed by exilic and post-exilic prophets, implemented to a degree by the building of the Second Temple, and the missions of Ezra and Nehemiah? Yoder brushes these aside as "inappropriate deviations from the Jeremianic line" leading into God's future.[45]

What does one say to Yoder's Jeremianic model and its buttressing by embedding it in the Old Testament canon as reimagined by him? Peter Ochs, the Jewish coeditor of the volume containing Yoder's essay, responds very bluntly in his appended commentary: "But the image they [Zweig and Yoder] have of Jeremiah is not Jeremiah's own."[46] I concur. Jeremiah's letter, when interpreted in the context of the canonical book of Jeremiah, turns out to have a very different import than Yoder attributes to it. The exile is pictured throughout that book as God's judgment on Judah—its king, priests, prophets, wise men, and people—and not only the kings. Already in his call, Jeremiah is commissioned in a formula that is also repeated later:[47]

"See, today I [God] appoint you [Jeremiah] over nations and over kingdoms, to pluck up and to pull down, to destroy and to overthrow, to build and to plant" (Jer 1:10). Jeremiah's own role is to identify and suffer with his people (for example, 16:1–13). The only positive word Jeremiah has to offer them is the sober promise that they will be spared if they surrender to the Babylonians (for example, 21:8–10).

Nowhere in Jeremiah is there a word to the effect that the exiles are sent on a mission to Babylon, or to start a new era of dispersion according to God's primeval and now reasserted will. Survival is all that God has to offer to the exiled generation. Those who surrender to Babylon "shall live and shall have their lives [nothing more!] as a prize [i.e., booty] of war" (21:9). In this light, Jeremiah's letter to the exiles can only be interpreted as a strategy for survival, and nothing more.[48]

---

44. Yoder's vision of synagogue-centered Judaism gains an ironic aspect if one recalls that these scattered communities longingly and hopefully read and studied in their synagogues precisely those Scripture texts that proclaim God's land promises, the laws for faithful life in the land, the restoration of Israel, the Davidic kingship, the centralized priestly tabernacle/temple worship, and other aspects that, according to Yoder, God wants them to leave behind in the new Jeremianic era.

45. Yoder, *Jewish-Christian Schism*, 193–94. The widespread view that the center of Jewish life eventually returned to Jerusalem and Palestine is historically wrong, Yoder claims. This center remained in Babylon for a thousand years, and what went on in Palestine was simply an abortive attempt to repeat the Davidic failure.

46. Ibid., 204.

47. See Jer 12:14–15; 18:7–8; 31:28; 45:4.

48. In a concise but superb analysis, Kathleen M. O'Connor has shown that Jeremiah's own role as a representative of, and a model for, his people is that of "model survivor"; see O'Connor, "Book of Jeremiah."

For the future, however, Jeremiah has a word of promise in the very same letter to the exiles:

> For thus says the LORD: Only when Babylon's seventy years are completed will I visit you, and I will fulfill to you my promise and bring you back to this place. For surely I know the plans I have for you, says the LORD, plans for your welfare and not for harm, to give you a future with hope . . . I will restore your fortunes and gather you from all the nations and all the places where I have driven you, says the LORD, and I will bring you back to the place from which I sent you into exile. (Jer 29:10–14)

This is not simply a return to old ways, but to a new life of closeness and faithfulness to God (Jer 31:31–34). Neither does it mean an ongoing mission through diaspora; to the contrary, it promises a return to the land of Palestine, just as Jeremiah had prophesied earlier through the symbolic act of buying a field while Jerusalem was already under siege, saying: "Houses and fields and vineyards shall again be bought in this land" (32:15). This will be God's way "to build and to plant" (1:10).[49]

What shall we say? Is Yoder simply wrong in his interpretation of Jeremiah's letter? No, not altogether. The letter does prescribe God's way for the people of God with respect to their relationship to a society of radically different religion and culture.[50] Yoder's mistake is to see in this way a prescription for faithful life *for all time*. Had he allowed for its specific applicability to that specific time and situation, he might have been open to other models in the Old Testament, applicable to other times and circumstances.

Peter Ochs points out the basic task that Yoder failed to shoulder: "the embarrassment, burden, and unreasonable complexity of Israel's landedness. For both Zweig and Yoder, there is no middle between Israel's exilic separation from the land and the Maccabean strategy for remaining in it."[51] Throughout the Old Testament, the land, belonging to God, promised to Abraham, given to Israel, constituting the "heritage" of the people to be administered justly by covenant law, lost through God's judgment on unfaithfulness, promised to the exiles as God's future for them, and partially received again—that land is a *sine qua non* of the Old Testament's theology, and it carries over, in a new key, to the New Testament.[52]

A part of Yoder's problem originates, as Ochs points out, in Yoder's refusal to see a middle ground between exile and Maccabean-like monarchy. If one accepts Lindbeck's argumentation—as I think one should—for the early church's self-understanding as shaped by the image of Israel, including both Israel's faithful and unfaithful aspects (the latter as

---

49. For a study of Jeremiah's and Ezekiel's promises of a return of the exiles to their land as centrally belonging to these prophets' understanding of Yahweh, see Martens, "Motivations for the Promise of Israel's Restoration to the Land."

50. It must be noted, however, that the exhortation to seek Babylon's welfare is ultimately motivated by Israel's need for survival, rather than by a "missionary concern" for Babylon.

51. In Yoder, *Jewish-Christian Schism*, commentary by Peter Ochs, 203. In the same volume, Michael G. Cartwright, Ochs's Christian coeditor, with reference to other Jewish and Christian scholars, offers a much longer and multifaceted analysis of Yoder's misapprehension of the later Old Testament canonical books and his insufficient entering into the hermeneutics of Rabbinic Judaism (205–40). He calls for a more adequate struggle with Christian supersessionism, drawing on—among others—the thought of George Lindbeck.

52. See Janzen, "Land."

warnings), then a canon radically cleansed of "Constantinian" elements is not an adequate Old Testament resource for understanding the church.

Is there a better way? A broader acceptance of "Israel" as truly the people of God, constituted by election rather than perfection, would allow God's calling and God's grace to emerge clearly in many other texts besides Jeremiah 29 as well. What would stand out would not be one form of a faithful remnant community but the faithfulness of God, who is not limited to any one socio-political reality in Israel's history.[53] Instead, God's willingness to work in and through many forms of socio-political existence, all of them part of the "fallen order," would then be the "good news" of Israel's story. Faithful living in a socio-political context almost the opposite of that of the exiles addressed in Jeremiah 29 is modeled, for example, in the book of Ruth. The story is well known: Naomi and Ruth return from "diaspora" (Moab) to the "promised land" (Bethlehem) and experience the protection and care of a Torah-abiding community (observing the laws of inheritance, gleaning, and levirate marriage), and therewith the leading of God within the frame of the Abrahamic blessing of land and descendants, while the Davidic monarchy appears as a promise for the future. No socio-political structures lay beyond God's reach and God's plans.[54]

God's Revelation in Both Testaments: Deliverance and Blessing

Some forty years ago, Claus Westermann published a small but significant study tracing two interwoven yet distinct modes of God's dealing with humanity: "From the beginning to the end of the biblical story, God's two ways of dealing with mankind—deliverance and blessing—are found together. They cannot be reduced to a single concept because, for one reason, they are experienced differently. Deliverance is experienced in events that represent God's intervention. Blessing is a continuing activity of God that is either present or not present. It cannot be experienced in an event any more than can growth or motivation or a decline of strength."[55]

Westermann wrote at a time when biblical theology was focused strongly on historical events or "acts of God" (whether in deliverance or in judgment) like the exodus, the occupation of the promised land, the establishment and the end of kingship, the exile and

---

53. Just as there was no faithful period of humanity (or golden age) between humanity's creation (Gen 1–2) and fall (Gen 3), there was never a golden age of covenant keeping on the part of Israel between the covenant conclusion (Exod 24) and its breaking by Israel at the foot of the mountain (Exod 32), while Moses is still receiving covenant instructions from God on the mountain (Exod 25–31). In both instances, God's continuing relationship with humanity and to Israel, respectively, is moved from a basis of perfect obedience to one of grace. See Rendtorff, "'Covenant' as a Structuring Concept in Genesis and Exodus," in *Canon and Theology*, 125–34.

54. What Duane K. Friesen says in a somewhat different context essentially applies to the Old Testament also: "[C]ulture is not to be viewed as a monolithic entity but is to be related to in a discriminating way. So . . . the church's position as the 'embodiment' of Christ in the world will vary—sometimes in sharp conflict with the dominant culture, sometimes in harmony with it, other times simply neutral, sometimes seeking to transform it." Friesen, "Toward a Theology of Culture," 43.

55. Westermann, *Blessing in the Bible*, 3–4. See also Westermann, *What Does the Bible Say about God?* 25–52, 84–85.

return, and so on. God's ongoing sustaining of life seemed to lie outside the "red thread" of salvation history, as then understood; it includes the birth and growth of children, the gift of rain and sunshine and the growing of crops, healing and feeding. And yet, claims Westermann correctly, this vast area of life (the realm of nature and of daily living associated with family and land) does belong to God's dealings with humanity and the cosmos.

The era emphasizing salvation history that dominated biblical-theological thinking was the time when John Howard Yoder (like me a little later) received his theological training and developed his basic theological approach. In retrospect, I recognize the conduciveness of that theological context to Yoder's rereading of history from the vantage point of the "true believers' church," recognizable as a red thread, however thin, running throughout church history in sociologically discernible "believers' churches" clearly distinguishable from the "Constantinianism" of world history and the churches that had capitulated to it. The result was a continuous dualism engaged in ongoing confrontation, with little room for God's dealings with humanity (including the church) in the mode of blessing. Westermann notes further that the neglect of God's presence in blessing in favor of God's mighty acts of deliverance and judgment tended to be associated in biblical scholarship with a one-sided emphasis on prophetic texts and themes, to the neglect of Scripture's priestly and wisdom concerns.[56]

Due attention to the biblical emphasis on God's work of blessing (of Israel, but with a view to extension to the nations) need not lead to a neglect of emphasis on God's acts of judgment and deliverance, but these themes would find a measure of counterbalance in texts and situations highlighting God's less historical yet equally pervasive dealings with Israel and humanity in the mode of blessing. Westermann shows that this theme is also richly present in the teachings and actions of Jesus, not only where the vocabulary of blessing is specifically used, but wherever Jesus concerns himself with such topics as the well-being of children, the care of aged parents, a living wage for workers, the feeding of the hungry, the healing of the sick, and so on.[57]

The proper attention to God's dealing with humanity—believers and unbelievers—in the mode of blessing is not highlighted here in order to deflect attention from the delivering or saving mission of Jesus that results in confrontation with the anti-godly "principalities and powers" and requires the followers of Jesus to take a firm stand and "take up the cross." These anti-godly powers, however, are not only encountered in political rulers and self-serving religious systems; they are at work in a sinful humanity generally, outside *and within* the church. To draw the front line in the battle between God's kingdom and its adversaries politically-sociologically in the manner of Yoder's "Constantinian split" is to superimpose the spiritual warfare, to which Christians are indeed called, too exclusively and schematically onto the teachings of Jesus. Jesus asked believers themselves to pray continually "Your kingdom come, your will be done," knowing that they were not yet an embodiment of that kingdom. The church is not *the sign* of the kingdom of God, not even

---

56. For my attempt to balance these realms in the search for the Old Testament's ethical message and its continuation and transformation in Jesus, see Janzen, *Old Testament Ethics*.

57. Westermann, *Blessing in the Bible*, 24–26, 64–101.

when it understands its separateness as a call to model the kingdom *for the nations*;[58] it is the community of followers of Jesus who consciously strive in all their weakness to live out *signs* (plural) of the kingdom, trusting God's love in Christ for forgiveness and grace.[59]

In sum, all that which made me object inwardly when I read Yoder's first *Concern* article, and which accompanied me through life, has been counterbalanced for me in the story of Israel, the people of God, and continued in the church—a story that embraces *both* deliverance and blessing. I can now better appreciate the clear call of Yoder to radical discipleship and to bearing the cross when necessary, since I know that the God who blesses is with us as we experience the blessings of the kingdom even while we bear the cross. In other words, we can joyfully receive foretastes of the kingdom—in our families, our homes, and our churches, as well as in a measure of peace, security, and order in society—in this life already, even as we attempt to live out signs of the kingdom, with the resurrection and the fullness of the kingdom as the hope before us (Mark 10:29–30).[60]

---

58. I am aware that Yoder intends the "anti-Constantinian" stance of the believers' churches to be a witness *for* the nations' benefit (shalom, blessing), but the sharp dualism in his stance obscures for me the common humanity and sinfulness of all people, since all live by God's blessing and all are in need of God's forgiveness.

59. Fernando Enns helpfully distinguishes between the "believed church" and the "experienced church": "Her [the church's] very being is determined by her calling. In the midst of this historical reality she is constantly challenged by the truth to which she has been called." Enns, *Peace Church*, 1, and throughout.

60. Jesus himself, in his human capacity, was not only a doer of God's works, but also a recipient of God's blessings at the hands of others—the people who hosted him, the woman who anointed his feet, and so on. He was both host and guest, a giver to others, but also a receiver of their gifts, from a borrowed manger to a borrowed tomb. See the section on "Hospitality" in Janzen, *Old Testament Ethics*, 206–9.

Bibliography

Bender, Harold S. "The Anabaptist Vision." *Church History* 13 (1944) 3–34.

Doerksen, Paul. "Beyond Suspicion: Post-Christendom Protestant Political Theology in the Thought of John Howard Yoder and Oliver O'Donovan." PhD diss., McMaster University, 2006.

Enns, Fernando. *The Peace Church and the Ecumenical Community: Ecclesiology and the Ethics of Nonviolence*. Translated by Helmut Harder. Kitchener, ON: Pandora, 2007.

Friesen, Duane K. "Toward a Theology of Culture: A Dialogue with John H. Yoder and Gordon Kaufman." *Conrad Grebel Review* 16 (1998) 39–64.

Gerbrandt, Gerald E. *Kingship According to the Deuteronomistic History*. Society of Biblical Literature Dissertation Series 87. Atlanta: Scholars Press, 1986.

Harrington, Daniel J., S.J. *God's People in Christ: New Testament Perspectives on the Church and Judaism*. Overtures to Biblical Theology. Philadelphia: Fortress, 1980.

Hossfeld, F.-L., and E.-M. Kindl. "lhq [*Qahal*]." In *Theological Dictionary of the Old Testament*, edited by G. Johannes Botterweck, Helmer Ringgren, and Heinz-Josef Fabry, 12:551–56. Grand Rapids: Eerdmans, 2003.

Huebner, Harry. "The Christian Life as Gift and Patience: Why Yoder Has Trouble with Method." In *A Mind Patient and Untamed: Assessing John Howard Yoder's Contributions to Theological Ethics and Peacemaking*, edited by Ben C. Ollenburger and Gayle Gerber Koontz, 23–38. Telford, PA: Cascadia, 2004.

Janzen, Waldemar. "A Canonical Rethinking of the Anabaptist-Mennonite New Testament Orientation." In *Reclaiming the Old Testament: Essays in Honour of Waldemar Janzen*, edited by Gordon Zerbe, 3–21. Winnipeg: CMBC Publications, 2001.

———. *Growing Up in Turbulent Times: Memoirs of Soviet Oppression, Refugee Life in Germany, and Immigrant Adjustment to Canada*. Winnipeg: CMU Press, 2007.

———. "Land." In *The Anchor Bible Dictionary*, edited by David Noel Freedman, 4:143–54. New York: Doubleday, 1992.

———. *Old Testament Ethics: A Paradigmatic Approach*. Louisville: Westminster, 1994.

Lind, Millard C. *Yahweh Is a Warrior: The Theology of Warfare in Ancient Israel*. Scottdale, PA: Herald, 1980.

Lindbeck, George A. "The Church as Hermeneutical Community: Jesus, Christians, and the Bible." J.J. Thiessen Lectures, Canadian Mennonite Bible College, 1992.

———. *The Church in a Postliberal Age*. Edited by James J. Buckley. Grand Rapids: Eerdmans, 2003.

Martens, Elmer A. "Motivations for the Promise of Israel's Restoration to the Land in Jeremiah and Ezekiel." PhD diss., Claremont Graduate School, 1972. Ann Arbor: University Microfilms International, 1976.

O'Connor, Kathleen. "The Book of Jeremiah: Reconstructing Community after Disaster." In *Character Ethics and the Old Testament: Moral Dimensions of Scripture*, edited by M. Daniel Carroll R. and Jacqueline E. Lapsley, 81–92. Louisville: Westminster, 2007.

Reimer, A. James. "Mennonites, Christ, and Culture: The Yoder Legacy." *Conrad Grebel Review* 16 (1998) 5–14.

———. "Theological Orthodoxy and Jewish Christianity: A Personal Tribute to John Howard Yoder." In *The Wisdom of the Cross: Essays in Honor of John Howard Yoder*, edited by Stanley Hauerwas, Chris K. Huebner, Harry J. Huebner, and Mark Thiessen Nation, 430–448. Grand Rapids: Eerdmans, 1999.

Rendtorff, Rolf. *Canon and Theology: Overtures to an Old Testament Theology*. Translated and edited by Margaret Kohl. Minneapolis: Fortress, 1993.

Schlabach, Gerald. "Deuteronomic or Constantinian: What Is the Most Basic Problem for Christian Social Ethics?" In *The Wisdom of the Cross: Essays in Honor of John Howard Yoder*, edited by Stanley Hauerwas, Chris K. Huebner, Harry J. Huebner, and Mark Thiessen Nation, 449–71. Grand Rapids: Eerdmans, 1999.

Schmidt, K.L. "ἐκκλησία [ekklesia]. F. Old Testament and Judaism." In *Theological Dictionary of the New Testament*, edited and translated by Geoffrey Bromily, 3:527–29. Grand Rapids: Eerdmans, 1965.

Shaw, Joseph M. *The Pilgrim People of God: Recovering a Biblical Motif*. Minneapolis: Augsburg Fortress, 1990.

Westermann, Claus. *Blessing in the Bible and the Life of the Church*. Translated by Keith Crim. Overtures to Biblical Theology. Philadelphia: Fortress, 1978.

———. *What Does the Bible Say about God?* Edited by Friedemann W. Golka. Atlanta: John Knox, 1979.
Yoder, John Howard. "The Anabaptist Dissent: The Logic of the Place of the Disciple in Society." *Concern* 1 (1954) 45–68.
———. "The Authority of the Canon." In *Essays on Biblical Interpretation: Anabaptist-Mennonite Perspectives*, edited by Willard Swartley, 265–90. Elkhart, IN: Institute of Mennonite Studies, 1984.
———. *Body Politics: Five Practices of the Christian Community before the Watching World*. Scottdale, PA: Herald, 1992.
———. *For the Nations: Essays Public and Evangelical*. Grand Rapids: Eerdmans, 1997.
———. *The Jewish-Christian Schism Revisited*. Edited by Michael G. Cartwright and Peter Ochs. Grand Rapids: Eerdmans, 2003.
———. *The Original Revolution: Essays on Christian Pacifism*. Scottdale, PA: Herald, 1972.
———. *The Politics of Jesus: Vicit Agnus Noster*. Grand Rapids: Eerdmans, 1972.
Zimmerman, Earl. *Practicing the Politics of Jesus: The Origin and Significance of John Howard Yoder's Social Ethics*. Telford, PA: Cascadia, 2007.

5

Living in the Light of Time
Historicism in Troeltsch and Yoder

J. Alexander Sider

HOW DO THINKING AND LIVING CHANGE WITH THE PASSAGE OF TIME? WHAT DO WE DO with ways of thinking and being in the world that feel old and used up? How do we negotiate our ties to the past, to traditions we have inherited but often have not sought out, especially given the deep extent to which they have made us what we are? Few theologians in the twentieth century asked these questions with more insistency than Ernst Troeltsch did. But Troeltsch and the historicism he represented are often discredited within current "postliberal" theological circles as reductive and anti-ecclesiological. Consequently, many theologians with postliberal sensibilities who encounter the sorts of questions Troeltsch asked about historicity turn to the theology of John Howard Yoder to provide answers.

Yoder may seem like an unlikely source of answers for the questions Troeltsch asked, because he is often seen as opposing the typological brand of Christian ethics Troeltsch represented. And to some extent this is true. Mennonites drank at Troeltsch's well in the last century, as a series of theologians grappled with the status of "sectarian" that Troeltsch and the Niebuhrs conferred upon them.[1] Those theologians, represented by Guy F. Hershberger and, somewhat later, J. Lawrence Burkholder, attempted to see a way past Troeltsch while nevertheless accepting the epithet as sociologically accurate.[2] At roughly the same time, however, Yoder was involved with a group of Anabaptist theologians who started publishing a pamphlet series called *Concern*, in which they attempted to clarify the relationship between the sociological designation "sectarian" and the church's sociopolitical witness. Yoder's first published book, *The Christian Witness to the State*, was itself a *Concern* pamphlet in its first incarnation and represents the beginning of his career-long task of relocating the church at the center of Christian ethics.

However, while Yoder opposed Troeltsch's typological approach to Christian ethics, it is crucial to see him as an heir to Troeltsch in another respect, namely, in trying to think through the implications of a non-reductive historicism for Christian theology.

---

1. See Keim, *Harold S. Bender*, and Bush, *Two Kingdoms, Two Loyalties* for overviews of Mennonite academia during Yoder's lifetime.

2. See Hershberger, *War, Peace and Nonresistance*, and Burkholder, *Problem of Social Responsibility from the Perspective of the Mennonite Church*.

Christian ethicists have never been done grappling with Troeltsch, but Yoder shifted the terrain of the debate from typology to history in a way that has been underappreciated. I find Troeltsch more important as a source for Yoder's thought about history than for understanding the impulses behind Yoder's careful rejection of a typological approach to Christian ethics.

As a growing number of scholars have recognized, Yoder's theological reflection on history asks us to naturalize irresolvability: we live in a world where we cannot control the way things turn out, where our calculations about effectiveness are much less accurate than we pretend, and where prayer often provides a more fulsome response to the perplexities of our lives than do attempts to methodologize our outlooks. It is an approach Yoder learned by reflecting on Troeltsch. Irresolvability is not the problem; it is just the way things are. Consequently, our attitudes toward history and irresolvability need to change. If there is a difference between Troeltsch's and Yoder's historicism, it does not have to do with their views of irresolvability. Rather, it has to do with their understandings of eschatology and the church.

That is not a startling claim. Troeltsch thought that the church had largely failed in its capacity to make Christianity credible under the conditions of modernity, whereas Yoder thought the church was uniquely positioned to provide a way of negotiating those very conditions. However, my point in this essay is somewhat different. Yoder's ecclesiological thought has roots in his critical appraisal of Troeltsch's attempt to mediate Christianity to modernity. Thus where Yoder's attention to the church's life in time is concerned, his indebtedness to and criticism of Troeltsch cannot be overlooked in a search for roots of his thought.

How does an awareness of belonging to history shape the church's conception of its political faith and activity? How do we locate anew—how do we consciously cultivate—the transformative potential of reflection on history, the sense of dispossession that comes with a recognition, as Hans-Georg Gadamer put it, that "history does not belong to us," but that "we belong to it"?[3] These questions and anxieties animated Troeltsch. Derivatively, then, they shape the way Yoder engaged in reflection on the church. Because I want to sketch an environment in which Yoder's thought about the church found fertile soil, I will limit my discussion of Troeltsch to the following question: How does his thought about history configure reflection on Christianity's political (ir)relevance? Even this, however, is a large question, so a few comments about the scope and order of this essay are in order:

a. *Absoluteness and equivocation.* I begin by discussing Troeltsch's historical method and conception of the absoluteness of Christianity. Troeltsch's historicism was a methodological attempt to facilitate the equivocation (and therefore wisdom) appropriate to encountering that which is historically distant and strange.[4] Because Troeltsch found the tension between the absolute and the individual insoluble, he was stymied in his attempt to find a fitting register of equivocation and was ultimately committed to a necessitarian reading of history.

---

3. Gadamer, *Truth and Method*, 276.
4. See Rose, *Mourning Becomes the Law*, 3: "Wisdom works with equivocation."

b. *Eschatology*. This showed itself most clearly in Troeltsch's eschatology, which assumed that the concept of a final end is necessary for an ethics to be successfully executed, and yet had to prescind from all material considerations about the nature of such an end. Troeltsch's historicism therefore led him to develop the link between eschatology and ethics that Yoder thought was essential to Christian ecclesiology.

c. *History, hope, and publicity*. Nevertheless, because Troeltsch conceived of history as an arena of conflicts to be mastered and overcome, or at the very least, ameliorated and controlled, he could not "read" the church as an alternative to the history of security and dominance that funded his social ethics. He could not, in other words, see the church as a history that refused, in Yoder's pregnant phrase, "seizing Godlikeness."[5]

Absoluteness and Equivocation

Fritz Ringer, in *The Decline of the German Mandarins*, paints a compelling picture of the academic milieu within which Troeltsch operated both as a systematic theologian at the University of Heidelberg and then, later, as a philosopher of culture and history in Berlin. Ringer argues that academics like Troeltsch found a position of relative cultural importance in late Wilhelmine Germany, which they then sought, unsuccessfully, to maintain in the face of German modernization. Once they lost their toehold as the purveyors of *Bildung*, they began to lament the degeneration of German society, to diagnose a chaotic ateleology unleashed within and by technological society, and to prescribe remedies for the spiritual downfall of German culture.[6]

Fritz Stern, in his study of Germany between 1850 and World War II, notes that after the November revolution of 1918 Germans in general looked to a "religious" movement to bring unity to the Republic and to reground Germany's political and cultural hegemony in Europe.[7] Troeltsch was no exception. Already in 1903 a purely secular German society had become inadequate for him. Troeltsch wrote, "The great religious movement of modern times, the reawakened need for religions, develops outside the churches, and by and large outside theology as well."[8] For him this was at once a sign of great hope and the cause of considerable unease. Could this religious movement possibly address the "vast and complicated" social problems of the day? "It includes the problem of the capitalist economic period and of the industrial proletariat created by it; and of the growth of militaristic and bureaucratic giant states; of the enormous increase in population, which affects colonial and world policy, of the mechanical technique, which produces enormous masses of material and links up and mobilizes the whole world for purposes of trade, but which also treats men and labor like machines."[9] Capitalism, industrialization, militarism, bureau-

---

5. Yoder, *Priestly Kingdom*, 145.
6. See Ringer, *Decline of the German Mandarins*.
7. Stern, *Politics of Cultural Despair*, 87.
8. Troeltsch was noting the immensely popular influence of Paul de Lagarde. See Troeltsch, "Die theologische und religiöse Lage der Gegenwart," 20–21; also quoted in Stern, *Politics of Cultural Despair*, 88.
9. Troeltsch, *Social Teaching of the Christian Churches*, 2:1010.

cracy, colonialism, the technological imperative, and globalism: these are just some of the forces that conspired to challenge the vision of the world held by Christians in Troeltsch's day. How could Christianity be seen as credible under those conditions?

Throughout his career, Troeltsch phrased and rephrased this question; sometimes he even did so as a point of academic autobiography. In "My Books," for instance, Troeltsch described the development of his thought on historicism and its problems. Reflecting back on *The Absoluteness of Christianity*, Troeltsch wrote, "At this point [1902] I had to come to grips with *the relationships of the historically relative and the substantively absolute*; that is, with the key issue in all philosophy of history as I had learned to understand it through exposure to critical historiography."[10] As Troeltsch familiarized himself with Marxist theory through the influence of Max Weber, he reformulated the problematic that drove his thought: "To what extent are the appearance, the development, the modification, and the modern impasse of Christianity sociologically conditioned, and to what extent is Christianity itself an actively formative sociological principle?"[11] The result of asking that question was *The Social Teaching of the Christian Churches*, which he described as having "shortcomings and gaps" that made him feel "rather uneasy."[12] When he moved to the University of Berlin, Troeltsch took up problems in the philosophy of history. He noted how far the implications of his work on the history of Christian social doctrine reached:

> The attempt actually to trace the historical development of religion in a select period brought me right to the center of all sociological problems; and in thus moving beyond religion to civilization as a whole, I, like Schleiermacher, found myself obliged to bring philosophy of history and ethics closer. From all these considerations there grew up in me, as basic to my present situation, concern for the theoretical and philosophical aspects of history—its relation to empirical professional research on the one hand, and to a theory of cultural values, or of ethics, on the other.[13]

The fruit of this problematic was the first volume of *Der Historismus und seine Probleme* (Historicism and Its Problems), which asked "how the way to valid cultural values is to be found when one starts with the historically relative," and thus broadened the horizons of the fundamental question broached in *The Absoluteness of Christianity*.[14]

From this brief appraisal of his own thought we see that throughout a period of twenty years, over three large books and numerous shorter studies, Troeltsch cycled around the same set of issues regarding the relationship between history and ethics. As he did so, he set in tension a drive to systematize on the one hand, and a drive to individuate and relativize on the other, a dualism Troeltsch refused to resolve, as his remarks, again in "My Books," on the nature of his "system" indicate:

> All my works up to now have only resolved specific issues, very concrete particular questions, that had to be settled before the system itself could emerge. After the first

---

10. Troeltsch, "My Books," 370 (emphasis added); cf. Troeltsch, "Meine Bücher."
11. Troeltsch, "My Books," 372.
12. Ibid., 373.
13. Ibid., 374.
14. Ibid.

> youthful dreams of a system, I committed myself to a way of thinking that proceeds from positive knowledge and that is saturated with reality. Such a way of thinking must first settle many concrete questions of detail... To be sure, such work can only have philosophical meaning and significance when it is undertaken with the conscious aim of clarifying or substantiating an important part of the system. In short, it requires a systematic philosophical foundation that will dictate what kinds of questions are asked and in what direction the results will be pointed. But on the other hand, the systematic foundation itself will also be greatly advanced and influenced by this progressive clarification of individual issues and presuppositions. To be sure, a system that keeps on reforming itself will not be quickly finished, and it will suffer from a certain liability; and it is bound to strive for precision, sharpness of outline, and universality... Of course, such a view of the role of the system rests on a certain view of the nature of thought and its relations to life, matters about which there has been, and continues to be, much dispute. But such a fundamental view of theoretical thinking is itself a vital part of the system and it can only arise out of extensive personal engagement in the problems of the various positive disciplines.[15]

One might ask what it means to speak of a *system* that is always reforming itself; that is, one might justifiably wonder whether Troeltsch's thrust toward reformation does not undermine the intelligibility of his claim to systematicity. Troeltsch's explicit recourse, in the paragraph cited above, was to methodology, to a sense of guiding questions that shape historical inquiry and are themselves revised over the course of investigations but never radically revolutionized. So to Troeltsch's mind, the problem with writing history was not revisability or fallibilism. Nor was the problem constructivism, the historian's imposition of a constructed system upon "reality." Rather, the danger was always that the historian would impose a false and prematurely final unity on history, or that the unity a historian found would fail to correspond to reality. There are always further questions to be asked.

Perhaps his sense of the questions that remained to be asked accounts for Troeltsch's ending *The Social Teaching of the Christian Churches* on a note of perplexity: "Christian social philosophy will bring to the [contemporary] task both its common sense and its metaphysical individualism; but it will have to share the labor with other builders, and like them it will be restricted by the peculiarities of the ground and of the material." He then continues, "Under these conditions it is impossible to give a description of the present situation, and to deduce from it principles for the future. Even if the undertaking were restricted to a mere description of the different Christian endeavors, schemes and associations of the present day, the whole situation is so complicated that the subject would have to be treated in a separate work."[16]

In summary: while Troeltsch always sought a Christian ethic adequate to the conditions of modernity,[17] he also found that modern life made it "still less possible to find an unchangeable and absolute point in the Christian ethic, since this also means the mastery of an existing situation, which is determined pre-eminently by social conditions and the establishment of an ideal which corresponds to this situation."[18]

---

15. Ibid., 376.
16. Troeltsch, *Social Teaching of the Christian Churches*, 2:992.
17. Ibid., 2:1002.
18. Ibid., 2:1003.

Eschatology

"Mastery" is a key concept when considering Troeltsch's influence on Yoder, especially as Troeltsch came to see that "mastery of an existing situation" could not be had under the conditions of modernity. Although his historicism led him to recognize Christianity's dominance as a matter of contingent fact, the need to ensure Christianity's relevance to modernity led Troeltsch to argue throughout his career for Christianity's cultural durability. Arguably, in *Der Historismus und seine Probleme*, as well as in *Christian Thought*, the tension between historical contingency and durability dissolved into a formal hope in a better future that motivated the present search for practical answers to socio-political problems.[19] In other words, for Troeltsch the question of developing an ethic adequate to the relativities and contingencies of modern social life (that is, of crafting a historicist ethic) was linked to eschatology. Yoder developed that link without succumbing to Troeltsch's assumption that ethics had social stabilization as its first task.

As I have already suggested, Troeltsch sensed the challenge historicism posed to Christian faith. Yet his sense of this challenge changed throughout his career, as Troeltsch found it increasingly necessary to adopt an ironic style, in large part because the historical method he adopted created difficulties for his ethical and political aspirations. Troeltsch thought one should be able to draw normative conclusions from history, but the sheer contingency of any given event meant that "normative" meant something less stable than he was entirely comfortable with. In *The Absoluteness of Christianity*, Troeltsch put his philosophy of history in a nutshell: "The scientific study of history does not exclude norms. On the contrary, its most important task is that of discerning norms and striving to see them as a unified whole. But the norms themselves, as well as the way they are conceptually unified, remain individual and temporally conditioned entities throughout every moment of their existence. They always represent a situationally informed striving toward a future goal, a goal that is not yet completely realized and has not yet become absolute."[20]

A study of history that systematically repressed norms would be partial and incomplete, amounting to a failure of nerve that shirked the full burden of the historian's responsibility and undid the anxiety of his task. However, the alternative that Troeltsch advocated, namely, accepting the onus of "discerning norms" in history, committed the historian to bear her task as one of strife, as the struggle of envisioning those norms "as a unified whole." Envisioning those norms as a whole, moreover, could not come without its own risks, because without constant vigilance the idea of a "whole" could foster a false discursive clarity that released the tension of its subject matter in a forgetfulness of its own implication in time, its own failure to recognize its "merely potential" absoluteness. The historian's task therefore had to be seen as a limited engagement, one involving skeptical self-criticism that refused to uncouple itself from the anxiety of beginning and beginning

---

19. See Troeltsch, *Christian Thought*. Originally published in German as *Der Historismus und seine Überwindung*.

20. Troeltsch, *Absoluteness of Christianity*, 90. For the German text, see Troeltsch, *Die Absolutheit des Christentums und die Religiongeschichte*.

again to take account of its own situation and effort, and to strain toward a wholeness of vision that always retained the character of a question.

How one approached that question, whether as a threat or as a promise (and it might be both), would depend on a variety of factors that rarely admit of neat arrangement and classification. And that left room for hope, a point for which Troeltsch's own life proved illustrative: from the outset of his career, his political hopes, his restlessness with the accepted canons of theological, philosophical, and historical inquiry, and his almost "pastoral" apologetic concern to make Christian faith credible combined to induce in him a profound confidence that the more one engaged in historical investigation the more it would become apparent that history is edifying. Mark Chapman, in *Ernst Troeltsch and Liberal Theology*, comments on the hopeful character of Troeltsch's writing: "Troeltsch's . . . combination of realism and optimism, where there can be no easy solutions within history, no immediate perception of absolute truth, but where nevertheless there is always the hope that history might be moving to its goal, perhaps better reflects the continued need not to escape or to evade but to transform history; that is, to discipline it ethically. For Troeltsch, it is the dare to accept the meaningfulness of history that ultimately provides the justification for religion."[21]

Troeltsch maintained that Christianity's validity could never be guaranteed via a conception of absoluteness "as a humanly realizable and exhaustible idea." Instead, he sounded a cautionary note: "The modern idea of history, as it has taken shape in connection with the object of its inquiries, knows no concept of a universal principle that embodies a law governing the successive generation of individual historical realities."[22] Moreover, he wrote, "The Christian religion is in every moment of its history a purely historical phenomenon, subject to all the limitations to which any individual historical phenomenon is exposed, just like the other great religions. It is to be investigated, in every moment of its history, by the universal, verified methods of historical research."[23]

The overall point, Troeltsch thought, was that because Christianity is subject to historical investigation, and because historical investigation concentrates on individual events, any conception of absoluteness that proved durable to modern historical thought had to be characterized only in terms "of a goal discernible in outline and general direction."[24] Here the eschatological horizon of historicism emerged into view. Ultimately, for Troeltsch, the only way to speak confidently of meaning in history was via eschatology.

Troeltsch's difficult balancing act between history and hope provoked an eschatology that was divested of all "primitive," "dogmatic," and "progressivist" elements. "Eschatology" stood for hope in a better and more inhabitable future. As a theme, eschatology enjoyed but a shadowy life in *The Absoluteness of Christianity*, wherein Troeltsch consistently limited himself to talk of history's "final goal" or "consummation." In contrast, his dogmatic theology lectures of 1912 and 1913, published in English as *The Christian Faith*, as well as his article on eschatology in *Die Religion in Geschichte und Gegenwart*, discussed specific

21. Chapman, *Ernst Troeltsch and Liberal Theology*, 136.
22. Troeltsch, *Absoluteness of Christianity*, 64.
23. Ibid., 85.
24. Ibid., 100.

aspects of Christian teaching on the last things.[25] In both texts, Troeltsch argued that eschatology was analytically related to religious thought. He wrote, for instance, that

> [e]very religion that seeks to achieve a clear self-understanding and self-expression has a doctrine of last things, an eschatology (to use the technical term), however mythical its form may be. More than a poetic impulse gives rise to it; it proceeds from the religious idea itself. For religion itself is, if not a doctrine, yet surely a sense of "last things"; that is, of ultimate realities and values that are absolute and unconditioned, uniform and inherently necessary, in contrast to finite realities and values that are relativized more and more by reflexion.[26]

Troeltsch argued that gaining a sense of the last things is a matter of course for any inquiry into the nature of reality that involves itself with questions of what is ultimate. That sense would be inchoate and metaphorical, a poetic representation of what lies beyond the limits of human knowledge rather than a matter of strict exposition. Indeed, any attempt to specify, circumscribe, or describe the last things would be a kind of dogmatism, a premature bid to tame history's complexity by a "deliberate misrepresentation" of "the relational nexus." That kind of eschatology needed chastening by modern historicism.[27] But once the last things were passed through the sieve of modern historical consciousness, once eschatology had been purified of its superstitious elements, its subject matter could competently be limited to two finally unanswerable questions: "(1) the question of the essence of the consummation, or the question of a definitive redemption; and (2) the question of whether all or only a few will participate in this final salvation, or the question of the universality and particularity of grace."[28]

Because these questions are unanswerable, Troeltsch thought that it was irresponsible and ahistorical to approach religious convictions with either thoroughgoing certainty or despair. Yet he did want to talk about religious certainty. Particularly, he said that "[t]he religious man needs . . . the certainty that he is on the right path, that he is following the right star."[29] The certainty that Christian eschatology can give cultivates openness to the future, but it does not need to speculate as to the specific shape of that future. But because he refused to use eschatology to imagine any future in particular, Troeltsch cut his theology off from any potentially countercultural narration of history and made it not so much the servitor of the dominant culture as entirely incidental to that culture, whatever it happened to be.

History, Hope, and Publicity: Yoder's Response to Troeltsch

Troeltsch's historicism, by a circuitous route, can therefore be seen as epistemologically imperialist—not primarily in the sense that he developed a set of sophisticated strate-

---

25. See Troeltsch, *Christian Faith*, 300–304; and "Eschatologie: IV Dogmatisch," translated into English as "Eschatology."
26. Troeltsch, "Eschatology," 146.
27. Ibid., 147.
28. Troeltsch, *Christian Faith*, 302.
29. Troeltsch, *Absoluteness of Christianity*, 120–21.

gies that allowed him to acknowledge the evidence of "incompleteness" in the writing of Christian history while retaining the idea of a general historical movement culminating in modern European (German) Christianity, but in that he claimed to have uncovered the necessary conditions for and limits of thinking in the light of time. In this he exhibited tendencies Yoder criticized as "Constantinian." Indeed, it is at the intersection between eschatology and history, rather than in a typological account of Christian ethics, that Yoder's thought most clearly responds to Troeltsch. However, Yoder can also be seen as picking up a set of tasks bequeathed to him by Troeltsch. Yoder, like Troeltsch, thought that Christianity had to be political (though they would not have agreed on what constitutes the "political"), that the gospel must be "hearable" in whatever context it is found, and that the search for a distinctively Christian epistemology denies the fundamentally historical nature of the faith.

Yoder took these tasks in directions Troeltsch could not, at least in part because Yoder was not concerned to secure Christianity's cultural hegemony. That is to say, the apologetic aspects of Troeltsch's project were absent in Yoder's theology. Yoder did not think to ask, much less answer, how Christianity could be legitimated in light of modernity. Instead, it might be said that Yoder rendered aspects of Troeltsch's theology more consistent than Troeltsch was able to on his own terms in at least two interrelated ways: (1) Yoder uncoupled Troeltsch's conception of history from its idealist undercurrents (for example, the constitutive tension between the absolute and the individual); and (2) he reinscribed Christian content into the eschatological hope that Troeltsch had reduced to a purely formal source of motivation.

To take each of these points in turn: In "But We Do See Jesus," Yoder responded to the problem of "Lessing's ditch" ("Accidental truths of history can never become the proof of necessary truths of reason"), out of which Troeltsch took himself to be working. The first thing to notice is that Yoder did not allow the tension between the absolute and the individual to go unquestioned:

> It would be wrong to think that the issue of the credibility of particular claims is best represented only by some quite recent reformulation of historical skepticism, or religious pluralism, or the death-of-God language, or by the gap between contingent facts of history and necessary truths of reason posited by Lessing, the dean of modern ditchdiggers. Each of those formulations is important. Yet none of them is at the bottom of our problem. None of them can find *beyond the ditch* a place to stand which would be less particular, more credible, less the product of one's own social location.[30]

That insight ought in a sense to be credited to Troeltsch, for Troeltsch's historicism labors in the ditch. The difference between Troeltsch and Yoder is that Troeltsch allowed the terms of the question to remain unchallenged. However, Yoder showed that one never encounters a problem of the absolute and the individual in general, but only by dint of the background of comparison enabled by an often-excluded third term. So Yoder, in contrast to Troeltsch, particularized (that is, located temporally and spatially) and politicized

---

30. Yoder, *Priestly Kingdom*, 46.

the terms of the question: the life of any particular community one encounters is always characterized by the movement from "smaller worlds into wider ones," always threatened by the assimilative force or "psychic dominance" of the "next wider world" it encounters.[31] This is not to claim that some people are less modern than others, or that some are legitimately anxious about a period of preparation they need to undergo before encountering perceived cultural elites as peers. It is not, in other words, to assume a progressivist paradigm, as the movement from small (parochial) communities to wide (cosmopolitan) ones might seem to suggest, because Yoder coupled such movement with the claim that the "wider world, in any one person's experience or pilgrimage or in any interface between two groups, is still a small place."[32] Rather, it is a challenge to look, for if we examine the life of any community we find that it is always in flux, always encountering that which is different, new, and unprecedented. Consequently everyone, even the representatives of various "wider worlds," lives, so to speak, in the green room of history.

In shaping the issue this way, Yoder released the tension between the absolute and the individual. If, he argued, we attend to how debates, conflicts, and movements in time actually occur, we find that claims in favor of absoluteness are often ideological, that is, arguments that characteristically mask some degree of provincialism. The question Yoder asked was therefore neither Lessing's nor Troeltsch's: he did not ask how one could claim absoluteness for this or that particular view. Rather, he asked, "How can particular truths be proclaimed publicly?"[33] For Yoder, publicity, not absoluteness, is the *telos* of the Christian message.[34] If every wider world is one more ghetto, then the "certainty that one is following the right star" is not at stake. What is at stake is a challenge to proclaim the gospel as good and as news. Thus, Yoder described the Christian relationship to the history of movement from smaller to wider worlds as "evangelical":

> I take the term in its root meaning. One is functionally evangelical if one confesses oneself to have been commissioned by the grace of God with a message which others who have not heard it should hear. It is *angellion* ("news") because they will not know it unless they are told it by a message-bearer. It is good news because hearing it will be for them not alienation or compulsion, oppression or brainwashing, but liberation. Because this news is only such when *received* as good, it can never be communicated coercively; nor can the message-bearer ever positively be assured that it will be received.[35]

In conceiving of the Christian's task as publication, Yoder displayed the relationship to the past as a question of and responsibility for the future, but not as one that attempts to guarantee the shape of that future. Rather, he argued, "What we are doing now . . . leads to where we are going."[36] As part and parcel of his picture of salvation as the creation of a community of Jesus's followers, "where we are going" was an admittedly complex concept

---

31. Ibid., 47.
32. Ibid., 49.
33. Ibid.
34. Ibid., 56–57.
35. Ibid., 55.
36. Yoder, *Politics of Jesus*, 241.

for Yoder. It both presupposed a spatial and/or experiential site of departure (what we are doing now) and had a "revolutionary" edge, where the destination is not a return to an original state but to a state transformed unpredictably and given to us as anamnetic renewal, which means that the (present) memory of our wandering, of our turning and turning again (*metanoia*), of our seeking to actualize, repress, extinguish, and use "what we are doing now" will no longer be recognizable except under the signs of promise—all of which is to say that Yoder recognized the extent to which the continuity that pertains to where we are going, that "leads" there, will also involve revolutionary discontinuity with what we are doing now.

Chris Huebner has referred to the revolutionary character of Yoder's thought, and particularly to his rejection of absoluteness or some other conceptual machinery that would underwrite the outcome of history, as his "methodological non-Constantinianism."[37] Here, and as the second site of commonality/difference between Yoder and Troeltsch, I want to supplement Huebner's discussion with a consideration of the non-Constantinian registers of Yoder's substantive eschatological claims.

At the beginning of "Peace without Eschatology?" Yoder noted that "Christian thought is learning to give increasing attention to the importance of the Christian hope for the Christian life."[38] He continued, "Christian thought in the decades prior to the Second World War was strongly influenced by thinkers and preachers who hoped for the brotherhood of man just around the corner and who therefore thought they had no time to waste on eschatology. The very word frightened them; it seemed to suggest weird speculations and wild-eyed fanatics out of touch with the world's real needs."[39]

The reference to the brotherhood of man in this passage makes it seem unlikely that Troeltsch was on Yoder's horizon here. The target was much more likely Walter Rauschenbusch and the social gospellers, which seems to be confirmed when Yoder goes on to speak of "[t]heir simple confidence that they could be sure of the meaning of life" as itself an eschatology, "a doctrine of what is ultimate."[40] Troeltsch, however, was in no way sure he could say what is ultimate; his confidence lay rather in the fact of the necessity of the question of ultimacy, of eschatology, for ethics.

Here too, then, Troeltsch's and Yoder's thought moved in the same direction, at least initially. Yoder indicated as much when he cited approvingly the World Council of Church's recognition that "[t]here is no significance to human effort and, strictly speaking, no history unless life can be seen in terms of ultimate goals."[41] Yet in another sense, Troeltsch was as much the target of Yoder's criticism as Rauschenbusch and liberal pacifists were, for when Yoder defined *eschatology*, he called it "a hope which, defying present frustration, defines a present position in terms of the yet unseen goal which gives it meaning."[42] This (to be sure) complex definition holds together a stance in the present (which may often be

37. Huebner, "Unhandling History," 192–285.
38. Yoder, *Original Revolution*, 55–90.
39. Yoder, *Royal Priesthood*, 144.
40. Ibid., 144–45.
41. Ibid., 145.
42. Ibid.

obstructed) with a "yet unseen goal" that does no more than let the present make sense. Yoder's unspoken premise is that if the present is to make sense, the goal that gives it its meaning must be specifiable. Troeltsch's "following the right star" "in outline and general direction" and Yoder's eschatology do therefore diverge. For Yoder, eschatology was not simply or merely a question of futurity as it was for Troeltsch. Rather, Yoder claimed that the gospel is "from beginning to end eschatological, a declaration about events and their place in the unfolding of God's purposes."[43]

In other words, what it means to speak of "history" has been transformed in the victory of the Lamb that was slain. Christ's activity is what history is for. Yoder's mantra in this regard is that the meaning of history is displayed in the church's obedience to and suffering with Christ. To be historical in this sense means to have time for God, to receive history in praise as God's gift.[44] History, received (and only thus seen) in the light of Christ's resurrection, cannot be based on an epistemology of dominance and security that harbors some sort of reservation about the future, because if the church thinks in terms of mastering time and contingency, or even in terms of ameliorating the threat they pose to its (self-generated) hopes, then it fails to participate in history as the promise of the gospel. For Yoder, our uses and conceptions of history are false and unhistorical to the extent that they generate an ethos of political and epistemological mastery, because they do not imitate the faithful obedience and self-denying patience of Christ.

In summary: I have argued that although Troeltsch thought modernity placed insurmountable constraints on the Christian faith, he never gave up on the project of securing Christianity's cultural durability. His historicism grew out of an attempt to find a religiosity adequate to the social situation of early twentieth-century Germany, which demanded an emphasis on historical contingency and particularity. Troeltsch tried to hold this emphasis in tension with the need to speak of ultimate values and final ends, but in order to do so he had to evacuate those ends of any specific content. But Troeltsch did draw the link between eschatology and ethics, and he did articulate a powerful vision of what it means to think in and with a sober recognition of historical finitude. In both of these respects he needs to be reconsidered as a source for Yoder's theology, as more of a ghost haunting that theology and less as a marker pointing down a road Yoder refused to take. The questions Troeltsch raised and the anxieties he faced, his sense that intolerable uncertainty about what comes next is what makes life possible, deserve to be engaged by theologians and ethicists writing today rather than avoided or explained away.[45]

---

43. Yoder, *Original Revolution*, 57.
44. See ibid., 64, and Balthasar, *Theology of History*, 34.
45. See LeGuin, *Left Hand of Darkness*.

Bibliography

Balthasar, Hans Urs von. *A Theology of History*. New York: Sheed & Ward, 1963.

Burkholder, J. Lawrence. *The Problem of Social Responsibility from the Perspective of the Mennonite Church*. PhD diss., Princeton Theological Seminary, 1958. Reprinted by the Institute of Mennonite Studies, Elkhart, IN, 1989.

Bush, Perry. *Two Kingdoms, Two Loyalties: Mennonite Pacifism in Modern America*. Baltimore: Johns Hopkins University Press, 1998.

Chapman, Mark D. *Ernst Troeltsch and Liberal Theology: Religion and Cultural Synthesis in Wilhelmine Germany*. Oxford: Oxford University Press, 2001.

Gadamer, Hans-Georg. *Truth and Method*. 2nd rev. ed. Translated by Joel Weinsheimer and Donald G. Marshall. New York: Continuum, 1997.

Hershberger, Guy F. *War, Peace, and Nonresistance*. Scottdale, PA: Herald, 1944.

Huebner, Chris K. "Unhandling History: Anti-Theory, Ethics and the Practice of Witness." PhD diss., Duke University, 2001.

Huebner, Harry J. *Echoes of the Word: Theological Ethics as Rhetorical Practice*. Kitchener, ON: Pandora, 2005.

Keim, Albert N. *Harold S. Bender, 1897–1962*. Scottdale, PA: Herald, 1998.

LeGuin, Ursula K. *The Left Hand of Darkness*. New York: Penguin Putnam, 2000.

Ringer, Fritz K. *The Decline of the German Mandarins: The German Academic Community, 1890–1933*. Hanover, NH: Wesleyan University Press, 1990.

Rose, Gillian. *Mourning Becomes the Law: Philosophy and Representation*. Cambridge: Cambridge University Press, 1996.

Sider, J. Alexander. "'To See History Doxologically': History and Holiness in the Theology of John Howard Yoder." PhD diss., Duke University, 2004.

Stern, Fritz. *The Politics of Cultural Despair: A Study in the Rise of the Germanic Ideology*. Berkeley: University of California Press, 1961.

Troeltsch, Ernst. *The Absoluteness of Christianity and the History of Religions*. Translated by David Reid. Richmond, VA: John Knox, 1971.

———. *Die Absolutheit des Christentums und die Religiongeschichte (1902/1912): Mit den Thesen von 1901 und den handschriftlichen Zusätzen*. Vol. 5 of *Kritische Gesamtausgabe*. Edited by Trutz Rendtorff and Stefan Pautler. Berlin: De Gruyter, 1998.

———. *The Christian Faith*. Edited by Gertrud von le Fort. Translated by Garrett E. Paul. Minneapolis: Fortress, 1991.

———. *Christian Thought: Its History and Application*. Edited by Baron F. von Hügel. New York: Meridian, 1957.

———. "Eschatologie: IV Dogmatisch." In *Religion in Geschichte und Gegenwart*, 2:622–32. Tübingen: J.C.B. Mohr, 1910.

———. "Eschatology." In *Religion in History*, edited by James Luther Adams and Walter Bense, 146–58. Minneapolis: Fortress, 1991.

———. *Der Historismus und seine Probleme*. Vol. 3 of *Gesammelte Schriften*. Tübingen: J.C.B. Mohr, 1922.

———. *Der Historismus und seine Überwindung: Fünf Vorträge von Ernst Troeltsch*. Berlin: Rolf Heise, 1924.

———. "Meine Bücher." In *Aufsätze zur Geistesgeschichte und Religionssoziologie*, 3–18. Vol. 4 of *Gesammelte Schriften*. Tübingen: J.C.B. Mohr, 1913.

———. "My Books." Translated by Franklin H. Littell. In *Religion in History*, edited by James Luther Adams and Walter Bense, 365–78. Minneapolis: Fortress, 1991.

———. *The Social Teaching of the Christian Churches*. Vol. 2. Translated by Olive Wyon. Louisville: Westminster, 1992.

———. "Die theologische und religiöse Lage der Gegenwart." In *Zur religiösen Lage, Religionsphilosophie und Ethik*, 20–21. Vol. 2 of *Gesammelte Schriften*. Tübingen: J.C.B. Mohr, 1913.

Yoder, John Howard. *The Original Revolution: Essays on Christian Pacifism*. Scottdale, PA: Herald, 1971.

———. *The Politics of Jesus: Vicit Agnus Noster*. 2nd ed. Grand Rapids: Eerdmans, 1994.

———. *The Priestly Kingdom: Social Ethics as Gospel.* Notre Dame, IN: University of Notre Dame Press, 1984.
———. *The Royal Priesthood: Essays Ecclesiological and Ecumenical.* Edited by Michael G. Cartwright. Grand Rapids: Eerdmans, 1994.

The Young Karl Barth's Critique of Anabaptism

Arnold Neufeldt-Fast

THOUGH MORE THAN THIRTY YEARS HAVE PASSED SINCE THE DEATH OF KARL BARTH, interest in his theological work has not abated, especially in the English-language world. The Karl Barth Archive in Switzerland continues to make new volumes of heretofore unpublished Barth sermons, lectures, papers, and letters available to scholars of twentieth-century theology. On the basis of some of these newly available documents, I want to examine Anabaptism as one of Barth's conversation partners—especially in his early years as a young professor in Göttingen, where he lectured on Zwingli. I will offer an initial summary and critical evaluation of Barth's 1922 account of sixteenth-century Swiss Anabaptism, and also trace briefly Barth's changing presentation of Anabaptist beginnings and of those theological themes that were of crucial importance to the Anabaptist witness to the Gospel. It is my hope that this exercise in historical theology will make a contribution to the church's ongoing ecumenical task of giving witness to the gospel in the shadows of modernity.

Until recently the writings of Karl Barth have suggested that he had only a very limited knowledge and understanding of sixteenth-century Anabaptism. The 2004 German publication of his 1922–1923 lectures in Göttingen on the "Theology of Zwingli"—specifically the section on "Zwingli's Struggle with the Anabaptists"[1]—shows otherwise. In 1921 the young Swiss pastor was appointed Honorary Professor of Reformed Theology at the University of Göttingen, Germany, a position he held for four years. In Göttingen, Barth was assigned to teach Reformed doctrine and church life. He prepared and taught a cycle of five courses on historical theology. The first course in the cycle was "An Exposition of the Heidelberg Catechism" (1921–1922). Then Barth turned to the masters of the Reformed tradition, offering courses on "The Theology of Calvin" (1922) and "The Theology of Zwingli" (1922–1923). In the following year he lectured on "The Theology of the Reformed Confessions" (1923) and then on "The Theology of Schleiermacher" (1923–1924). In each semester Barth also taught shorter New Testament courses. Six years after arriving in Göttingen, Barth admitted that he "did not even possess the Reformed confessional writings, and had certainly never read them, quite apart from other horren-

---

1. Barth, "Zwinglis Kampf mit den Täufern," in *Theologie Zwinglis*, 231–51. This volume has not yet been translated into English; translations from German publications throughout this essay are my own.

dous gaps in my knowledge."[2] It was under this pressure to teach Reformed theology that Barth first engaged Anabaptism with any seriousness.

Barth's preparations for the Zwingli lectures began in the summer of 1922 and proved to absorb almost all his energies until the course's conclusion early in 1923. In the same semester he also offered an exegetical course on the Letter of James. Only a week after lecturing on Zwingli's struggle with the Anabaptists in December 1922, Barth wrote in a circular letter, "Really since the beginning of the semester there has not been a quiet hour. Again and again, Zwingli, Zwingli, James, Zwingli."[3]

To date, the first German publication (2004) of Barth's 1922–23 lectures on Zwingli have only received limited commentary and evaluation. John Webster has written an excellent introduction and evaluation of the text;[4] missing, however, is a commentary on the section titled "Zwingli's Struggle with the Anabaptists." This section is Barth's only extensive reflection on sixteenth-century Anabaptism, and as such, it is worthy of commentary and analysis.

The section begins with an introduction that is extremely odd—even for Barth. Barth begins with a lengthy description of our capacity to "grimace" when we expend energy, experience joy and sorrow, or when we suffer sickness or death. Then Barth comes to his point, namely that

> Anabaptism [*Täufertum*] is the grimace of the Reformation. Each of the essential insights of the Reformation—its understanding of the Word of God in the unity of letter and Spirit, its understanding of faith which alone justifies before God, its understanding of good works which flow necessarily from faith, its understanding of church as the community of believers established by the Word of God, its understanding of God as the Holy One, who is merciful, and above all as the one who is unfathomably free, glorious, and who goes his own way—this all reappears in the differing variations of the Enthusiasts [*Schwärmertum*]—the same, but yet not the same; incredibly contorted as in curved mirrors, brought to its most extreme conclusions—first to the one side and then to the other.[5]

Barth recognizes that the Swiss Anabaptists, specifically those around Zwingli, were in agreement with all of the essentials of Reformation, but characterizes them as extremists and enthusiasts who contorted the "real face" of the Reformation. Notably, Barth holds here to the longer tradition of Protestant hostility toward Anabaptism and uses the terms *Schwärmer*, *Schwärmerei*, and *Schwärmertum* sweepingly. In contrast, Barth's contemporaries—liberal Protestants like Ernst Troeltsch, for example— refrained almost completely from the use of the largely derogatory and polemical term *Schwärmer* (Enthusiasts), and sought generally to distinguish carefully between ecclesial Anabaptists and free, individualistic spiritualists. But more significant for our purposes, as I will show, this difference

---

2. Barth, "Appendix 38: Autobiographical Sketches (Barth)," 156.

3. Karl Barth, circular letter written December 18, 1922, in *Barth-Thurneysen Briefwechsel*, 120. This was a very hectic year for Barth; many speaking engagements had to be declined, including one on "Christianity and the Enthusiasts," about which Barth writes: "the formulation shows insight; the opportunity is important and promising" (74).

4. Webster, "Theology of Zwingli."

5. Barth, *Theologie Zwinglis*, 233.

reveals something more basic to Barth's own program of the 1920s: Barth's overwhelming concern at this time was to create a space over against the Protestant liberalism of his day, and his evaluation of Anabaptism becomes an important, if in the end flawed, part of that strategy.

Barth admits that there are countless overlapping and mixed forms of Reformation and *Schwärmertum* in "a most intimate, indissoluble complexity." Yet *Schwärmertum* for Barth is "the sickness of the Reformation, and it is the Reformation itself which is sick."[6] The sickness manifests itself as a "splinter movement" from which the Reformers had no choice other than to "defend themselves," according to Barth. He writes: "One can justify the Reformers' stance; indeed one must. But one should not overlook the fact that here the human—the earthly—limit becomes concretely visible, even in the Reformation. It was precisely with and in response to the *Schwärmer* that this breaks through."[7] In this context Barth repeats the common political-tactical argument for Zwingli's defense: if Zwingli had not put the church under the protection and administration of the state, it would not have survived. Consequently the move against the Anabaptists was justified for the health of Zurich. Unfortunately, but necessarily, the Anabaptists became the "scapegoats" of the Reformation. "While it may cause anger and repugnance in us," Barth writes, "fear and sympathy would be most appropriate when we see the manner in which the light of the Reformation in Zwingli was followed by its unavoidable shadow in its struggle with its 'grimaces.'"[8] The concern for the unity of Zurich-Christendom made purging all that which contorts the face of the Reformation a *theological* necessity.[9]

In the Zwingli lectures, as well as in his other writings of the 1920s, Barth uses the term "Anabaptism" to cover positions that are logically opposed to each other. On the one hand, Barth describes the Anabaptists as enthusiastic spiritualists unfettered by objective revelation. On the other hand, he describes the Anabaptist movement as a "renunciation of the world," a "new monasticism, a new works righteousness represented by adult baptism."[10] Anabaptists holding to these positions are related in their "struggle for a pure life," Barth suggests, in contrast to the Reformers whose struggle was for "pure teaching." Specifically, in his account of Zwingli's struggle with the Anabaptists, Barth examines the Zurich Disputations, quotes Balthasar Hubmaier's writings, knows that Conrad Grebel and Felix Manz were humanistically trained, and is aware of Hans Denck and Ludwig Haetzer; nonetheless, Barth judges that the Anabaptist movement "for its part never produced a really superior mind."[11] In contrast to Zwingli, these Anabaptists shared in common a lack of "healthy moderation,"[12] according to Barth. Conrad Grebel, for example, is presented as a "typical new convert—young and excessive—who, with a sudden turn renounces the world, and moves beyond the narrow bounds of duty to which Zwingli

---

6. Ibid., 234.
7. Ibid.
8. Ibid.
9. See Yoder, "Turning Point in the Zwinglian Reformation," 140.
10. Barth, *Theologie Zwinglis*, 235, 239.
11. Ibid., 247; see also 235 and 239.
12. Ibid., 233–34, 235, 239.

sought to point him, toward an extreme position of exclusive opposition."[13] Zwingli, by contrast, consistently acted in a measured and evenhanded manner, Barth tells us, even as those around him were impatient, independent, audacious, and impudent.[14] In that context Zwingli's churchmanship impresses Barth: compared to Luther, who dealt harshly with the concerns of the German peasants, Zwingli implemented public disputations and was willing to negotiate with the peasantry about their concerns. Barth notes that "it is quite extraordinary that the Zurich Council managed with only one single execution" in 1525.[15] Whoever—like Zwingli—stands in the light will necessarily cast a shadow, according to Barth: "Greatness without culpability and shadow is an excluded possibility in human history, even where the desires and aspirations are pure."[16] Barth praises Zwingli as the Reformer who presented "a soberly moral understanding of Christianity balanced by the emphasis on God's powerful solidarity with us in Christ."[17]

With this comment we begin to sense the kind of light Barth sees shining around Zwingli. On the one hand, Barth notes that Zwingli was "only too united with these Radicals in rejecting a magical-sacramental understanding of baptism."[18] Yet while rejecting the salvific significance of pedobaptism, Zwingli energetically opposed the Anabaptist protestation that was framed publicly in terms of a "valuation of the salvific significance of the *experience of conversion*."[19] Zwingli judged this understanding of the Christian life as "another attack on the sole causality and honor of God."[20] Barth adopts this criterion—"the sole causality and honor of God"—for assessing the kind of witness that the church is called to give. For Zwingli the Word of God was a unity of inner and outer witness, and the latter is a two-edged sword: the testimony of Scripture and of the sacramental sign. Against the Catholics, Zwingli employed the "outer witness of the biblical Word," and against the Anabaptists, the "outer witness of the sacramental symbol." The "line of thought is the same," namely, the "emphasis on the singular authority of God."[21] Baptism for Zwingli was an expression that the people of God is a whole, testifying that Christ has indeed cleansed the church by his blood, and that the goal of redemption in Christ "is found not simply in the eternal bliss [*Beseligung*] of individuals, but in the building of a kingdom of God on earth," to which children also belong.[22]

Barth finds Zwingli a most helpful mentor at this point. Years later Barth employed almost the exact same language in the section on the "Unity of the Word of God" in the *Church Dogmatics* I/1 to criticize the private individualism of modern Protestant theolo-

---

13. Ibid., 235.
14. Ibid., 235, 247.
15. Ibid., 242.
16. Ibid., 247.
17. Ibid., 250. Many years later Barth will state the opposite; cf. *Church Dogmatics*, IV/3:29.
18. Barth, *Theologie Zwinglis*, 237.
19. Ibid. (emphasis mine).
20. Ibid.
21. Ibid., 250.
22. Ibid., 249–50.

gy.²³ Again, it gives us a hint at what Barth understands as central, on the one hand, and as a real hindrance to faith, on the other. It was in the 1920s, however, that Barth first began to think of baptism as a form of the Word of God. In this period he became a vocal advocate of infant baptism, especially because "official Protestant dogmatics" had virtually let the notion of sacraments "go to seed," making the doctrine appear peripheral.²⁴ In response, the young Barth is convinced that the recovery of a robust theology of infant baptism is a remarkably vivid depiction of the free and omnipotent grace of God, independent of all human thought and will, belief, and unbelief. Although four decades later Barth came to the exact opposite conclusion on infant baptism,²⁵ his criterion—the call for the community of faith to depict and give witness to the grace of God—remained the same.

In the Zwingli lectures Barth assumes without much argumentation that the roots of the "problem" of private, individual faith and its emphasis on experience can be found within Anabaptism and its high esteem for "the salvific significance of the conversion experience."²⁶ Whence this reading of Anabaptism? It is helpful to notice that in the context of the Zwingli lectures Barth was fighting on two fronts. With the four-hundred-year anniversary of the Lutheran Reformation in 1917, German scholarship had rediscovered Luther in his self-understanding and historic importance as a theologian; with this came a polemical and one-sided Lutheran reception of Zwingli. Barth's first aim in the Zwingli lectures was to rehabilitate Zwingli in the context of the Luther renaissance.²⁷ The second front for Barth was the battle against the modern privatization of faith in its Protestant liberal and Pietist forms. Anabaptism, rightly or wrongly, became a target for Barth on each of these larger battle fields.

On the one front, many Luther scholars simply followed Luther's lead and dismissed the witness of Zwingli to the *Sache* of the Reformation as *Schwärmerei*.²⁸ Barth sought to rectify this. In the context of that confessional debate Barth had no need for a more nuanced and fair presentation of Anabaptism. It did not help that Barth himself was accused of *Schwärmerei* by his Lutheran colleagues in Göttingen: Emanuel Hirsch was convinced that Barth's early account of ethics built on an understanding of the divine Word as the "great disturbance," "crisis," or "interruption" led inevitably to empty, "spiritualistic enthusiasm."²⁹ Carl Stange told him that the "Reformed Church in Hanover [which appointed Barth] has no more significance than the millennial sects."³⁰ Consequently,

---

23. Barth, *Church Dogmatics*, I/1:124, trans. G.W. Bromiley. Bromiley translates "Beseligung" as "saving."

24. Barth, "*Unterricht in der christlichen Religion*," 3:200, 199.

25. Barth, *Church Dogmatics*, IV/4 (fragment): 189-90.

26. Barth, *Theologie Zwinglis*, 237. Cf. Barth's later engagement with German and Swiss Pietists: "Gespräch mit Vertretern der Gemeinschaften," 18–19. For the Anabaptists, however, it was not at all the significance of "experience" that was at issue, but rather Zwingli's decision against the use of Scripture as norm, his denial of appeal by threat of force, and his granting to city council the authority for deciding matters of faith and their enforcement that brought about the breaking point. See Yoder, *Anabaptism and Reformation in Switzerland*, 28; also 149.

27. Barth, "Zwingli im Urteil des Luthertum," in *Die Theologie Zwinglis*, 3–36.

28. Ibid., 3; Barth, "Ansatz und Absicht in Luthers Abendmahlslehre, 1923," 298.

29. See Hirsch, *Deutschlands Schicksal*, 158. "The Great Disturbance" is Barth's section heading for chaps. 12 ("The Problem of Ethics") and following in *Epistle to the Romans*, 424.

30. Barth, letter dated May 17, 1922, in *Barth-Thurneysen Briefwechsel*, 77.

Barth's colleagues refused to approve his proposed course on "dogmatics," arguing that only *Lutheran* dogmatics could have the dignity of that generic (non-confessional) title.[31]

For Barth that debate was much more than denominational posturing. Barth was convinced that modern theology continually reaffirmed Feuerbach's conclusion that theology is in essence anthropology; both in its liberal and Pietist forms, Protestant theology had shifted "attention from what God is in himself to what God is for men."[32] In part, the seeds for this reversal were, according to Barth, Luther's understanding of faith "as an almost divine hypostasis," the doctrine of the Real Presence in the Lord's Supper (versus Zwingli), and the Lutheran doctrine of the *communicatio idiomatum* (interchange of attributes in the two natures of Christ).[33] Allowed to develop into semi-Pelagianism in the soil of rationalism and Pietism, the reversal was complete in the conclusion drawn by Feuerbach.

On these fronts against both Protestant liberalism and Pietism, Barth had cause to attack Anabaptism directly. Continental liberal scholarship had identified Anabaptists as the pioneers and forerunners of the modern religious spirit, and specifically as the forerunners of Pietism and the Enlightenment, and thus of Friedrich Schleiermacher. Troeltsch praised the Anabaptist emphasis on (1) the separation of church and state, (2) voluntarism in the formation of church bodies, and (3) the inviolability of the inner personal life by the state. "What the world today understands as Protestantism is indebted more to the legacy of Anabaptism than to the legacy of the Reformers,"[34] according to Troeltsch. Barth comments that if this is the case, "(and there is something to it) then it is time to turn around and acquire the legacy of the Reformers, whose name and intentions we claim."[35] Indeed, Barth notes that he would "feel more at home in [Catholicism's] world and among its believers than in a world and among believers in which the concern of the Reformation has become an unknown or almost unknown quantity."[36] Barth's ultimate concern is for the sovereignty of the Word of God: just as the Reformers charged both the Roman hierarchy and *Schwärmertum* with an immediacy that bypassed the incarnate Word of God, now Protestant liberalism, Pietism, and religious socialism must be charged with the same theological error, according to Barth. "[W]e operate with the Spirit as if we ourselves were Christ, as if we had him [the Spirit] in our pocket in the form of our science, our bit of

---

31. See Barth, letter dated December 27, 1923, in ibid., 213–14.

32. Barth, "Ludwig Feuerbach," 223.

33. Barth came across this key Christological insight in 1925 ("§28 Christus Jesus: seine Person," in "Unterricht in der christlichen Religion," vol. 3); this became significant above all for "§64 The Exaltation of the Son of Man," in *Church Dogmatics*, IV/2, esp. 73ff.

34. Barth, "Das Schriftprinzip der reformierten Kirche," 529.

35. Ibid. In "Protestantisches Christentum und Kirche in der Neuzeit," 305, Troeltsch argues that in the sixteenth century "the time was not yet ripe for the Anabaptists nor the Anabaptists for the time. But the Anabaptists' hour and their global historical success arrived with the English Revolution and Pietism . . . Schleiermacher's doctrine of religion in his *Speeches* is a . . . proclamation of the Anabaptist theory of religion and congregation; contemporary Protestantism stands closer to Sebastian Franck than to Luther." Barth makes a similar statement about the "Schleiermacher–Ritschl–Troeltsch" line of understanding the legacy of the Reformation in "Der römische Katholizismus," 339.

36. Barth, "Der römische Katholizismus," 318.

ethos, our religious consciousness—or as if we could get him into our pocket through an upsurge of activism."[37] In this regard Barth uncritically accepts the line of influence that Troeltsch drew from the Anabaptists to the English Revolution, the Pietists, and to Schleiermacher—and then attacks that root cause accordingly.

Barth himself also draws a line from Tolstoy back to the Anabaptists. Both, according to Barth, employed a "biblicistic" ethic that identified the relatively concrete biblical imperatives as directly applicable divine commands for us. *Nachfolge* (discipleship) is no straightforward matter, for it rests in the indicative of being "in Christ,"[38] Barth writes. Such a reduction of ethics to discipleship assumes, according to Barth, the "intolerable humanizing of Christ that triumphed under the aegis of Schleiermacher in the 19th century."[39] Barth's writings regularly takes Schleiermacher to task for the impetus he gave to the type of Christocentrism associated with the life-of-Jesus theology of liberal Protestantism: "To honor heroes, even the man Jesus of Nazareth, is to deny revelation, for it forgets the *Deus dixit* [that God has spoken], the divine nature in Christ, to which alone honor and worship belong."[40] In one passing comment, Barth blames this deficient Christology on the "*Schwärmer* blood flowing through Schleiermacher's veins"!ature[41] Working with the questionable assumption that sixteenth-century Anabaptism is a common ancestor—either historically or in spirit—of both Pietism[42] and liberalism, Anabaptism became a most worthy target in Barth's historical theological work of the 1920s.[43]

A few remarks are now necessary to tie together the loose ends and attempt an evaluation. To begin with, it is disappointing that Barth's engagement with Anabaptist sources during this period was not as serious or rounded as we would later come to expect from

---

37. Barth, "Schriftprinzip der reformierten Kirche, 529. Curiously, Barth appropriates here the structure of Ritschl's argument against Roman Catholicism and Anabaptism. Barth summarizes Ritschl's view (whose thought Barth otherwise despises): "Christianity is an outlook upon life and it is morality, but in no way is it an immediate relationship with God. Roman Catholicism and every form of Anabaptists' faith is finished off at one blow by virtue of the fact that they think they know Christianity, and perhaps indeed of a more perfect Christianity beside that provided by the consciousness and realization in the moral sphere of the fact that we are children of God." Barth, *Protestant Theology in the Nineteenth Century*, 644 (translation slightly altered). This was likely written in 1926 in Münster.

38. Barth, *Ethik*, 1:134. Biblical imperatives "are not direct revelation, but like the Bible as a whole, they are a *witness* to revelation. In this very specific sense—which excludes their application as general moral truths—they are God's Word to us" (pp. 134–35). For Barth's early account of "discipleship," see *Ethik*, 2:132–33. For the mature Barth, see *Church Dogmatics*, IV/2:533ff.

39. Barth, *Theology of Schleiermacher*, 106.

40. Barth, *Göttingen Dogmatics*, 1:62. In the *Göttingen Dogmatics* Barth is already developing a specifically Trinitarian theology based on the recovery of classical Christology.

41. Barth, *Theology of Schleiermacher*, 106. Barth is thinking here of mystics in the line of Zinzendorf; he is, however, very aware that Schleiermacher's brazen justification of war and harsh critique of pacifist Christian groups "like Mennonites and Quakers," for example, cannot be explained from the notion of "mysticism"; see Barth, "Brunners Schleiermacherbuch," 415.

42. See Busch, *Karl Barth and the Pietists*.

43. A number of Swiss, German, and Russian Mennonite preachers were trained at the pietistic Evangelische Predigerschule in Basel, which Barth's father, Fritz Barth, directed between 1886–89. See Crous, "Anabaptism, Pietism, Rationalism and German Mennonites," 246. Under the influence of Pietism, Mennonites in many areas of Europe rejected traditional Anabaptist convictions, including nonresistance, as hindrances to spiritual renewal. See Friedmann's detailed historical study, "Anabaptism and Pietism."

him. We know that much of the historical support that Barth offers, including his account of the Second Zurich Disputation in 1523, is copied *verbatim* (without citing his source) from his father's 1903 lecture manuscript on "Zwingli's Life and Writings."[44] Consequently, Barth is not forced to comment on the newer Zwingli materials that were prepared for the four-hundred-year anniversary of the Reformation in Zurich (1919), in particular the important historical studies by Walther Köhler—notably a "liberal Zwingli researcher" but also a foremost authority on Anabaptism.[45] A number of weakness result from this deficit.

First, while Barth strives to avoid the combative style of historical theology that he believed marred the Lutheran reception of Zwingli,[46] he does not assume that Anabaptist beliefs can or need to be grasped as a meaningful whole, and he shows only very limited willingness to understand their key concerns and intentions as contingent witnesses of the Reformation.[47] This diminishes the quality of Barth's work.

Second, Barth does not grapple with Zwingli's eschatological assumptions that lead Zwingli to protect the Christendom unity of Zurich at all costs. These assumptions leave Zwingli unprotected from the dangers of subjectivism and opportunism, and allow him to let the sinful present situation be its own norm.[48] Barth (more than anyone) is otherwise very perceptive to the manner in which the Word of God unsettles and challenges the self-evident quality of our present world. And Barth is indeed fascinated by Zwingli's theocentrism, but this does not allow Barth to challenge Zwingli's "Eusebian and Augustinian interpretation of the millennium" in which the "*corpus Christianum* is the *regnum Christi.*"[49] Zwingli can say that while the apostles separated themselves from the world, true Christians will now separate from no one, for the entire world confesses Christ.[50] Paradoxically, Barth is very aware at this time that all ethics is inescapably "millenarian anticipation"—from Plato to Calvin, Kant, Schiller, and Ragaz. However, "[t]here is nothing in the whole range of human possibilities . . . which is capable of realizing the moral objective, the goal of history."[51] In this context Barth is very anxious about identifying God's Word to us with any specificity lest it become simplified and reified as in cultural Protestantism; he is very concerned not to repeat the liberal Protestant mistake of

---

44. See Freudenberg, "Vorwort" to Barth, *Theologie Zwinglis*, xiv–xv; also 236n. Karl Barth's father, Fritz Barth, was a professor at the University of Bern.

45. As the doctoral supervisor of three leading twentieth-century Mennonite historians—including Harold S. Bender, longtime mentor to John Howard Yoder—Köhler was instrumental in the rebirth of Anabaptist studies in Europe. See Neff and Bender, "Köhler, Walther"; see also Freudenberg's comments in his "Vorwort" to Barth, *Theologie Zwinglis*, ix.

46. Barth, *Theology of John Calvin*, 99, with explicit reference to the combative manner in which modern Lutheran scholars dealt with Zwingli.

47. These are Barth's own criteria for judging Luther's assessment of Carlstadt, Zwingli, and Oekolampad. See Barth, "Ansatz und Absicht in Luthers Abendmahlslehre, 298.

48. For a larger discussion, see Yoder, "Peace without Eschatology?" Yoder wrote this essay in 1954 while studying with Barth in Basel.

49. Yoder, *Anabaptism and Reformation in Switzerland*, 258. Indeed, Barth saw *corpus Christianum* (the idea of the unity of church and state) as an unfortunate temptation that the church was not prepared to resist; see *Church Dogmatics*, I/2:334.

50. Zwingli, as referred to by Yoder in *Anabaptism and Reformation in Switzerland*, 258.

51. Barth, "Problem of Ethics Today," 161, 166.

identifying specific historical movements with God's saving action. Thus it is not surprising that Barth's ecclesiology at this time does not move toward a theological examination of the church that practices discipleship faith. For the Anabaptists, baptism became that sign that commitment to Christ requires a concrete social embodiment of the gospel difference; and as such non-conformity, but not distance, is crucial to its calling to witness. In the 1920s Barth was very concerned about any claim of concretely embodying the gospel. In this regard John Howard Yoder was correct when he suggested that Barth's 1920s "Theology of the Word" was "not *explicitly* anti-establishment,"[52] though with its careful reading of Scripture and reappropriation of the Reformation, it can be seen as the beginnings of a "post-Christendom reconstruction" of theology. While ethical absolutism remains idolatrous for both the young and old Barth, toward the end of his life Barth does see the problem of Constantinianism clearly, and he praises Mennonites and early Anabaptists for getting it right.[53]

Indeed, despite all of the weaknesses identified above, there is something very positive in these early lectures. First, Barth remarks that with a fresh examination of the Reformers, he hopes to acquire the tools and orientation necessary to thoroughly dismantle the liberal theological tradition determined directly or indirectly by Friedrich Schleiermacher.[54] Barth makes large strides toward that goal in the Zwingli course. We have already pointed to Barth's discovery of the sole causality and glory of the Word of God. In the early writings his primary concern is to "chasten the pretensions of the then-authoritative moral theory" by beginning with the in-breaking Word, which begins to clear the space necessary for "the right sort of status for the human agent."[55] This approach gave Barth the leverage in the 1920s to call into question the entire liberal Protestant vision constructed by Ritschl, Troeltsch, von Harnack, Hermann, and Schleiermacher; consequently, Barth understood his own writings as "signposts for the reconstruction of theology and church."[56] These signposts from the 1920s remain important beacons for the church in the shadows of modernity.

Second, despite the deficiencies in his historical work, Barth learns that what distinguishes the Swiss magisterial Reformers from Luther is an understanding that the church is more than a spiritual community of worship, prayer, and Scripture reading. In contrast to the Lutheran tradition, the Reformed had always accorded a high place to morals. Their ecclesiology refused to divide intellect from practice. What is important here is not the polemical debate with Lutheranism on this point *per se*, but the manner in which Barth discovers a theologically satisfying way of reconstructing the moral earnestness of liberal Protestantism.[57] This is precisely the point that a later Mennonite student—John Howard Yoder—praises in Barth's work: "The very concept of a split between belief and action is

---

52. Yoder, "Karl Barth, Post-Christendom Theologian," 176.
53. Barth, "Gespräch mit den Mennoniten," 426–27.
54. See Barth, "Appendix 38: Autobiographical Sketches (Barth)," 158.
55. Webster, "Ethics and Politics," 147.
56. This is the subtitle to the German original of his *Theology and Church: Shorter Writings 1920–1928*.
57. See Webster, "Ethics and Politics," 159–60. Webster's writings on Barth's ethics show well how Barth subverts and reestablishes the ethical projects of Kantian and Ritschlian theologians, including their key ideas, conventions, and terms: command, freedom, agency, responsibility, and the good.

itself a doctrinal error . . . [I]f we were to deal systematically with theology in a specifically biblical stance or Anabaptist stance, then there would have to be some way of restoring ethics into every section of it. Few theologians have tried to do this. Karl Barth did, although we could still debate whether he had done it consistently or correctly."[58] In these historical-theological studies Barth was coming to understand that the primary task of Christian theology and ethics is to describe that which *is*—namely, the nature of reality as it is constituted in Jesus Christ—and then to live accordingly. John Webster gives a characteristically insightful summary of Barth's earlier writings that applies to the materials on Barth, Zwingli, and the Anabaptists above: "Barth's basic instinct in his earlier ethical writing was to insist that culture, politics and individual moral subjectivity are not autonomous or primordial realities but functions of the presence and purposive action of God. In this way, he sought to undo a metaphysics of morals which made ethical consciousness or the work of culture and politics into first principles, and to replace it by a trinitarian moral ontology of the command of God."[59] This was to be a lasting theological discovery for Barth—something gained in the space cleared by his early work in historical theology.

Unfortunately, Karl Barth never returned to do further work on sixteenth-century Anabaptism or Anabaptist-Mennonite theology. Curiously, however, the later Barth did come to a very different assessment of sixteenth-century Anabaptist beginnings, some of which was due to his encounter with young Mennonite students in Basel in the 1950s, including John Howard Yoder.[60] When Anabaptism is mentioned in the *Church Dogmatics* IV/3 (composed in 1959), Barth does not charge Anabaptists with exclusive separatism as he did in 1922. Rather, he recognizes that "Anabaptism itself was segregated and suppressed . . . both externally by the political authorities and internally by the Evangelical congregations."[61] Moreover, Barth notes that in contrast to the Reformers and the various evangelical awakenings since the Reformation, the Anabaptists were among the only ones whose understanding of mission (including church and eschatology) challenged the "dominant orders and disorders" of the status quo. "We cannot but admit that in this respect, for all the shortwindness, over-haste and general weakness of their teaching and attempts to structure life, the Anabaptists and Spiritualists, the so-called Enthusiasts of the Reformation period, saw much further than the Reformers themselves. Unwilling merely to accept the validity of existing relationships, they wanted to test them in the light

---

58. Yoder, *Preface to Theology*, 391.

59. Webster, "Ethics and Politics," 150.

60. Karl Barth was an internal reader of John Howard Yoder's 1957 doctoral thesis, which has only recently been translated and published in English as *Anabaptism and Reformation in Switzerland: An Historical and Theological Analysis of the Dialogues between Anabaptists and Reformers*. The dissertation was published in German in two separate volumes in 1962 and 1968; key pieces of the research appeared in English in three essays published between 1958 and 1969. If space allowed, I would develop the following double claim: (1) that the manner in which Yoder unlocks the diasporic, missional logic displayed so well by sixteenth-century Swiss Anabaptism owes more to Karl Barth than to the "Anabaptist Vision" school of Harold Bender (who was trained under Köhler); and (2) that Yoder's dissertation, as well as the fifty-page critique of Barth's views on the problem of war, which he presented to and discussed with Barth for more than three hours in July 1957, had at least a small influence on Barth's post-1957 reflections on Anabaptism, baptism, the problem of war, and the missionary nature of the church. Yoder's personal reflections on his 1957 encounter with Barth are detailed in a presentation given later that month: "Karl Barth und christlicher Pazifismus."

61. Barth, *Church Dogmatics*, IV/3:29.

of the Gospel. Were they altogether wrong when they said that Luther had been moving in the same direction in his 1520 writings?"[62]

Exactly one year before his death, Barth had a very amicable meeting with Swiss Mennonites at the European Mennonite Bible School (Bienenberg) in Liestal, Basel-Land, Switzerland, on December 13, 1967. Barth was asked by one of the Mennonite instructors[63] about the strengths of the Anabaptist movement of the sixteenth century. Barth immediately pointed to the challenge that Anabaptists posed to the Constantinian arrangement between church and society—and connected that to the challenges of the church in a post-Christendom context. According to Barth, the Anabaptists were those people

> who noticed that there is something not in order in the church—namely, that it had allied itself so with state and society. In one shot the whole Canton of Bern should be one Christian people! No, no, it can't be that simple. In one shot all of Europe should be Christian. And how should that happen? Well, you baptize the little children, and then they are Christian and then we have a Christian world. Wonderful! This is how it has been since the fourth century. It was the Emperor Constantine who declared Christianity to be the state religion. The Anabaptists recognized that there is something wrong with that. Christianity is neither a state religion nor a religion of society in general. Rather Christianity is something that comes as a gift—here to the one, there to another; here to a group, there to another . . . And for this reason they opposed infant baptism because, they said, the baptismal waters are being wasted, as it were. One should baptize those people (as it was in the New Testament) who say that they would like to be baptized, who request it, who take it upon themselves as a responsible matter, and who are thus accepted by the congregation, and then they are baptized. But not to a small baby which cannot be asked! One should not be surprised . . . that the church is so secularized: it is because of infant baptism. For if everything is simply taken care of with that—and one makes the person into a Christian (it is taken care of simply with the water, and one claims that it is the new birth and the acceptance into the covenant of God and inclusion in the body of Christ, that they are baptized!), then one cannot be surprised when these people later say "No one asked me," and then go their own way and live without being Christian. So I would say that the Anabaptists stood up and helped to recall how it was still done in the first and second centuries—this was their strength.[64]

This lengthy quote should be compared with the whole of Barth's "Doctrine of Baptism as the Foundation of the Christian Life" (*Church Dogmatics* IV/4), which had just been published a few months prior to this 1967 meeting.[65] For our purposes the above quotation indicates clearly that Barth had come to an entirely different assessment of sixteenth-century Swiss Anabaptists than the position he had held forty-five years earlier. Moreover, Barth's understanding of baptism had also shifted radically during this time toward believers' baptism. We already noted above that beginning in the early 1960s, Barth began to develop a theology of baptism that brought him to reject infant baptism for the sake

---

62. Ibid., IV/3:28 (translation altered).

63. Interview with Helmut Doerksen (questioner), July 2009, Muttenz, Switzerland. Doerksen had taken a number of courses with Barth in Basel.

64. Barth, "Gespräch mit den Mennoniten," 426–27.

65. Barth, *Church Dogmatics*, IV/4 (fragment).

of the mission of the community of faith,[66] namely, in order for the church to depict and give witness to the grace of God. This development is of major significance for Barth studies, and Barth affirmed in 1967 that sixteenth-century Swiss Anabaptists got this part right—and emphasized that this has some significance for the witness of the church in a post-Constantinian, post-Christendom context.[67]

In his Gifford Lectures, Stanley Hauerwas provides a sympathetic account of "The Witness That Was Karl Barth."[68] However, Hauerwas remarks that "[A]ttractive accounts of the world can often turn out to be no more than fantasies. The needed incentive not just to entertain but to live Christian convictions requires the display of a habitable world exemplified in the life of the Christian community."[69] Hauerwas argues that Barth offers an "over cautious" presentation of the church in the economy of God's salvation. The latter requires churches like those represented by "John Howard Yoder and Pope John Paul II," which embody the "kind of witnesses who must exist if Christians are to recover the confident use of theological speech that Barth exemplifies so well."[70] In this initial study of recently published materials from the Karl Barth Archive on Anabaptist beginnings, we have been able to see that there is concrete support for both claims. On the one hand, through Barth's early engagement with sixteenth-century Swiss Anabaptist history, we have a unique perspective on Barth's early search for theological speech (appropriate to the twentieth century) that corresponds to the reality that "God speaks." Barth's method during the 1920s was to search historically for tools to faithfully, confidently, and unapologetically witness to an unbelieving world about the way things really are if God has really made himself known in the life, death, and resurrection of Jesus Christ. Barth recognized that authentic theologizing is not an alternative to contemporary pertinence, but its precondition.[71] On the other hand, we have also traced Barth's initial critique and his growing appreciation of the concrete, ecclesial witness of this reality in the testimony of the early Swiss Anabaptists.[72] When already firmly established as the most significant theologian since Schleiermacher, the old Barth pointed to Anabaptists as one group whose communal witness spoke eloquently that "Christianity is something that comes as a gift."[73] And within a post-Christendom context, as Hauerwas suggests, this kind of witness is "not just something Christians 'do' but is at the heart of understanding how that to which Christians witness is true."[74]

---

66. Ibid., IV/4 (fragment): 189–90.

67. In 1994 Yoder noted that Barth was "epistemologically post-Constantinian" insofar as he appeals to the early church as a model for present practice. See Yoder, "Karl Barth, Post-Christendom Theologian," 179.

68. Hauerwas, *With the Grain of the Universe*, chap. 6.

69. Ibid., 214.

70. Ibid., 216–17.

71. See Yoder, "Karl Barth, Post-Christendom Theologian," 176.

72. I think that it is unhelpful to say, as did Yoder, that "Barth's incomplete pilgrimage can best be understood as being on the way to what Anglo-Saxon ecclesiological thinking calls the Free Church"; see "Karl Barth: How His Mind Kept Changing," 168–69. George Hunsinger, in "Karl Barth and the Politics of Sectarian Protestantism," has strongly challenged this claim. Arne Rasmusson's notion of "diaspora politics" and "diaspora theology," however, may prove much more helpful; see his "Politics of Diaspora," 110.

73. Barth, "Gespräch mit den Mennoniten," 427.

74. Hauerwas, *With the Grain of the Universe*, 217.

Bibliography

Barth, Karl. "Ansatz und Absicht in Luthers Abendmahlslehre, 1923." In *Vorträge und kleinere Arbeiten, 1922-1925*, edited by H. Finze, 248-306. Zurich: TVZ, 1990.

———. "Appendix 38: Autobiographical Sketches (Barth)." In *Karl Barth-Rudolf Bultmann: Letters 1922-1966*, translated by G. W. Bromiley, 150-58. Grand Rapids: Eerdmans, 1981.

———. *Barth-Thurneysen Briefwechsel II, 1921-1930*. Edited by E. Thurneysen. Zurich: TVZ, 1974.

———. "Brunners Schleiermacherbuch, 1924." In *Vorträge und kleinere Arbeiten, 1922-1925*, edited by H. Finze, 401-25. Zurich: TVZ, 1990.

———. *Church Dogmatics*. 4 vols. Edited by G. W. Bromiley and T. F. Torrance. Translated by G. W. Bromiley. Edinburgh: T. & T. Clark, 1956-76.

———. *The Epistle to the Romans*. 2 vols. Translated by E. C. Hoskyns. New York: Oxford University Press, 1968.

———. *Ethik*. Edited by D. Braun. Zurich: TVZ, 1973-78.

———. "Gespräch mit den Mennoniten (13.12.1967)." In *Gespräche 1964-1968*, edited by E. Busch, 418-34. Zurich: TVZ, 1997.

———. "Gespräch mit Vertretern der Gemeinschaften (6.10.1959)." In *Gespräche 1959-1962*, edited by E. Busch, 13-41. Zurich: TVZ, 1995.

———. *Göttingen Dogmatics: Instruction in the Christian Religion*. Translated by G. W. Bromiley. Grand Rapids: Eerdmans, 1991.

———. "Ludwig Feuerbach." In *Theology and Church: Shorter Writings, 1920-1928*, translated by L.P. Smith, 217-37. London: SCM, 1962.

———. "The Problem of Ethics Today [1922]." In *The Word of God and the Word of Man*, translated by D. Horton, 136-82. New York: Harper, 1957.

———. *Protestant Theology in the Nineteenth Century*. Translated by B. Cozens and J. Bowden. Grand Rapids: Eerdmans, 2002.

———. "Der römische Katholizismus als Frage an die protestantische Kirche, 1928." In *Vorträge und kleinere Arbeiten, 1925-1930*, edited by H. Schmidt, 303-43. Zurich: TVZ, 1994.

———. "Das Schriftprinzip der reformierten Kirche, 1925." In *Vorträge und kleinere Arbeiten, 1922-1925*, edited by H. Finze, 500-544. Zurich: TVZ, 1990.

———. *Die Theologie Zwinglis: Vorlesung Göttingen, Wintersemester 1922/1923*. Edited by M. Freudenberg. Zurich: TVZ, 2004.

———. *Theology and Church: Shorter Writings 1920-1928*. Translated by L. P. Smith. London: SCM, 1962.

———. *The Theology of John Calvin*. Translated by G. W. Bromiley. Edinburgh: T. & T. Clark, 1995.

———. *The Theology of Schleiermacher: Lectures at Göttingen, Winter Semester of 1923-24*. Translated by G. W. Bromiley. Grand Rapids: Eerdmans, 1982.

———. "Unterricht in der christlichen Religion." Vol. 3, *Die Lehre von der Versöhnung/Die Lehre von der Erlösung, 1925/1926*. Edited by H. Stoevesandt. Zurich: TVZ, 2003.

Busch, Eberhard. *Karl Barth and the Pietists: The Young Karl Barth's Critique of Pietism and Its Response*. Translated by D. W. Bloesch. Downers Grove, IL: InterVarsity, 2004.

Crous, Ernst. "Anabaptism, Pietism, Rationalism and German Mennonites." In *The Recovery of the Anabaptist Vision*, edited by G. Hershberger, 237-48. Scottdale, PA: Herald, 1957.

Freudenberg, M. "Vorwort" to Karl Barth, *Die Theologie Zwinglis: Vorlesung Göttingen, Wintersemester 1922-1923*. Zurich: TVZ, 2004.

Friedmann, Robert. "Anabaptism and Pietism." In *Mennonite Piety through the Centuries*, 2-88. Scottdale, PA: Mennonite Publishing House, 1949.

Hauerwas, Stanley. *With the Grain of the Universe: The Church's Witness and Natural Theology*. Grand Rapids: Eerdmans, 2001.

Hirsch, Emanuel. *Deutschlands Schicksal*. 2nd ed. Göttingen: Vandenhoeck, 1922.

Hunsinger, George. "Karl Barth and the Politics of Sectarian Protestantism: A Dialogue with John Howard Yoder." In *Disruptive Grace: Studies in the Theology of Karl Barth*, 114-30. Grand Rapids: Eerdmans, 2000.

Neff, C., and H. S. Bender. "Köhler, Walther." In *Mennonite Encyclopedia*, 3:212. Scottdale, PA: Herald, 1957.

Rasmusson, Arne. "The Politics of Diaspora: The Post-Christendom Theologies of Karl Barth and John Howard Yoder." In *God, Truth, and Witness: Engaging Stanley Hauerwas*, edited by L. Gregory Jones et al., 88–111. Grand Rapids: Brazos, 2005.

Troeltsch, Ernst. "Protestantisches Christentum und Kirche in der Neuzeit." In *Die Kultur der Gegenwart*, edited by P. Hinnebert, 253–458. Leipzig: Teubner, 1906.

Webster, John. "Ethics and Politics." In *Karl Barth*, 141–63. New York: Continuum, 2000.

———. "The Theology of Zwingli." In *Barth's Earlier Theology*, 15–39. New York: Continuum, 2005.

Yoder, John Howard. *Anabaptism and Reformation in Switzerland: An Historical and Theological Analysis of the Dialogues between Anabaptists and Reformers*. Edited by C. Arnold Snyder. Translated by David C. Stassen and C. Arnold Snyder. Kitchener, ON: Pandora, 2004.

———. "Karl Barth: How His Mind Kept Changing." In *How Karl Barth Changed My Mind*, edited by Donald K. McKim, 166–71. Grand Rapids: Eerdmans, 1986.

———. "Karl Barth, Post-Christendom Theologian." In Yoder, *Karl Barth and the Problem of War and Other Essays on Barth*, edited by Mark Thiessen Nation, 175–88. Eugene, OR: Cascade, 2003.

———. "Karl Barth und christlicher Pazifismus." Bericht der zweiten Konferenz, Iserlohn, July 28–August 1, 1957. In *Puidoux Series of Theological Conferences on the Lordship of Christ over Church and State*, Section E, 66–73. Bechlinghoven bei Beuel, 1960.

———. "Peace without Eschatology?" In *The Royal Priesthood: Essays Ecclesiological and Ecumenical*, edited by Michael G. Cartwright, 143–67. Grand Rapids: Eerdmans, 1994.

———. *Preface to Theology: Christology and Theological Method*. Grand Rapids: Brazos, 2002.

———. "The Turning Point in the Zwinglian Reformation." *Mennonite Quarterly Review* 32 (1958) 128–40.

Anabaptist-Mennonite Political Theology

Conceptualizing Universal Ethics in Post-Christendom

A. James Reimer

I AM PLEASED TO CONTRIBUTE THIS CHAPTER TO A BOOK IN HONOR OF HARRY HUEBNER'S work. This occasion has allowed me to look more closely at Huebner's writings as I develop my own "Anabaptist-Mennonite Political Theology." I first got to know Huebner in the halls of the University of Manitoba in the 1960s, where he was finishing a philosophy degree and I was pursuing a combined history and philosophy degree. He was interested especially in Immanuel Kant, whereas I was drawn to Hegel and Marx. After receiving my master's degree in European intellectual history at the University of Toronto, I enrolled at the University of St. Michael's College for a PhD in theology. Here I again met Huebner, who had transferred from the University of Toronto, where he had virtually completed a doctorate on Kant, to St. Michael's to write a thesis on Ernst Troeltsch. Both of us had the Canadian theologian Gregory Baum as our advisor and were influenced by his passion for social justice. I have always been impressed with Huebner's commitment to the church, his intellectual rigor, and his ability to inspire students. Two of my children studied with Huebner at Canadian Mennonite Bible College.

More recently, I have undertaken a comprehensive study of Christian political theology, a project that shapes the broader context of this chapter. My present purpose is to investigate the possibility of conceptualizing universal moral principles without surrendering the particularities of Christian theology.[1]

Conceptualizing Universal Moral Principles for Social Ethics

It is generally acknowledged that, in the West at least, we have moved from a modern to a postmodern way of looking at the world. Whereas in the modern period it could be assumed

---

1. This chapter is the third in a series of articles that began with "An Anabaptist-Mennonite Political Theology: Theological Foundations," in which I lay out my Trinitarian assumptions and consider some foundational biblical texts. The second article was "Anabaptist-Mennonite Political Theology: Historical Manifestations and Observations," which concentrates on the Constantinian turn of the fourth century, with some discussion of the medieval, Reformation, and modern periods. The present essay draws on a paper I presented at a conference on Islamic ethics in Qom, Iran, entitled "Conceptualizing Universal Moral Principles for Social Ethics: The Pros and Cons of Global Ethics." Muslims have a high view of natural theology—that is, of the role of human reason in theological work—and my paper was written with this in mind.

that there was a common rationality undergirding public morality, as in Kantian ethics (sometimes referred to as foundationalism), in the postmodern period such universal understanding of reason can no longer be presupposed (non- or even anti-foundationalism). Instead of one foundational rationality presupposed by all public discourse, postmodernism offers multi-rationalities with differing views of justice. Alasdair MacIntyre's book *Whose Justice? Which Rationality?* illustrates precisely this approach. MacIntyre situates rationality in the context of linguistic and moral traditions with continuities over time, which he calls "narratives." Ethicists like Stanley Hauerwas have aligned themselves with this so-called narrative school of thought. I have appropriated some aspects of this view (e.g., the importance for theology of the language of narrative, metaphor, symbol, and parable) while maintaining a role for universal principles that transcend narrative, as in some forms of natural law. I continue to explore new (or premodern) ways of understanding natural law (as in Aquinas's hierarchy of divine law, eternal law, natural law, and civil law) and universal rationality (as in the ancient *logos* and wisdom traditions).

My strong conviction as a Christian theologian is that theology has political ramifications. Although theology is political, it is not *only* political, nor is good theology defined by political correctness. Good theology must have its own prior grounding in a certain view and experience of God—in Trinitarian monotheism. In short, behind a good social ethic is a good theology. Here Harry Huebner's understanding of political theology is basically sound, although, as the following quotation makes clear, he may be linking theology and politics too closely, even if it is an alternative politics: "This essay... asks what Christian theology has to say politically, which is different from asking what it has to say *to politics*. It is written against the common temptation to give too much credence to political givens and then be left only to sprinkle faith onto the secular imagination. Such an approach may well give politics a Christian 'flavour' but it is not yet political theology. The challenge is to let theology be the discourse that informs how we structure our social and political existence."[2] Huebner refines this broad statement further by proposing that the church develop alternative structures to the world: the church is called, he says, to "conscientiously develop an alternative life-sustaining tradition with new social structures: structures related to economics, health care, management/labour relations, responses to criminals, international relations, poverty, violent conflict, and so on."[3] Granted, there are times when the church is called to develop counter-structures, both religious and political, to the dominant culture—as, for example, the alternative seminary system of the Confessing Church in Nazi Germany in the 1930s, or the Christian Peacemaker Teams' effort at mediation between opposing sides in situations of conflict and war. Nevertheless, when the overarching image of the church is an alternative community with separate and parallel structures in virtually every facet of life, I begin to sense that the other dimensions of the gospels such as "love of the world" and "solidarity with the world"—its suffering, its tragedy—and even humanistic rationality are in danger of being lost. To make theology primarily a new form of politics is a form of reductionism, and does not take seriously enough the inner, spiritual, existential, experiential, and sacramental nature of the Gospel.

2. Huebner, "Nation: Beyond Secular Politics," 258.
3. Huebner, "Church Made Strange for the Nations," 102.

A study of German theology in the Nazi period can bring these exact issues to view. My doctoral work focused on two German theologians, Paul Tillich and Emanuel Hirsch, friends with similar backgrounds and educations who read and reviewed each other's books in the 1920s, struggled with the same philosophical and theological issues, but parted ways politically. Toward the end of World War I, Hirsch became a religious nationalist, and Tillich a religious socialist. In 1933 Hirsch was a strong supporter of Hitler and National Socialism, on both theological and political grounds, while Tillich lost his job at the University of Frankfurt for his opposition to Hitler. I closely examined their open debate in German periodicals in 1934–1935,[4] where it becomes clear that Tillich and Hirsch both *politicize* theology, one on the left and the other on the right. In this politicization of theology they are formally similar, even though ideologically they are opposed. Their contemporary, Karl Barth, refused to ally theology with politics of any stripe and claimed that while all theology is political, it must always give priority to dogma. My study of German theologians in the 1920s and 1930s has confirmed my belief in the importance of theology for social ethics, and, at the same time, the dangers of identifying theology too uncritically with politics either on the left or the right, or the liberal center, for that matter. It has also made a new form of political theology that sees Christianity primarily as alternative social-political-economic structures seem suspect.

My current research project, tentatively titled "A Theology of Law, Order, and Public Life in a Multicultural World," a historical survey of the Western development of legal and political thought from a religious-theological perspective, seeks to apply these findings to contemporary multicultural and multi-religious societies, in which traditions with competing truth claims seek to live peacefully alongside each other. For such diverse, even competing, traditions to coexist peaceably within one society requires some minimum agreement on the basic legal and political principles to which all groups can subscribe without compromising their fundamental ideological and religious commitments. This becomes a special problem in postmodern societies where shared, universal values can no longer be presupposed, as they were in premodern and modern cultures. My interest in this larger project is to explore how a minimum of universal principles can be identified as the *raison d'être* for a legal system within which competing minority groups can coexist under what might be called a "public orthodoxy" (Jon Levenson), represented by the dominant tradition that carries the given culture.

My involvement in Christian-Muslim dialogue over the past decade with Iranian doctoral students studying in Toronto and in a series of four academic conferences (2002 in Toronto, Ontario; 2004 in Qom, Iran; 2007 in Waterloo, Ontario; and 2008 in Qom, Iran) have convinced me that agreement on universal moral and religious principles cannot be arrived at in abstraction but emerges through particular encounters between different communities of belief. In other words, *one gets to the universal through the particular*. The success of our Mennonite Christian and Shi'a Muslim exchange is based on the dialogue between members of two believing communities, out of which emerged some commonalities and differences, not by first establishing abstractly some universal norms upon which we could agree and then basing our dialogue on these. Any global ethic, if

---

4. See Reimer, *Emanuel Hirsch and Paul Tillich Debate*, and *Emanuel Hirsch und Paul Tillich*.

such a thing exists, will have to evolve through the authentic and open encounter between particular religious and cultural traditions.

Stackhouse and Company: What about Global Ethics?

In "The Church Made Strange for the Nations," Huebner rightly stresses the fact that no one can occupy a neutral public or private space; we all speak from a particular, culturally and religiously mediated point of view. In our case this is the biblically based Christian perspective. Here Huebner reflects the anti-foundationalism and rational perspectivalism of postmodern and post-liberal thought. However, public space is always defined by a "public orthodoxy" of one kind or another, not by neutrality.[5] I have repeatedly made the point that we get to the universal *through* the particular; we ought not to fixate on the particular but to strive for the universal. We do this through encounter with the other, not through the imposition of our particularity on the other.

Much is being written currently about the phenomenon of globalization and its implications for social ethics. In much of this literature, the universal surfaces too quickly, at the expense of the particular. In a four-volume series under the general title *God and Globalization*, edited chiefly by Max L. Stackhouse, various specialists make the case for such a religiously based global ethic.[6] While the authors differ on the meaning and implications of globalization, none questions the fact of globalization itself. All of them accept, as Stackhouse describes it, that "[t]oday, the world as a historical interaction of people and societies is undergoing a dynamic transformation called 'globalization,' one that has many implications for the world as a biophysical planet and for the world as a philosophical-theological concept" (*God and Globalization*, 1:1).

Furthermore, while it is generally recognized that "globalization is disrupting many aspects of traditional religion, ethics, culture, economics, politics, and society," there is a pervasive sense in these volumes that religion, the sense of the holy, can generally ally itself positively with forces of globalization (1:6). Such a positive alliance allows us to "use ethics to assess the assumptions and implications of every theologically approved practice and dogmatic claim. We may demand further that valid ethical criteria find ultimate sanction in what is truly universal and enduring, and not only in what is religiously and temporarily 'mine' or 'ours' at the moment" (1:7). According to Stackhouse, global developments in business, technology, ecology, and universal human rights "seem now to be leading humanity toward the possible creation of a global civilization that will alter every community and tradition" (1:8). In the words of Stackhouse again: "The process that we call globalization seems to be creating the conditions for a new super-ethos, a worldwide set of operating values and norms that will influence most, if not all, peoples, cultures, and societies. It is quite possible that most of the contexts in which humans now live, and their

---

5. For a discussion of what is meant by "public orthodoxy," see Reimer, "Public Orthodoxy and Civic Forbearance."

6. *God and Globalization*, vol. 1, *Religion and the Powers of the Common Life*; vol. 2, *Spirit and the Modern Authorities*; vol. 3, *Christ and the Dominions of Civilization*; vol. 4, *Globalization and Grace*. Volume and page references will appear parenthetically in the text.

roots in particular sets of values and norms, will be modified by a new comprehending context that owes its allegiance to no particular society, local ethos, or political order, even if it is advanced by 'Western' influences" (1:19). It is not entirely clear whether Stackhouse and other authors in *God and Globalization* are simply *describing* the inevitability of globalization or *welcoming* it as a positive development to be supported by religious ideologies. In the contributions of some of the writers, at least, there also appears to be a relativization of the truth claims of particular religions in favor of a watered-down set of global values. This relativization of particularity is the fundamental threat of globalization.

There is some acknowledgment in these volumes of the dangers of globalization and the opposition movements to it. One of the more important critical challenges to globalization comes from those who claim that it is a force for *sameness* and *homogenization*, erasing traditional and local differences. However, others such as Roland Robertson disagree. Optimistic about the future of religion and culture in a globalized world, he maintains that globalization in fact enhances traditionally distinct cultures. Robertson considers "the homogenization-versus-hetereogenization dispute as the core feature of globalization" (1:56). He argues that globalization spreads sameness and difference simultaneously; in fact, globalization breeds a sense of difference that he calls "localization."

Robertson admits that one aspect of globalization that represents a threat to traditional religions and cultures is *relativization*—the challenge that comes with the coexistence of different and sometimes clashing cultures. According to Robertson, "relativization refers to the ways in which adherents to cultural traditions come to feel threatened by existence alongside rival or alien identities or traditions in an increasingly interdependent world" (1:61). Clearly revealing his prejudices, he calls the various "fundamentalist" opposition movements to globalization "globaphobic." "Cultural clashes and tensions," he says, "are an inevitable feature of globalization. What should be called the dark side of globalization involves the militance and, indeed, violence that not infrequently accompanies these clashes. Nothing about globalization should lead people to believe that it is leading to a more peaceful world" (1:61). One of the core values that would constitute a global morality would be *peaceful* and *nonviolent* coexistence. For Christians, this would have its root in the teachings and life of Jesus.

Yersu Kim, in "Philosophy and the Prospects for a Universal Ethic," recognizes the weakness of globalization. Acknowledging the triumphalism that accompanies much neo-liberal economics, he says: "It is clear that the benefits of globalization do not extend to all countries or social groups. Indeed, the dramatic extremes of wealth and poverty born of globalization menace both democracy and social stability in various regions. For many globalization signifies a race to the bottom, not only in wages but in standards of environmental regulation and social legislation" (1:77).

Despite these dangers, Kim too cites positively the many attempts by international commissions and agencies to develop a global ethic. He refers favorably to various commissions of the United Nations and other international bodies, particularly the 1995 statement by the Commission on Global Governance, *Our Global Neighborhood*, on the core values of a global civil ethic: "Such a global ethic comprises a minimum of core values shared by all cultures and religious traditions, and a set of rights and responsibilities constituting a 'civil code' based on these core values. These values include respect for life, liberty, justice, and equity; mutual respect; caring; and integrity. The values derive in one way or another from the principle of reciprocity known as the Golden Rule—that people should treat others as they would themselves wish to be treated" (1:79).

The Roman Catholic theologian Hans Küng has done much "to identify 'the minimum of what the religions of the world already have in common now in the ethical sphere' and professes to draw from them broad, ancient guidelines for human behavior. This process involves an understanding of the hermeneutics of religious texts, sociology of religions and morals, cultural anthropology, and other social sciences" (1:93).[7] Kim concludes that a global ethic will need to "guide humanity in its tasks of survival and flourishing." He adds that "since the aim is to forge an ethical statement acceptable to all societies and cultures, built on different perceptions and aspirations, it must accommodate the challenge of cultural diversity and polarities of values and principles" (1:103).

Surely globalization is taking place in our world. The global triumph of Western technology, the computer being its supreme symbol, is an instance of this globalization. I am not as happy about it, however, as most of the authors in these volumes. And although some universal values and moral commitments are needed for the peaceful coexistence of different religions and cultures in the modern and postmodern world, the above authors do not provide an adequate account of how to arrive at these commonalities, nor how they can be grounded in the metaphysical, ontological, and theological truth claims of particular traditions, including those of Islam and Christianity. Globalization is no doubt eroding the commitments of particular traditions, but this is an unfortunate consequence of the global village and ought to be resisted by all believing communities. Universal ethics are needed to meet the challenges of globalization, but ought to be conceptualized in such a way as not to devalue the particular; they need to emerge out of the respectful encounter between different faith groups.

Stout: A Common Morality without Metaphysics

While a strong case can be made for the growing need for a universal ethic (a "public theology"), there are some commonly perceived, and justified, critiques of the attempt to abstractly identify such a common morality, set of core values, and beliefs for all religions and all societies that will guide human behavior worldwide. First, there is the legitimate fear of triumphalism and imperialism (frequently enforced by violence) by one dominant religious-political culture, such as the Western world, or more specifically, North America ("Americanization"). Second, and related to the first, there is the distinct danger of such a common morality being simply a means of spreading Western-style capitalistic economy around the globe under the guise of so-called democratic values of "freedom." Third, globalization, like technology, may be a form of homogenization that threatens "otherness" and "difference," that is, traditional values and cultures (heterogeneity). Fourth, there is the tendency to ground a universal morality in a selected form of Enlightenment rational-

---

7. Quotation from Hans Küng taken from Küng and Kuschel, *Global Ethic*, 8.

ity, called "technical reason" by the Canadian philosopher George Grant and "purposive rationality" by Catholic theologian David Tracy.

Tracy, in his essay "Public Theology, Hope, and the Mass Media: Can the Muses Still Inspire?" in support of Jürgen Habermas's theory of communicative and inter-subjective rationality, makes this point when he says, "[Habermas's] central theory does seem to clarify how the problem of modernity—including the problem of rationality in our contemporary globalized situation, which has been named either late modernity or postmodernity—is one of selective and one-sided use of a purposive rationality appropriate for social systems like global communications technology, but inappropriate for, indeed devastating for, the communicative rationality necessary for a proper understanding of 'reason' in any contemporary theology or philosophy."[8] A universal ethic arrived at abstractly tends to be one based on forms of rationality devoid of metaphysical and transcendent grounds.[9]

In his book *Democracy and Tradition*, Jeffrey Stout strongly advocates democratic values, but in his chapters titled "The Ideal of a Common Morality" and "Ethics without Metaphysics," he argues against the attempt to establish abstractly a global ethic based on some form of natural law or metaphysics. Stout is not opposed to the notion that a common morality is desirable; what he rejects is the idea that such a common morality *preexists*, "a single way of talking and thinking about ethical issues that is already the common possession of humankind."[10] He rightly observes that "a common morality can only be achieved piecemeal, by gradually building discursive bridges and networks of trust in particular settings" (226).

While such a statement reflects the underlying conviction that one gets to the universal only through the particular, nonetheless Stout's dismissal of the natural law tradition as a whole is problematic. He distinguishes his approach from those philosophers and theologians who "appeal directly to a morality that is already, in their view, the common property of humankind." According to them, this morality "is not simply a common way of thinking and talking about moral issues (that is, a discursive practice) but a body of moral truths that need only be applied to yield concrete moral guidance on the questions currently under dispute. It is a law higher than, better than, the mores of any people. Traditional natural-law theorists take it that we all have cognitive access to this law, at least to some significant degree" (226). While on the practical, everyday level such universal moral principles are not as readily accessible as some would claim, I hold, in line with the Realist heritage, that some notion of universal or eternal laws do exist behind or beyond the practical agreements that parties achieve in particular contexts.

Stout makes the important distinction between truth and its justification. He does not advocate skepticism and moral relativism. There may well be truths that are common

---

8. *God and Globalization*, 1:239.

9. I also have been critical of this kind of universal, technical rationality in my work. See especially "Part One: The Crisis of Modernity," of my *Mennonites and Classical Theology: Dogmatic Foundations for Christian Ethics*.

10. Stout, *Democracy and Tradition*, 225. Subsequent page references to Stout will appear parenthetically in the text.

to all and transcend what each party in a controversy believes, but humility is required in relation to the possession of these truths, and these can be justified only contextually. Given a certain understanding of justice, for example, Nazism can be said to be wrong. "Using a relativist conception of truth to redescribe our differences would be to dissolve the conflict in which we take ourselves to be engaged" (239). Stout is a soft pragmatist (that is, truth has to do with practices) who wants "to combine a contextualist account of justification with a nonrelativist account of moral truth" (240). He says:

> Contextualist epistemology is compatible with the idea that there is a moral law in this sense: an infinitely large set consisting of all the true moral claims but not a single falsehood or contradiction. Being infinitely large and including truths cast in myriad possible vocabularies we will never master, this set boggles the mind. We will never believe, let alone be justified in believing, more than a tiny fraction of the truths it encompasses. Most of them are inaccessible to us—and therefore not truths it would be wise for us to pursue. (240)

What he calls his "minimalist" view of moral law does not require for Stout a theistic view of the world. He rejects the concept of an ideal rational system of moral laws that are accessible to human reason and ought to guide moral behavior and be able to adjudicate ethical controversies. However, natural law and divine-command theories based on revelation (for example, killing is wrong) can legitimately provide criteria for ethics in a way that is universalizable.

Stout wants to keep on talking about truth while shedding the baggage of metaphysics. He achieves this, he thinks, with a modest form of pragmatism based on how we use language. "Truth does not belong . . . to the furniture of the natural world (as conceived by natural science). So we cannot provide an account of it by turning our attention to some feature of the natural world and describing empirically in what that feature consists. The concept of truth is normative. It belongs to the practices in which we assess claims and beliefs as possessing or failing to possess a sort of status" (254). He adds, "Truth-talk is not an implicitly metaphysical affair, standing in need of metaphysical articulation and defense. It is an aspect of ordinary language use, to be made sense of in terms of an empirically oriented linguistic theory" (255).

Stout makes a distinction between metaphysics in the pejorative sense, based on a correspondence theory of knowledge (i.e., our rational truth claims correspond to external reality) and metaphysics in a non-pejorative sense (i.e., "a class of claims . . . [referring] to something beyond or above the ontological framework assumed in the natural sciences") (256). In other words, a non-theistic pragmatist like Stout could accept the "social-pragmatic theory of obligation" present in certain theist views—that is, the social-obligatory dimensions of divine commands—but not the ontological claims being made about a personal God who interacts with us (260). However, to base a theory of moral obligation on pragmatic (human practice) understandings of normativity alone is not robust enough to withstand moral relativism. Some metaphysical, ontological, theological foundation is necessary if ethics is not to be reduced to some form of historicism.

The most difficult thing to understand in Stout's argument is how he can make truth claims on purely pragmatic grounds without becoming totally relativist and subjectivist. He believes that the norms for ethical behavior emerge out of human practices: "We understand what excellence [the good] is, practically speaking, because we interact constantly with finite things that satisfy the interests and excellence that arise in the context of practices like child rearing, spiritual counseling, philosophy, science, the arts, athletics, and politics. These are all practices in which we are trying to improve on something; a child's behavior, our grasp of a concept, a set of institutional arrangements, or whatever" (264). He says further: "To understand excellence is thus to possess a kind of wisdom that is difficult or impossible to state propositionally. The metaphysical temptation, in this area of philosophy, is to think that an explicit, highly general propositional formulation would represent an advance on the practical understanding gained through experience of particular excellent things" (264). We come to understand excellences by learning the language and practices of our community. "In these practices we interact with instances of excellence, and learn to apply such expressions as 'good,' 'better than,' 'eloquent,' 'beautiful,' and 'virtuous' in accord with the norms of our community" (267).

Stout's quarrel is not with those whose ethics is shaped by belief in some transcendent being, but with those who believe that this God has revealed objective propositional truths that can be rationally understood and universally applied, the God of Descartes and analytic metaphysics: "[Pragmatism's] account of excellence, like its account of obligation, can accommodate whatever persons, social relationships, and practices there happen to be. Its purpose should not be to put theologically inclined citizens on the defensive. The purpose served by pragmatic ethical theory is rather to make clear that a society divided over the nature and existence of God is not thereby condemned to view its ethical discourse as an unconstrained endeavor" (268). I find Stout's disclaimer not totally convincing, for his particular pragmatic theory of moral obligation does not in fact require some higher source, which most religious people would hold.

Conclusion: Reconceptualizing Universal Moral Principles

Arguing strenuously for an ethic that is grounded in dogmatics, that is, in "modest" metaphysical assumptions about the nature of God (understood in Trinitarian terms), humanity, salvation, nature, and history sets me at odds with Stout.[11] Dialogue with my Muslim friends from Iran engenders an appreciation for the strong conviction within the Islamic faith that moral and ethical principles should be founded in a monotheistically based view of natural law. Muslims have a very high view of a God-given rationality's capacity to understand the universe, human beings, and moral obligation. In the light of these two factors (arguing for dogmatic foundations for ethics, and experience with dialogue between Mennonite Christians and Shi'ite Muslims), I propose that one can conceptualize universal moral principles rooted in a particular notion of transcendence.

Huebner's strong advocacy of a comprehensive set of alternative social, economic, and political structures alongside those already existing in many different and changing forms in the global community makes me intellectually claustrophobic. I hold with the *God and Globalization* series that the world is fast becoming a global village in which dif-

---

11. Reimer, *Mennonites and Classical Theology: Dogmatic Foundations for Christian Ethics.*

ferent and sometimes competing religious and cultural traditions live side by side and are required to interact with each other, whether they like it or not. This fact, and the further fact that we all face global challenges like climate change and the nuclear threat, makes it imperative that we come to some understanding about how we are to live together without destroying ourselves, each other, and the planet. I also believe with Stout that the common values and commitments that are necessary for such peaceful coexistence will have to develop piecemeal as we meet and encounter each other through, in David Tracy and Jürgen Habermas's terms, a communicative rationality. However, more importantly, for these common values and commitments to achieve sustainability and robustness they will need to be based on transcendent norms—in Islamic and Christian terms, some form of revelation, divine command, and a modest, theologically grounded natural law.

This can be conceptualized through what John Howard Yoder, a Christian ethicist from my own (Mennonite) tradition, has called "middle axioms." For Yoder, middle axioms mediate between a particular tradition and the political sphere (or the state). These axioms can be understood by society at large, whether Christian or not. They include normative concepts like "liberty, equality, fraternity, education, democracy, human rights."[12] For Christians, they have their transcendent foundation and receive their content from Christian revelation (Christology). For non-Christians they have their roots in so-called pagan sources. In Yoder's thought, they are not self-evident, however, or generically grounded in some theory of natural law or metaphysics available to all:

> Traditional social ethics attempted to apply principles which it was held were somehow built into the nature of man or of the social order. The approach sketched above will need to operate without such principles, not because definite and knowable understandings of God's will do not exist, but because such insights are known only in Christ and their application is therefore possible only mediately. Consequently, our speaking to the state will call for the use of middle axioms. These concepts will translate into meaningful and concrete terms the general relevance of the lordship of Christ for a given social issue. They mediate between the general principles of Christological ethics and the concrete problems of political application. They claim no metaphysical status, but serve usefully as rules of thumb to make meaningful the impact of Christian social thought. (32–33)

The concept of middle axioms, says Yoder, avoids ethical relativism on the one side, and metaphysical-natural law foundationalism on the other. "It permits meaningful communication of a significant Christian social critique without involving extended speculation about the metaphysical value of the principles appealed to" (33).

To reject all natural law and metaphysical foundation for social ethics is not necessary. There are good reasons for accepting some modified premodern version of natural law and metaphysics that is theologically grounded (as opposed to modern-enlightenment versions of the same). Nonetheless, Yoder's concept of middle axioms provides some possibilities for dealing with postmodern societies in which a diversity of competing religious and cultural communities exists side by side. The middle-axiom approach that Yoder uses to mediate between Christian social ethics and the state can be applied to any

---

12. Yoder, *Christian Witness to the State*, 73.

religious tradition in its relation to the public sphere. The theological languages of different traditions function as middle axioms, mediating between each tradition's fundamental religious convictions and the public realm. Take, for example, the concepts of love and nonviolence that are so important to a Mennonite understanding of what Christ taught. For Christians these core convictions are grounded in the Christian Scriptures, especially in the teachings of Christ. For Muslims similar core convictions would have their roots in the teachings of Mohammed the Prophet and in the Qur'an.

The core ethical convictions that we share would not have their foundation in some autonomous sphere but would in each case be grounded in particular traditions. We could arrive at shared understandings of the meaning of these middle axioms but would differ in how we justify them. This is the way that universal principles can be conceptualized and justified for social ethics. Whether these convergences that are arrived at through the encounters of different religions and worldviews could be said to be rooted in some more fundamental, universal, natural principles, only time will tell. Who is to say that there are not universal rational principles of some kind at the heart of the cosmos that are as yet not fully apprehended or articulated by any one religion?

Bibliography

Huebner, Harry J. "The Church Made Strange for the Nations." In *Echoes of the Word: Theological Ethics as Rhetorical Practice*, 84–106. Kitchener, ON: Pandora, 2005.

———. "The Nation: Beyond Secular Politics." In *Creed and Conscience: Essays in Honour of A. James Reimer*, edited by Jeremy M. Bergen, Paul G. Doerksen, and Karl Koop, 257–79. Kitchener, ON: Pandora, 2007.

Kim, Yersu. "Philosophy and the Prospects for a Universal Ethic." In *God and Globalization*, edited by Max L. Stackhouse, 1:69–104. Harrisburg, PA: Trinity, 2000.

Küng, Hans, and Karl-Josef Kuschel, editors. *A Global Ethic: The Declaration of the Parliament of the World's Religions*. New York: Continuum, 1993.

MacIntyre, Alasdair. *Whose Justice? Which Rationality?* Notre Dame, IN: University of Notre Dame Press, 1988.

Reimer, A. James. "Anabaptist-Mennonite Political Theology: Historical Manifestations and Observations." Paper presented at conference on political theology, Innsbruck, Austria, June 2009.

———. "An Anabaptist-Mennonite Political Theology: Theological Foundations." *Direction: A Mennonite Brethren Forum: Toward Anabaptist Political Theology* 38 (2009) 29–44.

———. "Conceptualizing Universal Moral Principles for Social Ethics: The Pros and Cons of Global Ethics." Paper presented at conference on Islamic ethics, Qom, Iran, spring 2008.

———. *The Emanuel Hirsch and Paul Tillich Debate: A Study in the Political Ramifications of Theology*. Lewiston, NY: Mellen, 1989.

———. *Emanuel Hirsch und Paul Tillich: Theologie and Politik in einer Zeit der Krise*. Berlin: de Gruyter, 1995.

———. *Mennonites and Classical Theology: Dogmatic Foundations for Christian Ethics*. Kitchener, ON: Pandora, 2001.

———. "Public Orthodoxy and Civic Forbearance: The Challenge of Modern Law for Religious Minority Groups." *Conrad Grebel Review* 21 (2003) 96–111.

Robertson, Roland. "Globalization and the Future of 'Traditional Religion.'" In *God and Globalization*, edited by Max L. Stackhouse, 1:53–68. Harrisburg, PA: Trinity, 2000.

Stackhouse, Max L., editor. *God and Globalization*. With Peter J. Paris, Don S. Browning, and Diane Obenchain. Vol. 1, *Religion and the Powers of the Common Life*. Harrisburg, PA: Trinity, 2000; Vol. 2, *The Spirit and the Modern Authorities*. Harrisburg, PA: Trinity, 2001; Vol. 3, *Christ and the Dominions of Civilization*. Harrisburg, PA: Trinity, 2002; Vol. 4, *Globalization and Grace*. New York: Continuum, 2007.

Stout, Jeffrey. *Democracy and Tradition*. Princeton: Princeton University Press, 2004.

Tracy, David. "Public Theology, Hope, and the Mass Media: Can the Muses Still Inspire?" In *God and Globalization*, edited by Max L. Stackhouse, 1:231–54. Harrisburg, PA: Trinity, 2000.

Yoder, John Howard. *The Christian Witness to the State*. Newton, KS: Faith and Life, 1964.

8

Making Strange

Harry Huebner's Church–World Distinction

P. Travis Kroeker

THE TITLE OF THIS BOOK MAKES ME THINK OF THOSE YOUNG CHILDREN—ONE OFTEN sees them in church—so attached to their parents that they cry when another person tries to pick them up or merely relate to them.[1] The child begins to cry, often quite frantically, much to the mortified embarrassment of both parents and "stranger." What is this "making strange"? And why is it so dramatic and visceral for all involved? Is it a highly expressive sign of awakening to the trauma of having a separate identity or personhood that nonetheless wants the security of an intimate community or a parental identity to cling to? And is this not an ongoing lifelong struggle for everyone in a family, including a so-called church family?

Harry Huebner quite rightly argues that the church is a place where becoming a self before God in the world is modeled and fostered.[2] As such, I want to argue, the church is both nurturing and "strange-making," a place of struggle, cries, and tears—not only tears of joy or penance but also squalls of panic, stress, and trauma, as people make overtures that upset each other's equilibrium and sense of well-being. I think that Huebner doesn't pay enough attention to this latter dynamic, insofar as he seems to favor a representation in which violence, trauma, and struggle usually happen "out there" in the world, when Christians who live out their visible strangeness encounter non-Christian others. That is, I think ultimately Huebner's church is too externally visible and therefore triumphalist, in a "radical orthodoxy" kind of way.[3]

But before pursuing this claim more closely, I can't resist another more personal reference to strange-making. I am technically a graduate of Canadian Mennonite University, as I completed a degree at what used to be called Mennonite Brethren Bible College—though I have noticed that my picture is not available in the graduation photos hung in CMU's hallowed halls. I suspect one reason my photo is not there is that I had a hard time graduating, not only because I didn't finish my music requirement (which was waived after

---

1. This essay began as an address given at Harry Huebner's retirement symposium, "The Church Made Strange," held at the Canadian Mennonite University in 2008, and has been left largely in its original form.

2. See Huebner, *Echoes of the Word*, section 2.

3. Huebner borrows the language of "the church made strange" from John Milbank, to whose approach he is clearly indebted; see *Echoes of the Word*, 97–98.

petition), but also because I had to undergo an orthodoxy interview. As an advanced undergraduate I was invited to participate in a debate on how to interpret the early chapters of Genesis, which was held at another Christian college, Winnipeg Bible College. I argued that the creation accounts ought not to be interpreted as historical or scientific accounts of cosmic origins, but as theo-poetic accounts countering the mytho-poetic creation stories of Israel's neighbors. That debate turned out to be a much larger public occasion than I had anticipated, and formal letters questioning my orthodoxy were sent to my church denomination and to my college. I remember being invited into the office of a biblical studies faculty member, who gently questioned me about my views of Scripture and faith. Although this is a story that can't be fully told here, I raise it not as a critical comment about my experience in the church (in this case represented by two Christian colleges) but as an experience in which my strange-making was treated both with mortified embarrassment and with respectful care and attention. This was an important formative experience for me, not because I am in favor of orthodoxy tests or interviews, but because it helped build what Kierkegaard calls "inwardness"—which is a different thing from "character."[4] As such I cannot describe it to you directly, since its meaning is of necessity both visible and invisible, and in and of itself it is not obvious whether such inwardness is harmful or beneficial. This is relevant to the argument I wish to make with regard to Huebner's sharp church-world distinction.

Harry Huebner's work is intricate and complex, and here I must be brief and to the point, thus ignoring much in his work with which I heartily agree. What I say here is meant to be a friendly even if strange-making gift exchange. I like Huebner's idea of theology as involving imagination, but I am less sure than he is that theology is best imagined as a tradition-based enquiry, nor indeed even as a narrative-based form. When Paul says, "Do not be conformed to this world, but be transformed by the renewal of your mind" (Rom 12:2; NRSV), I do not think he means that we should exploit the resources of an ecclesial or even biblical tradition in terms of rhetorical practice. I think Paul means something more active than this, more in keeping with the title of Huebner's earlier book coauthored with David Schroeder, *Church as Parable*,[5] and more in keeping with Karl Barth's statement in his Romans commentary: "The church is that visibility which forces invisibility upon our notice, that humanity which directs our attention toward God."[6] Such a church would seek to present itself as a living sacrifice to God in its service to the world, an embodied service that is properly related to the form of this world as "passing away" (1 Cor 7:31). I think this kind of service is not easily spoken about except in parabolic terms—that is, in terms of paradoxes that relate to both visibility and invisibility, temporality and eternity. The church is called not to point to itself, its structures, its teachings, its traditions, but rather to bear sacrificial witness to the passage of God in the world that is ever passing away. If it is to do this well, it seems to me, the church must learn to imitate the movement

---

4. In effect it is the God relation, which cannot be mediated in any finite or external relation or form. See Kierkegaard, *Works of Love*, 138–39; *Practice in Christianity*, 136–37, 214–15; *Concept of Anxiety*, 146–47.

5. Huebner and Schroeder, *Church as Parable*.

6. Barth, *Epistle to the Romans*, 337. For Barth's discussion of the church as parable, see his chapter on "The Great Disturbance," and especially 434–35.

of its anointed sovereign, the crucified Messiah, who does not cling to the perfections of the heavenly Father with possessive strength but empties himself and descends in weakness to an exilic, humiliating service in the world—not to its high places but to the lowest places, even to the things that "are not," that is, empty and nonexistent things (*ta me onta*, things lacking ontic being; 1 Cor 1:28)—and does not resist the embarrassment of making strange in doing so.

If this is true, then I am not as sure as Huebner seems to be that the church's calling is to develop "alternative structures" for business, medicine, gerontology, sex (Huebner's order),[7] as this puts too much emphasis on a visible church-world distinction in terms of an ontological difference. Just as Huebner, I think rightly, says our security as human beings is not to be found in the state, so too should he avoid implying that our security is in or with the church. Even if the church were to develop, as it sometimes has, wonderful strategies and structures and techniques of "peace-making," our security cannot rest in those (let us admit it) worldly attachments, and we dare not cling to them. Rather, those enactments must come from another, invisible (dare I say "spiritual"?) movement that can never be possessed—especially not as a "high ground" or moral tradition over against a sinful world. When Jesus stoops down and writes in the dirt while positioning himself between the adulterous woman and her accusers, is he doing something strategic that can be captured in a technique? René Girard will argue that Jesus is avoiding eye contact, which as a passive challenge would unleash the murderous fury of the accusers, so instead he looks down and away and thus gestures indirectly.[8] That may be, but Jesus does seem precisely to unleash such fury at other times in his ministry, even in his indirect speech. Is there an unambiguous visible structure to be found here or anywhere?

Let me try to show what I mean with reference to scriptural parable, the parable that is the complex relation between Jesus and John the Baptist (that indirect forerunning messianic witness par excellence) in Mark's gospel. The first word of the Gospel of Mark, the earliest of the four gospels, in the Greek is *archē*, translated as "the beginning" of the good news of Jesus the Messiah. A new beginning is signaled here as a new creation tied to the appearance of the Messiah. Like Isaiah, Mark sees the new beginning as taking place not in the center of things, the temple in Jerusalem, but rather in the wilderness. Israel's beginnings, like those of creation itself, emerge from the chaotic formlessness and deep darkness of the wilderness, where the people called out to holiness have had to learn always anew what it means to walk in the way of the Lord, the way of justice and mercy. Mark sees the need to enter that educative experience again, but not at the best scribal colleges under the tutelage of smart tenured professors and highly skilled professionals. Rather, he begins with a strange wild man, John the Baptizer, who is a voice crying in the wilderness beyond Jerusalem, away from conventional religious, social, and political authorities and structures.

John has no school, no sophisticated organization, no institutional location or authorization or credentials—indeed he doesn't even have a proper wardrobe or diet. To begin to prepare the way of the Lord means letting go of our closed visible markers about insid-

---

7. Huebner, *Echoes of the Word*, 55.
8. Girard, *Scapegoat*.

ers and outsiders, the elite and the rabble, the respectable and the vulgar. John preaches the renunciation of all closed claims, repentance for forgiveness of sins—and his rite of baptism is intended to open up the possibility of a completely new beginning. This baptism is not a special ritual code related to a creed and an insider community; it is a radical leveling and calls only for a complete turnaround of one's life, away from conventional and structural markers of success and failure, sin and holiness, health and illness.

Like Elijah, John the Baptist is no charismatic lapdog to power. Despite the fact that "all the people of Jerusalem" go out to see him and be baptized in the river Jordan, he remains a threat, especially to the religious and political establishment, and is eventually arrested by King Herod (Mark 6). So when John says, "After me comes one who is mightier than I, the thong of whose sandals I am not worthy to stoop down and untie," he does not mean Herod, though Herod would no doubt think so. Rather, he is referring to a man from Nazareth—literally "nowheresville" in Galilee—a man whose career will intersect with his at strategic moments in Mark's gospel. But John and Jesus are no power rivals; far from requiring John to stoop before him, Jesus invites John to baptize him in the river Jordan, a complete dispossession of privilege on the part of the Messiah. After this, Jesus too is "driven out into the wilderness" by the Spirit and wrestles with temptations concerning power and authority.

It is here that the parallels and intersections between Jesus and the Baptist begin. Jesus's public prophetic ministry begins when John is arrested by Herod, and he begins to preach the same message as John did: "The kingdom of God is at hand; repent and believe in the good news." Later (Mark 11), when Jesus goes to Jerusalem, he ties his authority to John's baptism, which traps the conventional religious authorities who question him. Jesus asks them, "Was the baptism of John from heaven or of human origin? And they argued with one another, "If we say 'From heaven,' he will say, 'Why then did you not believe him?' But shall we say 'Of human origin?'—they were afraid of the people, for all held that John was a real prophet" (Mark 11:29–32). By responding in this way, these religious leaders prove themselves characteristic of all conventional political and social authority—taking its cues from human beings, its desires shaped by the power games that accord status and respect in every culture through rivalry and domination: Who is the strongest, the brightest, the bravest, the richest, the most virtuous, the most beautiful rhetorician, the one with the best structures and traditions? Who commands control over our shared motivating worldly attachments, our collective imagination? This is not the power that authorizes and motivates either John or Jesus, and this fact is at the heart of the good news that reshapes desire and establishes a very different line of motivation and authority, the way of the sovereign Messiah.

Just as John the Baptist succeeds Elijah and Isaiah, so Jesus succeeds the imprisoned and then executed John the Baptist, even though their way of life is quite different. John and his disciples fast, neither eating nor drinking, while Jesus and his disciples eat and drink with notorious sinners—yet both of them preach repentance in a way that scandalizes the professional power classes. Those whose authority is not from other human beings are not concerned about their human reputations, and this gives them a very unsettling, strange kind of freedom and power. Mark gives us a series of vignettes early on that display this in confrontation with human authorities and conventional power structures, which are rooted in exclusion, rivalry, and violence. The miracle stories of Jesus's healing call into question the rigid boundaries around illness and health, clean and unclean, righteous and sinners, and reveal them to be power games tied to human authority—religious, educational, medical, legal, and political—and the professionals who control the definitions, the treatment, and the prestige that go along with that. Jesus's mighty works call those definitions radically into question by engaging them on a spiritual level that completely escapes professionals and indeed scandalizes them. He authorizes his disciples to do the same. In Mark 6 he sends out his ragtag and very unprofessional disciples and gives them authority over unclean spirits, charging them to take with them no symbols of conventional power—no bread, no bag, no money. Their message is repentance, a repentance that gets rid of demons and assorted illnesses but does not create new health care or social work or educational structures.

Interestingly, the career of John the Baptizer intersects again at precisely this point in the story. When King Herod hears about this ministry of Jesus and his disciples, he says, "John, whom I beheaded, has been raised from the dead." Then Mark tells a detailed story of John's imprisonment and death. It seems Herod had imprisoned John at the behest of his consort Herodias, who, it turns out, was Herod's brother's wife—an erotic power game that John the Baptist had the audacity to criticize publicly. The criticism especially enraged Herodias, who wanted John dead, but which Herod refused to act on because he feared John's spiritual power, troubling though he found it. No doubt the fact that Herod apparently gladly heard John while he was kept in the palace prison further worried Herodias—people mesmerized by the power game find it threatening when those players closest to them and complicit with them become open to questioning it. This famous violent story is itself about mesmerization.[9] Herod's birthday is the occasion, and he throws a sumptuous banquet for his courtiers and officers and the "leading people of Galilee" (Mark 6:21); all the power players are present. And the highlight of the party is the dance of Salome, Herodias's daughter. She is a very pleasing dancer, and she dances the dance of her life. Herod and his guests are mesmerized, each fantasizing about the motivating object of their desire and all it represents, inevitably with themselves at the top of the world, the pinnacle of power. Here is the false *imitatio dei*.

The king sees this and he makes the proper power gesture: "Ask me for whatever you wish, even half of my kingdom, and I will grant it" (Mark 6:23). Herod is a bit drunk. He gets a little carried away; after all, he doesn't have a real kingdom to divide—he's a tetrarch, a Roman lackey with limited powers. But his guests buy the illusion, and why not? It makes their own fantasies a little more real, a more powerful socially reinforced possession. Salome, of course, doesn't really know what she should desire (who of us really does?) and this is a big opportunity, so she consults with her mother Herodias, who knows exactly what she wants. Get rid of that fantasy-puncturing prophet in prison who could corrupt her man and carry the people with his message of radical repentance and turning away from the power game. She tells Salome: ask for John's head, and quick, before the mood breaks. Poor Salome, she's being danced as much as she is dancing, and after awhile

---

9. See the evocative discussion by René Girard in *Scapegoat*, chap. 11.

who knows the difference? But she adds a little twist of her own to this request, the literal *coup de grâce* right here and now that will make this even more a night to remember. "I want you to give me *at once* the head of John the Baptist *on a platter*" (Mark 6:25; emphasis mine). What a stroke of brilliance, the mother's figure of speech vividly realized in a violent display that reinforces the erotic one. King Herod is suddenly sober—this is out of control, and he fears and likes John (Mark 6:20). But he has made a power gesture and he is in front of all these important guests, the leading players in his power game—he can't back down. *At least not without a complete repentance.* The confrontation is exactly what Herodias wants; it requires Herod to make a public and visible choice about the source of his authority and power, and Herod chooses to save face, which requires John to lose his. One can imagine the violent spectacle, as many artists have done: John's now-silenced head drips eloquently from the platter. The human power game often ends this way, figuratively and literally, visibly and invisibly.

But the voice continues to cry in the wilderness in the person of Jesus and his disciples, who now also see more clearly, though only indirectly, what is at stake in the power struggle against the powers of violence and oppression. Their fates will intersect with John's as well—they will lose their lives by preaching repentance. It is a career move that makes sense only for those baptized with the Holy Spirit, that same Spirit that drove Jesus into the wilderness to struggle against the temptations of merely human power and glory that operate by setting up structures of exclusivity, rivalry, and visible domination. The authority of Jesus and John does not rely upon the centers of this kind of human power. They do not seek to hold such power and its symbolic possessions of human prestige, including traditions and rhetorical practices.

This eventually becomes more palpable also to Jesus's disciples, but this parabolic good news is sometimes hard to hear. In Mark 10 Jesus has been telling his disciples how hard it is to enter the kingdom of God—easier for a camel to go through the eye of a needle than for a professional to enter the kingdom—and they are astonished: Well then, who can get in? (Mark 10:26) Jesus then talks about the suffering brought about by the renunciation of human claims that is required, how the first will be last, and how he himself will be killed for this message. Immediately, two of his disciples come forward and ask Jesus to do something for them in this coming kingdom (and they haven't even danced), and Jesus says, "What do you want me to do for you?" (Mark 10:36). They say, let us sit at your right and left hand in your glory. Jesus tells them, "You don't know what you are asking," and asks them if they are able to be baptized with the baptism with which he is baptized (Mark 10:38–39). It is also John's baptism, the baptism of suffering. The other disciples get upset at this exchange, which really does imitate the scene in Herod's palace in crucial respects, a group of power players in rivalry about who will be greatest in this coming kingdom (fantasies of power and glory spring up quickly in the human heart, both in the church and the world). Jesus completely levels the ground. As Jesus showed by submitting to John's baptism even as John pointed away from himself, this is not a kingdom of rivals. The kingdom of God, says Jesus, is very different from human kingdoms, where people love to lord it over one another and exercise their professional authority—always for the most noble and benevolent of reasons. "But it shall not be so among you; but whoever would be great among you must be your servant, and whoever would be first among you must be slave of all. For the son of man also came not to be served but to serve, and to give his life for the many" (Mark 10:43–44).

This is the mind of the Messiah, and it does not take the erotic form of desire. It takes the humiliating and often invisible, strange-making form of sacrifice, which relates to the form of this world as a "passing away." Such witness—and I daresay it is a witness equally paradoxical in the church and in the world—bears testimony to the power of the Spirit that brings about not new human achievements but discloses the strange and strange-making passage of God in the world. It cannot be possessed; it cannot be restricted to the church; it can only be prepared for by repentance. "Here there cannot be Greek and Jew, circumcised and uncircumcised, male and female, barbarian, Scythian, slave and free [and, we might add, church and world], but Messiah is all in all" (Col 3:11; cf. Gal 3:28). If that is so, then perhaps we may hope one day to be no longer strangers but fellow citizens in a messianic structure that includes all penitent sinners.

Bibliography

Barth, Karl. *The Epistle to the Romans*. Translated by Edwyn C. Hoskyns. London: Oxford University Press, 1968.

Girard, René. *The Scapegoat*. Baltimore: Johns Hopkins University Press, 1989.

Huebner, Harry. *Echoes of the Word: Theological Ethics as Rhetorical Practice*. Kitchener, ON: Pandora, 2005.

Huebner, Harry, and David Schroeder. *Church as Parable: Whatever Happened to Ethics?* Winnipeg: CMBC Publications, 1993.

Kierkegaard, Søren. *The Concept of Anxiety: A Simple Psychologically Orienting Deliberation on the Dogmatic Issue of Hereditary Sin*. Edited and translated by Reidar Thomte. Princeton: Princeton University Press, 1981.

———. *Practice in Christianity*. Edited and translated by Howard V. Hong and Edna H. Hong. Princeton: Princeton University Press, 1991.

———. *Works of Love: Some Christian Reflections in the Form of Discourses*. Edited and translated by Howard V. Hong and Edna H. Hong. Princeton: Princeton University Press, 1995.

"To Serve the Dead"
Fidelity and Resistance in Antigone

Joseph Wiebe

AT FIRST GLANCE, ANTIGONE SEEMS TO BE A STORY OF ANTITHESIS—BETWEEN KINSHIP and state, private and public ethics, divine and civil laws. However, to see Sophocles' play as an image of opposing forces, of resistance and domination, one would have to ignore significant motivational forces in both Creon and Antigone. Antigone's fidelity is not best seen as the choice to resist Creon's political authority rather than be subordinate to it. Instead, her faithfulness destabilizes tradition itself as a site of pure opposition to whatever threatens its way of life.[1] Sophocles frustrates commitment and fidelity as the hope for continuity and coherence beyond human control. In short, he relieves the need to maintain a site of resistance come hell or high water.

    I am interested in exploring how *Antigone* attempts to subdue our tendency to control our place and surroundings. Specifically, its performance of a battle over a corpse is illustrative of an obsession with ascribing legitimacy to and ensuring meaning in tightly held commitments. The totality of traditions, the stories of which we are a part and to which we are committed, as well as their success, are essentially unknown. Any victory over our enemies, the overcoming of that which threatens future continuity and perdurance, cannot be known in advance; it is unclear what it means to be victorious or what our role is in that turbid triumph. And yet it is exactly moving into the unknown and being open to the divine that resists controlling current states of affairs to secure the future. I, through Sophocles, want to stress the loneliness of the unknown and of the openness to

---

    1. This reading, which sees Antigone as a politically informative destabilizing force of that which she supposedly represents, is indebted to Judith Butler's argument against interpreting *Antigone* as a straightforward conflict between kinship and ethics. See her *Antigone's Claim*. Although I find much that is compelling about Butler's argument, and agree with her that Antigone's incestuous lineage is integral for a complex understanding of the play, she almost entirely elides Antigone's religious sensibility. Butler assumes that theological appeals and justifications are closures to negotiating human dilemmas, which leads her to argue that Antigone receives the force of her argument from Creon's idiom of sovereignty and autonomy. While there is much Antigone and Creon share in common, Antigone relentlessly appeals to her piety and the gods as the source of her disagreement with Creon. Antigone's religious discourse opens up the possibility of conflict and negotiation while simultaneously exposing Creon's essentially nonreligious politics. Butler blinds herself to the significance of religion for Antigone, similar to the way in which she accuses others of blinding themselves to Antigone's incest. In both cases, the deprivation makes the respective interpretations and political conclusions more compelling.

the divine "elsewhere." I do not offer an exhaustive interpretation of *Antigone* but instead suggest that it offers an image of the strange and uncomfortable place the church is called to inhabit. Fidelity to and defense of one's heritage or community, not letting one's tradition be seduced by compelling forces of mastery, conjure images of an opposition between two rival agencies.[2] However, a sense of responsibility can blind our ability to see and interrogate the story to which we commit ourselves and the unborn. It may be that the only future faithfulness can produce is the possibility for a theological anthropology that is admittedly a degenerative, less-than-human subject that has the capacity to resist the obsession with mastery, but only because it risks losing everything—even the continuation of the heritage and tradition that makes this capacity possible.

~

Antigone and Creon equally find themselves bound to the dead: Antigone to legitimize her heritage, Creon to legitimize his rule. The difference between them is the way in which the corpse functions. Creon's political authority both draws on and is extended through an unburied, half-eaten corpse insofar as he denies it a resting place—even outside the city. Antigone is compelled by the corpse's claim to a tradition of divine law that is the basis for her life's meaning. Creon sees the corpse as a tool to prevent another rebellion, a device to forestall the potential for new conflict. Antigone sees the corpse as part of her family's story, a catastrophe that seems to have no end. Her desire to bury the dead body is driven by the shame of her lineage and the preoccupation to cease its perpetuation. Both Creon and Antigone try to lawfully justify and protect their futures through that which has passed away. Freedom, from anarchy or ignominy, is somehow linked to the dead. The tragic outcome of this story seems to be a message to its audience to release themselves from the dominion of the dead. And yet, according to the famous lines in the "ode to man," we are doomed to be in their service as the only material in nature that cannot be mastered.

Creon's desire for the totalized mastery of his rule is almost too obvious. His first words that prelude the decree against Polyneices's body and any would-be mourners declare loyalty to his country as the primary criterion for friendship. Creon likens his country, moreover, to a ship as a metaphor for the "safety" and "security" it offers when it is well maintained.[3] Nothing can threaten the order that makes this security possible, not even

2. Harry Huebner argues that "the primary moral task of the church is to concentrate on not being seduced by those forces that can undermine its character as a community of Christian virtues." *Church as Parable*, 195. The community is itself a "powerful force" that shapes the lives of its members, the God of whom authors and enacts the story in which the church participates and to which it remains faithful. Fidelity, for Huebner, instills the practice of any Christian virtue "that seeks to *build up* the Christian community." *Echoes of the Word*, 174 (emphasis mine). While Huebner does maintain the importance for the individual and community to be open to a hidden divine reality that is an active agent for profound change, it is not clear how such an emphasis on the reality of the invisible affects the visible structures and practices of the church. Huebner's attention to the transcendent, the cultivation of an openness to God, is meant to relieve the anxiety to control the situations of life. Yet there may be a sense in which the invocation of a hidden, more determinative agency can be a way of reinforcing—building up—preexisting activity if it only underwrites the current stance of the invocator.

3. Sophocles, *Antigone*, 204–8. All line references are from Grene's translation in Sophocles, *Greek Tragedies*, rather than from the Greek text. Further references will appear parenthetically in the text.

the political judgments of the people whom Creon rules. No one's advice is acknowledged, much less heeded, lest it question Creon's sole authoritative claims over the living and the dead. Creon is not only unwilling but also unable to listen; he transforms Haemon's diplomatic pleas for a more deliberatively democratic rule into disobedience toward authority, and Teiresias's prophetic counsel into a greedy, corrupted ploy. Indeed, Creon's whole interaction with Antigone can be interpreted as a refusal to allow public speech and action. Her appeals to a higher and more extensive divine law that enjoins an activity Creon's civic politics denies are excluded out of hand. Antigone's labor of mourning is a pollution to the city that must be expiated. That she is sentenced to death is an extension of Creon's tyrannical attempt to rule all within his grasp. Execution is Creon's act of *taking* Antigone's life, part of his desire to "have everything" (543).

But this is not the whole story. There are moments of transformation and reversal in Creon's judgment and character that are elided if he is seen *only* as a myopic, inflexible tyrant. The initial punishment for burying the forbidden corpse is execution by stoning—an unusually harsh sentence considering the type of action addressed. But after discovering the perpetrator is his niece, hearing her explanations, witnessing her debate with Ismene, and, perhaps most significantly, arguing with his own son over the correct political response, Creon inexplicably reduces the brutality of the sentence to being buried alive. At the same moment, Creon limits the culpability to Antigone alone, after the Chorus questions Creon's initial verdict that named both Antigone and Ismene guilty. Teiresias is able to persuade Creon to change his intentions, after which Creon admits it would have been best "in the end of life, to have kept the old accepted laws" (1190–91). All of which point to a flexibility that is latently present both in Creon and the *nomos*—a flexibility that demonstrates Creon should not be seen as a dictator. The extent to which he should be seen as a tyrant is only in the pre-pejorative sense as taking the throne by means other than direct bloodline. But even these means are malleable.

Creon manipulates his consanguineous ties to Thebes's preceding rulers in order to legitimate his authority. The elder gentlemen of Thebes that comprise the Chorus are gathered because of their loyalty to the throne heretofore. Instead of describing his current authorial role as regency, Creon locates himself biologically within the male lineage of monarchal succession. Furthermore, that to which the Chorus is loyal is carefully worded; Oedipus's throne is remembered in connection with his triumph over the Sphinx rather than his incestuous heritage. Of course, Creon's claim to the throne is through his sister Jocasta, and his reign is and has been intermittent between calamities in her family. In *Antigone*, Creon is only freshly governing Thebes because Eteocles' death has not long passed, and yet he claims to "hold all authority and the throne, in virtue of kinship with the dead" (192)—namely Laïus, Oedipus, Polyneices, and Eteocles.

Creon's claim to share in the bloodline of the dead is ironic. The statement is a pretense of Creon's self-perception that will ultimately reveal an unacknowledged aspiration. In short, it points to a tension between the way political authority is legitimized and the kind of rule that is enacted as a result. The blood of the dead that establishes the royal family is the locus of its downfall. Creon appears to know this, which is probably the reason why he does not attribute the Chorus's loyalty to Oedipus in terms of his blood relationship with Laïus. It may also be the reason that Creon initially places the fate of the city in the hands of the gods rather than directly blaming Polyneices and praising Eteocles.[4] Creon presents himself to the elders as one who simultaneously inherits authority and the throne and yet disinherits the form of his predecessors' rule. However, incest creeps into Creon's judgments and deliberations not biologically, but as a political sensibility that connects him to Oedipus's legacy more than he knows.

While the incest of Oedipus and its repercussions on his family are no secret to the inhabitants of Thebes, Antigone mediates it to Creon.[5] Her attachment to Polyneices's corpse goes to extreme lengths, even for Greeks. Political and moral philosophers have appealed to *Antigone* in various ways: Antigone enacts familial or clan virtues that conflict with those of the city;[6] she resolves this conflict with an inflexible, un-erotic, simplification of the world through divine law;[7] and she displays the action that brings newness to the totalized discourse of Creon's mastery.[8] And yet, there is more to her attraction—nay, obsession—with Polyneices's corpse itself than these political reflections account for. It is no surprise to find the act of burying declared to be an act of loving, but Antigone exaggerates the interconnection. She not only acknowledges Creon's mortal decree but also accepts it as her fate and looks forward to the *good* possibility—in both senses of favorable and likely—that they might lie together in love (84–85). Were this a description of two lovers, the connotations would be explicitly sexual. That she has her brother as her object may relativize the kind of love Antigone has for the corpse. Nevertheless, the reader cannot forget the incestuous heritage borne by all members of this family, whether Antigone admits it or not—either to herself or the reader. One can see this in her particular grief for Polyneices. It is only *him*—not *them*, or her *family*—that she desires to lie next to in death.[9] Incestuous descriptions of relations and the grave's beckoning are coextensive in Antigone's account of her circumstances.[10] She could not live with Polyneices so she will lie with him—a possibility only in death.

---

4. Benardete, *Sacred Transgressions*, 23.

5. That is to say, the reader can interpretively read Creon's dispositions through Antigone's incest. It may be that the interactions between Creon and Antigone themselves push Creon into a harder stance than he would have otherwise taken, but I doubt it.

6. MacIntyre, *After Virtue*, 144–45.

7. Nussbaum, *Fragility of Goodness*, 66.

8. Euben, *Corrupting Youth*.

9. On the cusp of her execution, Antigone announces her hope that upon her arrival in Hades, her father, mother, and brother (again, singular) will welcome her. Nevertheless, when the threat of death is only a possibility and not a reality, she only mentions her brother. The question is, which brother? There is a sense in which, by the end of the play, it could be that her love of Polyneices is a displaced love of her other brother, who is also her father. Her confused love reflects her confused kinship. Which brother, exactly, is she referring to when she says, "Brother, it was a luckless marriage you made, and dying killed my life" (923)? Judith Butler offers an excellent political analysis of Antigone's ambiguous kinship and the role in which that places her within Thebes. See *Antigone's Claim*, especially chap. 3.

10. See Benardete, *Sacred Transgressions*, 13: "the language of incest . . . coincide[s] with the language of the grave."

Incest is the only kind of love Antigone knows, and death is the only legitimate form it can take.[11] Antigone's familial orientation reveals incest to be coterminous with death to the extent that she denies her betrothed in favor of joining her brother's corpse in order to have a family reunion in Hades. Antigone is engaged to Creon's son, Haemon. Their children would have continued the royal lineage and brought together the divided factions of the city that had just engaged in civil war. In other words, Haemon, both in who he is and what he offers, is an alternative to Polyneices that promises much generative potential. Haemon appeals to both Creon's political sensibilities and pedigree in his attempt to assuage his father's decision to execute Antigone. He tells Creon that "the city mourns for this girl; they think she is dying most wrongly and most undeservedly of all womankind, for the most glorious acts" (747–49) and also that "nothing I own I value more highly, father, than your success" (755–56). In terms that resemble Creon's opening speech to the Chorus, Haemon suggests that it is possible to enable the "ship" to keep from capsizing with a slackened sail and concurrently reproduce the glory of success in himself as Creon's son and future leader of Thebes (758–73).[12] However, a political success and its continual propagation combine to form a conflict of interest within Haemon, one that illustrates what Antigone denies, namely, generation. Haemon's love for both Creon and Antigone tears him apart because he wants both to be reproductive—as strong leader, as fruitful mother—but here they are pitted against one another. Despite Haemon's steadfast advocacy, however, Antigone is simply "anti-generation," and Haemon does not seem to understand this position, her form of love.[13] Haemon's inability, or perhaps unwillingness, to accept love in Antigone's terms is delineated in his refusal to die by her side (825–29). Haemon reverses Antigone's form of love; he would rather live alone than die with her.[14] Antigone's commitment to an inanimate body over a living husband forecloses the possibility of renormalizing the family and finalizes her status as neither dead nor alive. Instead of creating a new family through marriage, Antigone joins the only family to whom she exclusively desires to belong.

Serving and lying with the dead are ways one can love one's own with nobility. Antigone tells Ismene that her "life died long ago, to serve the dead" (614–15). This servitude has constituted Antigone's entire life, and yet dignity escapes her and her family. Her

---

11. This is quite opposed to Martha Nussbaum's reading of Antigone, whom she sees as having no love for Polyneices that is out of the ordinary. Indeed, she says, "Antigone is as far from eros as Creon." Hers is simply a devotion to the family dead and is bound only to those "inside" the family circle. *Fragility of Goodness*, 64. For this to be the case, one would, I think, have to ignore entirely the family's incestuous constitution.

12. Indeed, Haemon's speech resembles Creon's initial address to the Chorus at a number of points: he is primarily concerned for the city, he uses the analogy of the city as a ship that needs to be kept afloat, and he encourages receptivity to counsel. Haemon appeals to his father on Creon's own terms, which is markedly different than Antigone's self-defense. Perhaps this is a further reason why Antigone cannot bring herself to live with Haemon and would rather die with Polyneices.

13. "Antigone" can mean more than just "anti-generation." It can also mean "unbending," or "against ancestors." Again, it is not my intention to provide an exhaustive interpretation of the play. Instead, I offer one avenue of thought provided by one interpretation of her name.

14. Of course, Haemon kills himself in the end—but only after a failed attack on his father. That he dies "in anger at himself" (1311) rather than being reunited with Antigone in Hades reveals his suicide to be much more bound up with his relationship with his father than with his dead betrothed. See Benardete, *Sacred Transgressions*, 139.

childhood consisted in caring for Oedipus, who gouged his eyes out so he would not have to look upon his abominable children, yet did not kill himself so he would not have to look upon his father and mother in death. Thus, Antigone's tending to Oedipus was already a reversed wardship of the living dead. Polyneices's death and unburied corpse exposes the hereditary ignominy that Antigone, at first, denies. In her first speech, Antigone does not connect the present problem of Polyneices's unburied body to Oedipus's evils, but rather places Polyneices's dishonor in the hands of Creon (25ff.). In fact, she claims that both she and her sister Ismene are of noble birth and nature, who will only become base should they refuse to bury their brother's corpse (141–43). Antigone continuously appeals to the divine laws to justify her desire to bury Polyneices, yet always articulates her case in terms of the dead and dignity. In her final pleas to the Chorus, she claims that it is her religious openness to what Creon closes—her piety that makes her impious, her reverence for what claims reverence—that enables her to legitimately love her dead family. Her appeal to the holy rests in her work with the dead. Antigone has already removed herself from the rest of humanity, without "a home in common—neither with the living nor the dead" (904–5). She describes herself to the Chorus as betrothed to "the Lord of Death" (877), that her tomb is her "bridal chamber" (945). Antigone bears a perverse relation—marriage—to the dead, one that forestalls any possibility for future generation. Thus, her speeches about Justice and Zeus that are meant to justify her opposition to the "mortal laws" of Creon are in continuity both with her understanding of her life as part of a disastrous legacy and with the desire to do whatever she can to salvage it. Antigone's obsession with burial has less to do with her commitment to the corpse as a locus for the representation of eternal and divine laws that are purely opposed to civil polity than with it being simply the family's only legitimate bond.[15] Antigone's incestuous love manifests itself through the practice of loving one's own, writ large. Marriage to another of one's own is out of the question, but to be wedded to death makes it possible. Antigone is just dying to lie with her family.

It does not seem to be the case, therefore, that Antigone can be read as simply appealing to kinship as opposed to the state, or to transcendent law as opposed to civic duty. She is not devoted to just any family, but to hers as an unstable, disordered relational catastrophe. She also admits that she would not have performed the burial if it were any other member of her family or under different circumstances. Antigone's claim is neither steady nor can it be consistently applied. The only thing that is clear is that she is bound to—cursed by—this ambiguous position in her family heritage, and that as a result, she has never had the chance to live life. She goes to her final grave "unbedded, without bridal, without share in marriage and in nurturing of children; as lonely as you see me; without friends; with fate against me I go to the vault of death while still alive" (974–78). Antigone was never fully alive; her death is not as much a disruption as it is a continuation of the character of her life. As such, Antigone marks a strange reversal of the so-called "ode to man" (368–411) insofar as the ode names the human condition as the propensity to bend every natural thing to its advantage except death. Only the power of death cannot be domesticated; it exceeds human attempts to tame and master nature. And yet Antigone is

---

15. Ibid., 110.

that human whose life has been formed by death, even if she interprets its impetus as fate rather than will. She knows all too well the ineluctability of death, for she bears it in her own body and lacks the cognitive capacity to invent a new way of life. She is stuck serving her incestuous family. Antigone, then, is not included in the Chorus's ode to humanity. That her exclusion is fatal and cursed reveals her to be less than fully human, something other than what the Chorus names, and she is thus unable to live the terrible/wonderful life of dominating nature. Others, such as Creon, try to cunningly escape death; Antigone desires to enter into it.

Antigone's incestuous love for her family informs a reading of Creon's incestuous love for the city. Incest is not merely a biological problem; it is a helpful metaphor for political domination as anti-generative. Creon's attempts to justly rule the city are frustrated by his temptations to a tyrannical command that refuses counsel. We as readers should suspend our judgment of Creon, however, even though he seems unreasonable. A civil war has just ravaged Thebes, during which Menoeceus, Creon's father, killed himself in order for Teiresias's prophecy of Theban victory to come to fruition. It is this kind of violence Creon is devoted to obviating. His slide toward mastery and the demurral of alternate advice and perspectives is in the name of peace and security. Creon opposes the burial of Polyneices precisely because of his duty to the just, the honorable defenders of the city's safety. It is the anarchy of civil war that Creon wants to preclude, that which his anti-generative position is set against. Creon's fidelity to the continued existence and flourishing of Thebes is not unlike Antigone's devotion to her brother's corpse—they are incestuous and in servitude to the dead. Put simply, fidelity and commitment are anti-generative.

Creon is a conflicted character, to say the least. The moments when his anger at divergent political orientations and desire to dominate flare up are clear contradictions of the kind of ruler he purports to be. Creon heaps accolades on the ruler that seeks counsel, yet he himself denies it at almost every turn. He advocates flexibility and "free speech," yet he himself is mostly inflexible and keeps the citizens too afraid to speak. He condemns Antigone's commitment to her family that supersedes her devotion to civic duty, yet he himself desires that Haemon have the same constancy. The impetus behind Creon's blatant inconsistency is his concern and love for Thebes. Creon's confident assertion that Antigone's love for her dead is "labor lost" (848) illuminates his preoccupation with progress. He is particularly future-oriented—trying to secure the ongoing safety and proliferation of Thebes. Security insists that there can be no rival love. Creon is well aware that there are still people within the city who disapprove of his rule, and laments that the love of money could rouse a party to disobey, deny, or betray its love of country. Greed is politically destructive and reduces one's humanity: "the worst currency that ever grew among mankind is money. This sacks cities, this drives people from their homes, this teaches and corrupts the minds of the loyal to acts of shame" (326–30). Even love of others, love between lovers, is at best secondary. The city does not consist in the fraternal love of a community; Thebes is a community of people bound together by their fraternal love for the city.[16] Thus, Creon's unsympathetic response to the death sentence of his son's

---

16. "The bond forbidden within the family is the indispensable bond for the city—it is what guarantees that its citizens be brothers." Ibid., 104.

wife—"there are other fields for him to plough" (627)—delineates his obligation and allegiance to the perpetuation of the royal family through the male line regardless of the spouse, which is in continuity both with his authorial pretense established in his opening address as well as his inflexible authorial position. The only purpose of marriage is the reproduction of raw materials—giving birth to the same citizenry that already agrees with Creon, those who are already loyal to the city. Put differently, Creon's perception of Haemon's marriage and generative potential demonstrates that authority should be fixed and that difference should not make a difference. Creon's Thebes is the organization of loving one's own, writ large.

Creon attempts to maintain Thebes's organization through the power of a corpse and his kinship with the dead. While Creon claims that the fortune and fate of Thebes ultimately lie in the hands of the gods—who both shake and cradle the ship—his politics seem to accord them only a nominal acknowledgment. His rage at the Chorus's concern that Polyneices's burial may have been the gods' forethought erupts from the assumption that Polyneices was exceptionally dishonorable in his plot to "burn their pillared temples, their dedicated offerings" (316–17). Hence, Creon presumes either a greedy person or a band driven by those who disagree with Creon performed the burial. Later, Teiresias accuses him of making a terrible mistake in that Polyneices's carrion meat covers the altars and prevents the gods' reception of sacrifice and prayer (1072–79). Again, Creon denies the gods in favor of denouncing greed; he even inculpates Teiresias's motives as proceeding from rapacity. Here Creon slips up; he is pushed to finally reveal his understanding of the divine-human relationship. He is "certain no human has the power to pollute the gods" (1104). Creon's decree against the corpse is not spoken out of reverence for Zeus but against greed and corruption; it is his way of swaying the ship of Thebes. The gods are just used as a name for people's actions. The failure of Creon's order for Thebes's organization is not due to the gods but to the corruption of human avarice. Thus, Creon's use of the corpse can be seen as an argument for a politics of religious nominalism. The exposure of the corpse denies the comfort burial brings to those in its presence. Creon depends on the sheer nakedness of decomposition, entrails, and rotten flesh to burn the nostrils, brand the retinas, and silence those who may want to honor Polyneices through hiding his dead body. The shame Creon inflicts on Polyneices is not limited to his person; it is public. Dishonor is not metaphysical and invisible, but palpable and present through the witnesses' spectatorial reception of the grotesque. Creon extends his authority in and through the dead.

The irony of Creon's locus of authority in his self-proclaimed kinship with the dead is that he uses Polyneices's corpse to legitimize and simultaneously expand his rule over the dead. It is not just the living people of Thebes but also the dead who are under Creon's jurisdiction. Honor is given to those who are "loyal to the state in death [and] in life" (228–29), and the Chorus accedes him the power "to use any legal means [that] lies in [his] power, both about the dead and those of us who live" (232–33). Death is denied redemptive power and has no claim over the quality of reverence in the present life. Death does not offer any bond greater than that which one's city already provides. To take and execute Antigone is the ultimate claim over both her life and her death—

Creon demands "everything," including the dominion of the dead; he desires the ability to make "even the stout of heart shrink" (638–39). Antigone, however, is not so easily subsumed and disrupts Creon's attempts at mastering the dead, as she herself is at the threshold of life and death—the place where Creon amplifies his authority. Antigone bears the kinship that Creon can only fabricate.[17] This kinship is the power of authority that is intimately connected to the dead, but which also contains its own incestuous self-destruction. Creon's pretense to claim the dead begins his life's mortification and leaves him in Antigone's ambiguous position of having a home neither among the living nor the dead. It is the preamble that adumbrates the final extreme image of the dead above ground and the living buried in a tomb.

The final showdown in the grave between Haemon and Creon depicts the lack of generation that an extreme obsession with the dead produces. Antigone's last speech is a strange specter of Creon's first speech. She addresses her country to reveal that it is she who is the last remnant of the royal line and is being exiled/executed for honoring the dead. Stated comparatively, Creon's use of Polyneices constitutes his reverence for his office; Antigone's love for Polyneices constitutes her reverence for the dead. When Creon places himself in kinship with the dead he unwittingly puts himself in their service; the attempt of mastery places him under the authority of the dead, which mediates not only their legitimacy but also their neuroses. Creon uses the corpse only to find out that it has used him. After the moment of Creon's transformative realization that he should have "kept the old accepted laws," he gives Polyneices's corpse a proper burial instead of immediately unbinding Antigone. Creon has become Antigone; he attends first to the dead and then the living. As with Antigone, this way of ordering care ends in tragedy. Creon finds Antigone hanging by a noose and his son, her betrothed, mad with grief. Haemon pierces himself with his own sword, splattering blood over Antigone's corpse. Sophocles' bloody conclusion delineates the eerie connection between the dead and the unborn. The final scene renders the tomb as a perverse womb: the unmarried virgin child wrapped in a noose-cum-umbilical cord, covered in the blood of the self-penetrated Haemon (hymen). Creon's incestuous necrocracy begets a political abortion.

⁓

The outcome of this tragic tale seems to echo the Chorus's ode to the terrible wonder of human mastery that is, despite any efforts to the contrary, ineluctably bound to the dead. *Antigone* offers different responses to this human condition through the performances of the characters and their interactions with each other. In other words, *Antigone* is not simply an argument to establish the form of humanity's mortality and the political causalities that produce gruesome deaths. The dramatic responses are extremes that could easily have been otherwise, and therefore, I think, *Antigone* does not call the reader to a specific

---

17. There is a sense in which Creon helps create the ambiguous yet exclusory conception of kinship that dooms Antigone. Insofar as he redraws the lines of possibility within kinship to his advantage, he takes Antigone's rightful place and pushes her to the periphery. Creon's use of kinship produces Antigone's displacement within it. Creon says more than he intends and dooms himself to the same kind of fate Antigone is curse to live out—namely, a living death.

judgment. Ismene tells Antigone that she is "in love with the impossible" (104–5). Perhaps the tragedy of this play lies in the decision to "hunt the impossible," that both Antigone and Creon act on illusory perceptions of the dead to preserve their commitments. Creon especially reveals the tragedy of hardening his position so as to pass it along, to keep the polis going. The decisions and principles intended to ensure the continued generation of the social reality from which they emerge actually contribute to the disaster, the *tragic* end to history and heritage.

Our attempts to both maintain and hand down may be hunting the impossible. That is, our desire to preserve may be based on the illusion that we have the ability to control the present—to articulate its truth and keep it from losing its significance and legitimacy. Perhaps the best advice we can take is Socrates' argument that "the same man should know how to make comedy and tragedy; and that he who is by art a tragic poet is also a comic poet."[18] It might be possible, albeit a stretch, to read *Antigone* as a comedy, or at least to see the humor in fighting over a corpse. Teiresias's intervention provides an alternative point of view to what has just transpired. Apparently, the altars cannot light because they are drenched in Polyneices's remains. Even the birds are all in a tizzy because they are so full from eating the corpse. Teiresias seems to say to Creon: "I can't do my job and this is a problem, but an easy one for you to fix—just clean up the mess. Look, we all make mistakes. This is no big deal and there is no sense in creating a big hubbub because of it, since all that is at issue here is carrion meat. What is the threat in remitting a judgment against dead meat? You can't harm a corpse." Neither Antigone nor Creon can agree with this perspective on the dead. It reveals their respective animating forces behind the corpse—incestuous love and political mastery—as absurdly connected to dead meat. Obviously, there is more at stake here; nobody loves or governs bodies as mere matter. And yet, were one to witness or imagine the performance of the struggle, its absurdity should bring some relief to the supposed transcendent or cosmological weight of each claim over the corpse.

This lighthearted reading reveals the locus of the tragedy in confident self-determination and the reliance on absolutely independent perspectives and standards for fidelity. Commitments to traditions and strategies, even those of dispossession and nonviolence, place us closer to Creon than to Antigone. Creon thinks that the dead are raw materials at his disposal, like the rest of nature, that he can use for his own ends. By controlling the discourse of those passed away, those who cannot speak for themselves, Creon attempts to control his city's movement toward the future. The dead are often used to justify and legitimate the politics of the present, to turn an illusion into a reality, despair into hope, the unknown into certainty. The energies that invigorate the behaviors and commitments of the present are driven by interpretations of the past—be it in continuity or for change.[19]

---

18. Plato, *Symposium*, 223D. The understanding that it is impossible to preserve and pass on the truth, that acting on an illusion is connected to attempts to rigidify the truth in ways that actually contribute to its death, as well as the possibility of finding a remedy in Socrates' suggestion to read the same play as a comedy and tragedy comes from Lear, *Open Minded*, 6. See also his reading of Oedipus in chap. 3, titled "Knowingness and Abandonment: An Oedipus for Our Time," 33–55.

19. Former American president George W. Bush made explicit the simultaneity of giving the dead a meaning that subsequently legitimates existing ambitions such that alternative objectives and procedures are rejected out of hand. As both the body count of American soldiers and the disapproval of the president's

Those who advocate a tradition-based politics can be especially committed to maintaining its continuity. Even when different practices or ways of articulating the tradition are welcomed, when change is allowed within the traditional community, it is seen to contribute to the overall continuation of the tradition itself. Should this tradition be threatened by another political force, advocates of the tradition articulate their hope for survival in terms of keeping it pure from the rival group. The tradition becomes a site of resistance that must not be overtaken or seduced by that which threatens the intelligibility of the lives of its constituents.[20]

Tending to the living as a priority puts the future of our stories, and those of the dead, at risk. Creon wants a consistent community ethic and Antigone wants a divine law to disrupt it. Their struggle portrays an image of tradition that exposes its instability and deformation rather than its potentiality as a pure opposition to whatever threatens its way of life. As incest destabilizes kinship, so too fidelity destabilizes religious tradition, as both are open to that which exceeds cultural norms. To the extent that we see fidelity as strengthening our position—invoking tradition and a *telos* to establish legitimacy and intelligibility such that only certain forms of life are livable and only certain forms of ethics are intelligible—we become Creon. Antigone's fidelity, her commitment to her heritage, exceeds the attempts to master culture and nature but only leads to an anti-generative end. Of course, the problem is that Creon will not let her enact her piety; Antigone is structurally excluded from the polis. However, to offer a counter-polis as a site of pure opposition, a more legitimate *Sittlichkeit*, is to simply reproduce Creon's control of humanity. A life trapped in a corpse is an image of humanity, one whose death and glory are immanent and perhaps less disposed to the terrible art of mastery. Antigone may be that person who disrupts the seemingly fixed human condition the Chorus articulates, but she can only do so through her fatal and incestuous love of the dead. In other words, we see in Antigone a depiction of one condition of generative possibility through a constructive disruption, but it is ugly. Perhaps we can avoid becoming depressed by this grotesque hope for newness if we can make fun of our love for the impossible—if we can both laugh and cry at the excesses and deficiencies of our desires.

---

invasion of Iraq rose, Bush attempted to gain public support through the resolve to "honor the fallen by completing the mission for which they gave their lives, and by doing so we will ensure that freedom and peace prevail." Reuters, "We'll Stick It Out in Iraq." This way of remembering the dead affects how one remembers the living. The current president, Barack Obama, solicited an optimism and legitimacy for American presence in Afghanistan through delineating that country as anarchic, corrupt—"the most dangerous place in the world"—and in need of stability provided by American-style state democracy. See Stewart, "Irresistible Illusion." Both Bush and Obama speak for those who are denied a place or unable to speak for themselves in order to justify and compel, to reduce the practicable courses of action.

20. One advocate of such politics who articulates the benefits of conflict in terms of strengthening the intelligibility and perpetuation of the tradition is Alasdair MacIntyre. He says that ethics is about "enabling us to overcome the harms, dangers, temptations and distractions we encounter, and which will furnish us with increasing self-knowledge and increasing knowledge of the good." *After Virtue*, 219. MacIntyre's account of tradition-based ethics, its intelligibility and conflicts, is more complicated than the extent of this sentence. For a more thorough engagement with this aspect of MacIntyre's work, see Lear, "Can the Virtuous Person Exist in the Modern World?" 25.

Bibliography

Benardete, Seth. *Sacred Transgressions: A Reading of Sophocles' Antigone*. South Bend, IN: St. Augustine's, 1999.

Butler, Judith. *Antigone's Claim: Kinship between Life and Death*. New York: Columbia University Press, 2000.

Euben, J. Peter. *Corrupting Youth: Political Education, Democratic Culture, and Political Theory*. Princeton: Princeton University Press, 1997.

Huebner, Harry. *Echoes of the Word: Theological Ethics as Rhetorical Practice*. Kitchener, ON: Pandora, 2005.

Huebner, Harry, and David Schroeder. *Church as Parable: Whatever Happened to Ethics?* Winnipeg: CMBC Publications, 1993.

Lear, Jonathan. "Can a Virtuous Person Exist in the Modern World?" *London Review of Books* 28 (2006) 24–25.

———. *Open Minded: Working Out the Logic of the Soul*. Cambridge, MA: Harvard University Press, 1998.

MacIntyre, Alasdair. *After Virtue: A Study in Moral Theory*. 2nd ed. Notre Dame, IN: University of Notre Dame Press, 1984.

Nussbaum, Martha C. *The Fragility of Goodness: Luck and Ethics in Greek Tragedy and Philosophy*. Rev. ed. Cambridge: Cambridge University Press, 2001.

Plato. *Symposium*. Translated by Seth Benardete. Chicago: University of Chicago, 2001.

Reuters. "We'll Stick It Out in Iraq: Bush." *ABC Online*, August 14, 2005. Online: http://www.abc.net.au/news/newsitems/200508/s1437090.htm.

Sophocles. *Greek Tragedies*. Translated by David Grene. 2nd ed. Chicago: University of Chicago Press, 1991.

Stewart, Rory. "The Irresistible Illusion: Why Are We in Afghanistan?" *London Review of Books* 31 (2009) 3–6.

10

Worship Made Strange

Irma Fast Dueck

Occasionally I take the students in a worship class I teach on a field trip. The distance is not far—just one building away on the university campus—yet each time we make the trip it feels as if we've entered a strange land. We journey to the archives of the university and search out a fifteenth-century worship book that originally came from a monastery in Spain. It looks like no other worship book the students have seen before. Approximately 2 1/2-by-1 1/2 feet in diameter, its covers are made of wood, its pages are vellum, and of course, it is written and illuminated by hand. I don a pair of gloves and carefully turn its pages as we examine the texts and observe the illuminations. The words of Scripture, songs, and prayers are all there. We imagine the monks gathered in the evening, all leaning over this one book to read or sing the texts together. And as strangers observing this foreign land, we are surprised by a few discoveries: a hymn that is also in a contemporary hymnbook that resides in twenty-first-century pews; phoenixes, dogs, and peacocks all giving expression to faith. Toward the end of the book, we discover a page where human faces are playfully caricatured as notes on the lines of the musical staff. Could it be that these are the faces of the monks, carefully drawn into their worship book?

For some students, the visit to the medieval worship book is like a visit to another land, a place far from the contemporary worship technology, the screens and PowerPoint presentations to which many of them are accustomed. Students frequently marvel at the work and time it took to prepare this book. For some, the book prompts feelings of gratefulness for contemporary technologies with which worship resources can be created more efficiently, or even downloaded with a click of a button. And yet, as strange as the book may seem, on a visceral level it frequently draws students into its pages.

In the church today, few topics receive as much attention as the relationship between worship and culture, and more specifically, the need for worship to be relevant and familiar, connecting to contemporary realities. At its best, the emphasis on worship and culture reflects a growing desire for hospitality and greater inclusivity by giving particular attention to the context of worship, in regard to both multicultural settings and the contemporary culture in which the church finds itself. This has included a creative rethinking of liturgical expression, of language and the use of idioms and images that enable the worshipper to enter into the worship of God and the Christian story.

At its worst, in its desire to become culturally relevant, the church has become seduced by contemporary culture in such a way that worship has become market driven. In the church's attempt to be pertinent and meet the "needs" and desires of its "consumers," worship has come dangerously close to being yet another form of entertainment, as attention shifts from the narrative of the Christian faith and its compelling challenges to those who walk in the Christian faith, to strategies that make worship more enjoyable and accessible for its participants. Worship risks becoming, as Paul Wadell claims, "a weekly massage for the ego, not the ritual that initiates us into the often unnerving disciplines of discipleship and the redemptive practices of God."[1] And as Wadell says so bluntly, when liturgy becomes entertainment, the risk is that "our worship becomes as trivial as our lives."[2]

Yet no matter why and how the church negotiates the earnest desire to ensure that worship is relevant to the contemporary context, there remains a peculiar reality within the worship of God that thwarts any attempt to contain it in familiar cultural forms. The reality is that worship, by its very nature, is strange and in many ways culturally incomprehensible. There is something irrational and illogical about worship that continually reminds us that God can never be domesticated or tamed. Catholic theologian Nathan Mitchell acknowledges this inexplicable nature of worship in the beginning of his book on liturgy and the sacraments when he claims that liturgical theology begins "not with historical reconstruction or even with our 'experience of worship's symbols, rites, and texts,' but with the sober recognition that *we don't know what we're doing*."[3] Worship at its very best should remind us that we are *not* in control, not masters of the universe nor even of our worship; on the contrary, worship invites a relinquishing of control, a letting go of our compulsion to control, master, and manipulate, to allow God to move us into holy presence. Again Mitchell writes, "[L]iturgies have no other content than the body itself in prayer, the body-as-prayer, and though we often heap them high with meaning, the fact remains that we don't 'mean' (control, determine) rites; rites 'mean' *us*. They are older than we are."[4] French Catholic theologian Louis-Marie Chauvet reinforces the unfathomable nature of the liturgy when he claims that after Vatican II, the first effect of using vernacular languages in Roman Catholic worship was to make the congregation "understand that they did *not* understand."[5]

What makes worship so strange and incomprehensible? I will suggest three reasons for this strangeness, all of which bear a particular witness to the peculiar relationship of worship to the world, reminding us that in our world the book of Christian liturgy will always be strange.

---

1. Wadell, *Becoming Friends*, 18.
2. Ibid., 19.
3. Mitchell, *Meeting Mystery*, xv.
4. Ibid.
5. Chauvet, *Symbol and Sacrament*, 328, quoted in Mitchell, *Meeting Mystery*, xv.

Purposeless Worship in a Purpose-Driven Culture

Worship is, in an odd way, purposeless. The incomprehensibility of the liturgy is compounded by a purpose-driven culture fixated on outcomes and results, in which worship is really, as Marva Dawn so provocatively claims, "a royal 'waste' of time."[6] Worship is purposeless in the same way some other activities might be considered purposeless: Why kiss someone you love? Why watch a sunset? Or read poetry? Marianne Micks says it succinctly when she compares worship with love: "People who worship and people who love generally suppose that they know what they are doing. They assume that other people are doing something similar under the same name. But worship, like love, is a curiously difficult activity to talk about. If one asks worshippers, 'What, precisely, is it that you are doing?' no one can say very clearly."[7]

Like love, worship is of terminal, not instrumental value. Worship is not validated to the extent that it is culturally relevant or personally meaningful or useful. It is a purposeless act in that its reason for being is not its utility; it is sufficient as its own end, requiring no purpose beyond itself.[8] This is not to say, however, that worship is meaningless. On the contrary, while worship by human standards of validation may be purposeless, it remains full of meaning. While the church may be a carefully organized and structured body, with a clear sense of purpose and with instruments and programs to accomplish its mission, there always remains a part of itself—its worship—that is in a particular sense free from purpose.

Romano Guardini develops this relationship between purpose and meaning in worship in his classic book, *The Spirit of the Liturgy*, where he considers the concepts of purpose and meaning as interdependent. Human life requires a sense of purpose; otherwise, Guardini argues, it "degenerates into pseudo-aestheticism." However, when human life is regulated only by purposeful behaviors and actions, it "droops and perishes." Human life needs both purpose and freedom from its tyranny. In worship, the church enters another sphere that is free from purpose. And while things may indeed be accomplished by worship, liturgy does not teach by means of "an artificial system of aim-conscious educational influences" but "simply creates an entire spiritual world in which the soul can live according to the requirements of its nature."[9] By analogy Guardini compares a gymnasium, in which every piece of apparatus and exercise is directed toward a particular calculated effect, to the open woods and fields, where life is lived within nature and "intergrowth takes place in her." Guardini writes, "The liturgy creates a universe brimming with fruitful spiritual life, and allows the soul to wander about in it at will and develop itself there. The abundance of prayers, ideas, and actions, and the whole arrangement of the calendar are incomprehensible when they are measured by the objective standard of strict suitability for a purpose."[10]

---

6. Dawn, *Royal "Waste" of Time*.

7. Micks, *Future Presence*, ix, quoted in Smith, *Where Two or Three Are Gathered*, 17.

8. For further development of this theme of the purposeless of worship, see Smith, *Where Two or Three Are Gathered*; Dawn, *Royal "Waste" of Time*; Clapp and Webber, *People of the Truth*; Willimon, *Bible*.

9. Guardini, *Church and the Catholic, and The Spirit of the Liturgy*, 177.

10. Ibid.

It is for this reason that Guardini is able to talk about the playfulness of liturgy. Worship has close affinities with play, for play is non-goal-directed activity. Children need to play in order to mature and develop and learn, yet they do not enter into it with the intention of maturing or learning. They simply play. And in play, actions acquire a coherence on their own discovered simply by engaging in it. Worship, too, invites an abandonment of the yearning to do something, accomplish something, solve something, and instead invites us to learn to squander time with God and "play the divinely ordained game of the liturgy in liberty and beauty and holy joy before God."[11] The play of worship will always be at odds with a purpose-driven world.

Strange to Say—Worship's Mother Tongue

Part of what makes worship strange is the language it speaks—a language spoken and comprehended as much by the body as the mind. While worship may utilize patterns and rituals that are familiar and repetitive, it is at the same time polyphonic in that it is able to speak in several voices simultaneously. When we enter into worship, we enter into the ambiguous language of ritual and symbol, vehicles for meanings far greater than their own immediate reality. Symbols and rituals are capable of conveying the realities of a spiritual world that extends beyond the material world and yet uses material existence to convey these meanings.

Nowhere is this more obvious than in the central worship rituals of the church: baptism and the Eucharist. We know that the accounts of Jesus's baptism in the Gospels, the washing of early Christian converts told of in the book of Acts, and Paul's baptismal descriptions are more than descriptions of cultural rites of passage—these became the charter for Christian baptism in the church. But more than pointing to the origins of baptism, the baptismal accounts also link the church to divisions that separate people on the basis of cultural identities and ideologies, race and birthright, and calls those very practices into question, seeking to redefine Christian identity on the basis of the Trinity in whose name the practice takes place.

In a similar way, Jesus's Last Supper with his disciples was more than simply a farewell meal with his friends—it became the origin of the Christian Eucharist. But the Last Supper was also more than the origin of the Eucharist, for the very story of this meal links the church to food practices in the ancient Mediterranean world, where meals were maps, structuring social relationships and designating "who ate what with whom." The story of the Last Supper calls into question those very practices both then and now, redefining community and social relationships. It also links the Eucharist to stories of human hunger and human need and economic disparity, and tells an alternative story.[12]

---

11. Ibid., 183–84.

12. This is testified to by one of the earliest accounts of the practice of the Eucharist in the early church, an account by Justin Martyr describing how believers brought gifts to the worship service and placed them on the table. From that one table came the offerings made by the whole congregation, as well as the bread, wine, and water for the eucharistic service, and the food distributed after the service to the needy within the community. Christian faith and life were intimately linked through the celebration of the Eucharist and the distribution of the bread to all who were in need of it. See Jourjon, "Justin."

It is because of the peculiar multivalent language of worship that we cannot help looking at the natural world differently. Material elements are not *only* or *merely* natural phenomena (water is never *just* water, bread is never *just* bread); they function as hierophanies, revelatory of the sacred, of God in Christ through the Spirit. Worship invites Christians to look differently at the natural world in order to enter another set of meanings than the utilitarian, technological, and/or scientific meanings immediately proposed by the physical elements. And when we in contemporary Western culture rob worship of its use of rituals and symbols, we rob it of its native language, its mother tongue.

But ultimately these gestures, words, symbols, and rituals of worship are not human constructions to teach or convey information or even to produce meanings, for as long as symbols are used there will always be ambiguity and fluidity of meaning. One last reason for worship's ambiguity, which may be the most significant reason, is that it takes place among God's people, in the church, the body of Christ, a community sustained by the Holy Spirit. The goal of liturgy is ultimately not to produce meanings, but *meeting*. The practices of baptism and the Lord's Supper clearly attest to this. Worship is about encountering the Trinity—God in Jesus Christ and each other through the Spirit—and the world in which we live. And in this *meeting* we discover not only who God is in Jesus Christ but who we are in God, as the body of Christ sustained by the Spirit. Nathan Mitchell writes that "at liturgy, we do not invent or assert our own identity; we *receive* it."[13] Worship is strange in that we discover our identity lies not primarily in the culture from which we come, the family into which we were born, or the church denomination that shaped us; our identity lies in the Trinity—in God through Jesus Christ and as revealed by the Holy Spirit. In worship we discover who by the grace of God we are, and who we are meant to be. This is an identity we do not earn or achieve or create, but receive as a gift. This identity is our inheritance as Christians. And in worship the creation of this identity requires the active and full participation of the congregation as a body. Again, Romano Guardini writes,

> The [liturgical] act is done by every individual, not as an isolated individual, but as a member of a body in which the Church is present. It is this body which is the "we" of the prayers. Its structure is different from that of any other collection of people meeting for a common purpose. It is that of a *corpus*, an objective whole. In the liturgical act the celebrating individual becomes part of this body and he incorporates the *circumstantes* in his self-expression . . . in the [liturgical] act the individual becomes conscious of the meaning of the words "congregation" and "Church."[14]

As Christians we receive our identity as the body of Christ through worship's rituals, symbols, and gestures—worship's mother tongue.

Strangers in a Strange Land

Worship begins with the gathering of the church. Typically, worshippers are scattered, both physically in their homes and spiritually in terms of their values and moral commitments. Worship begins as people enter the procession from where they are to assemble into a community. Worshippers are called *from* the world, and they gather as individuals

---

13. Mitchell, *Meeting Mystery*, 45.
14. Guardini, "Open Letter," 6–7.

from different cultures, settings, homes, and families; they bring their lives, indeed their "world" with them in order that they might become more than what they were: one "new" community, unified by its praise of God. This act of gathering is not unlike the scriptural accounts of Jesus calling his first disciples to follow him (Mark 1:16–20). Just as the original separating out of the disciples was disruptive to their normal flow of life, so, too, worship breaks through the ordinary, the mundane, and requires people to leave behind what is familiar and comfortable and enter into a new community, a new way of being and living in the world. In this way, the paradigm of Jesus calling a people provides a good canonical basis for gathering the people of God.

Gathering as an act of worship is basic to the pattern of most Christian liturgies. Many traditions begin with a procession, physically exemplifying this coming together. Catholic and Anglican traditions typically include a prayer called the *collect* that, as its name implies, functions to collect the faithful and focus their attention on why they have come together. What is clear is that this coming together is not by accident, nor is it preliminary to worship itself, like the warm-up before a hockey game; rather, it is more like the face-off at the beginning of a hockey game, an integral part of the game without which it cannot begin. Gathering itself is an intentional act of worship, reminding Christians that worship is something that is done together, not because Christians have things in common or because of some religious obligation, but because it is through the communal mode of remembering that the Christian faith and story—the story of a communal people—comes to be understood.[15] The Christian faith is a shared faith; faith in God is held together with other people. Gordon Lathrop, in his book on liturgical ecclesiology, roots the corporate nature of worship in the Trinity, which he describes as a "community of being." It is the Trinity that binds the community to God and to each other. He writes, "This Trinity, this God-for-us, is also known in a social way: God has created humankind as a race of social beings; Jesus has been at the center of a movement, a meal-fellowship, that still continues; and the Spirit enlivens communities today. From the liturgical point of view, that faith in the triune God comes into existence and comes to expression as the assembly meets, as the church which is the meeting for worship happens."[16]

In this sense worship has everything to do with what it means to be the church, or as Lathrop says, "[t]o interpret the meaning of the assembly is to interpret the meaning of 'church' and the church's faith."[17] To be concerned about the church is to be concerned about its worship, and vice versa.

The history of the church also attests to this symbiotic relationship of worship and church. Liturgical theologian Paul Hoon is so bold as to say that historically, to change

---

15. It cannot be assumed, however, that all who come to participate in worship are necessarily shaped by it. Don Saliers argues that the "concept of 'understanding' the world in and through the Christian story" in worship is complex. People can participate in the liturgy without full understanding or wholehearted sincerity. Nonetheless, corporate worship does articulate and shape how "they are to be disposed toward the world." See Saliers, "Liturgy and Ethics," 18.

16. Lathrop, *Holy People*, 8.

17. Lathrop, *Holy Things*, 9.

worship was to change the church.[18] Worship is not only a central practice of the church; at the heart of worship lies the identity and self-understanding of what it means to be the church. Hoon writes, "Worship, let it always be remembered, involves the very being of the Church. In the transaction between God and man through Jesus Christ in Christian worship, the Church is constituted, called into being, knows and confesses her true being, and reveals her true being. Indeed, worship is 'the epiphany of the Church,' the Church's 'pre-eminent self-realization.'"[19]

Having said this, however, it must be made clear that worship is not done for the sake of community, nor is the purpose of worship to create a communal identity. The community gathers not only for fellowship or for renewal of relationships, but because God is holy and calls together a holy people. Worship is not a private gathering of people who have things in common theologically, culturally, or personally. It is an event Christians participate in because of a relationship with one another through Jesus Christ and his reconciling work on the cross, breaking down barriers and creating a new humanity. The purpose of worship is first and foremost about God, in Jesus Christ and through the working of the Holy Spirit, as discovered through the actions of worship—through reading scriptures, singing, preaching and praying, participating in the table of Jesus Christ and in baptism as newcomers are welcomed into the church. The identity of the church in the Trinity is found in these "doings" of the church in worship. Gordon Lathrop writes, "The church begins to know itself not by contemplating its own identity, but by beholding the face of Christ in that word, bath, and table that manifest God's identity. In these things the church is filled with the power of that Spirit to bear witness in the world to the truth about God. The meeting for worship is itself the ground and beginning of such witness. The meeting for worship is the church becoming the church."[20]

The gathering together of the church in worship into one community is in itself a radical action marking the community as distinct, as an alternative if not strange community to the world around it. The church gathered from all the nations as a new people reminds the world that we are in fact one people. It is, as Stanley Hauerwas claims, "the foretaste of unity of the communion of saints."[21] It is an eschatological community whose identity is located in Jesus Christ, in whom those gathered experience their unity. Alexander Schmemann, an Orthodox liturgical theologian, reminds us that the original sense of *leitourgia* was an action through which a group of people corporately became something other than what they had been; through worship they became something different than merely a collection of individuals. He writes, "The *leitourgia* of ancient Israel was the corporate work of a chosen few to prepare the world for the coming of the Messiah. And in this very act of preparation they became what they were called to be, the Israel of God, the chosen instrument of His purpose. Thus the Church itself is a *leitourgia*, a ministry,

---

18. Hoon, *Integrity of Worship*, 33. Hoon cites numerous examples, but perhaps the best is that of Martin Luther's Ninety-five Theses, in which he condemned the corruption of the liturgy and appealed for the liturgy to be given back to the people, marking the beginning of the Protestant Reformation (33ff.).

19. Ibid., 34.

20. Lathrop, *Holy People*, 9.

21. Hauerwas, "Liturgical Shape of the Christian Life," 41.

calling to act in this world after the fashion of Christ, to bear testimony to Him and His Kingdom."[22] To gather in worship, then, is to help the church to become what it already is in Jesus Christ and in so doing be a witness in the world. The action of assembling worshippers together in one place signifies both who the church is and why it is here.

Furthermore, as the community gathers, it is reoriented. Worshippers readjust their time to the church's calendar. Worship directs its participants by creating a fundamental location and orientation within the world. Indeed, an ancient Christian practice oriented worshippers in the world through physically facing them toward the east. They thus located themselves in the world and were reminded that the four directions, the "ends of the earth," were all created by God. Worshipping while facing the east, the place of sunrise, was understood as standing for God's time and the coming day of God in the risen Jesus Christ. It was to bear witness to the risen Lord and the hope of his return one day.[23]

Not surprisingly, worship presupposes separation—that there is, in fact, a boundary created between the ritual practice of worship and worshippers' lives in the world. Worshippers leave their "homes," with all the symbolic attachments of role and biological identity, of comfort and security and all that is familiar, to enter into another place, a community that is dissimilar and peculiar. It is through gathering together in worship that the community is helped to understand that the church, the body of Christ, is a community different than any other, and it gathers those who are different from each other to become a community that has a particular identity and self-understanding. Part of what makes them particular is that they root and form their lives around a particular story, one centered on the life, death, and resurrection of Jesus Christ. Or as Galatians 3:26–28 describes it, "[F]or in Christ Jesus you are all children of God through faith. As many of you as were baptized into Christ have clothed yourselves with Christ. There is no longer Jew or Greek, there is no longer slave or free, there is no longer male and female; for all of you are one in Christ Jesus" (NRSV). This story of Jesus Christ is what gives shape to the kind of people they are and are to be. Such an understanding of the church assumes that different people, different gifts, and different stories come together into one.

The separation of the gathered worshipping community, however, does not necessarily imply an escape from the world. To enter into worship is to look at the world from another, fuller dimension—to comprehend the world more fully. Or as one writer says, "The liturgy 'makes conspicuous' the world as it is."[24] To gather in worship is to enter into a new way of seeing. Schmemann describes it as "the journey of the Church into the dimension of the Kingdom." He continues, "Our *entrance* into the presence of Christ is an entrance into a fourth dimension which allows us to see the ultimate reality of life. It is not an escape from the world, rather it is the arrival at a vantage point from which we can see more deeply into the reality of the world."[25] To look at the world more fully, more deeply, to see "what is really real" requires a real separation from the world but not a flight from it.

---

22. Schmemann, *For the Life of the World*, 25.

23. Lathrop, "O Taste and See," 41–42. In this essay, Lathrop develops his understanding of the relationship between worship and ethics around the theme of worship orienting its participants to the world.

24. Leo the Great, quoted in Willimon, *Service of God*, 52.

25. Schmemann, *For the Life of the World*, 27.

Such a perspective stands in sharp contrast to the desire of some congregations to minimize the separation between worship and contemporary life to such a degree that the Christian distinctions are diminished. Scripture is not read and prayers and liturgy are downplayed in an attempt to make worship acceptable and palatable to people today so that they will "hardly know that they are in a worship service at all." What such a practice of worship fails to comprehend is the radical nature of the gathered community as a countercultural community, called by God through Jesus Christ and by the power of the Spirit to another way of being, seeing, and living. Such a practice fails to comprehend that the church is itself a political reality that frequently stands in sharp discontinuity with the politics of the world. To gather together in worship is a political act; it is to enter a different and holy way of being.

Yet even as the lived reality of the church reflects a counter-politics, a strangeness, or a particularity, it is not "other-worldly." Alexander Schmemann writes, "This is not an 'other' world, different from the one God has created and given to us. It is our same world, *already* perfected in Christ, but *not yet* in us."[26] As Christians gather in worship, particularly as they gather around the Lord's Table, they become Christ's body. They enact and perform another way of living in the world. As William Cavanaugh writes, "The Eucharist is the true 'politics,' as Augustine saw, because it is the public performance of the true eschatological City of God in the midst of another City which is passing away."[27]

Worship Made Strange

Worship *is* worldly. It draws on the earth's bounty—water, bread, oil, light—and uses the world's technologies. The essence of worship is the praise of a God who not only meets us through history but continues to reveal Godself in the particularity of our present human situation, acknowledging that God is working in the very earthiness of present human lives and experiences. Worship is acted out in a very particular way, in a particular order, and at its best it engages all parts of our being: our bodies, our senses of sight, hearing, touch, taste, and smell, our hearts and minds. Human experiences of time and place are brought into the church. The Lord's Supper is a physical meal. As it is eaten, it reminds community members of their relationship with God and to each other. Furthermore, it is consistent with an ecological understanding of the world, as it points to the dependence of all of creation on God. In worship there is no dichotomy between something as mundane as eating and drinking (the Lord's Supper) and washing (baptism or footwashing) and the spiritual world, for the Spirit is at work in these earthly, bodily acts. The physical actions involved in the ordinances further embody connectedness with the world.

And all of worship is, in a sense, culturally conditioned—bound by a cultural context and shaped by a cultural environment. Worshippers are always products of a particular culture, with all its patterns of communication. Worship can never escape the influence of culture, nor should it try to. We, like the monks of the medieval worship book, are always drawing our own faces into the liturgical tradition that has been given to us.

---

26. Ibid., 42.
27. Cavanaugh, *Torture and Eucharist*, 14.

Yet despite the fact that worship takes place in particular communities in place and time, the identity of the community gathered is rooted not in ourselves but in something decidedly Other than us. We gather in the "name" of God, a name that is not self-assigned but is given to us. For this reason, Catherine Pickstock argues, Christian worship begins "only after all participants agree to act as impersonators, traveling to a 'strange land' under assumed identities, on another's passport: 'In the name of the Father, and of the Son, and of the Holy Spirit.'"[28] The first and last words of liturgy should remind us not first who *we* are, but should "inscribe us in Another."[29]

We are called into God's presence, not God into ours. And because of this, worship will always be strange. The worship of God is driven by forces that break apart culturally imposed expectations. Worship speaks a strange language—the language of gratitude and praise, the truthful language of confession and reconciliation, the language of Scripture, a normative story that can be contextualized but never relativized. Worship is a language too deep for only words and is comprehended as much by the body, which is worship's native language, as by the mind. But most of all, worship is strange because it belongs to the community of faith, the body of Christ—not to individuals in space and time nor to customers or consumers, but to an eschatological community. The practice of worship gives witness to an eschatological calling, a new social wholeness that is proclaimed through each baptism, through each sharing of bread and wine. Worship is the public performance of what Cavanaugh calls "the true eschatological City of God in the midst of another City which is passing away."[30] As such, worship is always a call to conversion, a call to transformation. If we enter worship with the assumption that it should make us feel good, that it should confirm our ideas of God and the Christian faith and affirm our lives and identities, then we have failed to comprehend its fullest meaning and enter into its strangeness. In worship we receive our inheritance, our identity in Christ. Our individual bodies are transformed to become part of the one body of Christ, setting us on a well-traveled though peculiar path that has always appeared strange to a watching world. But no stranger than a group of students looking in a fifteenth-century worship book and suddenly discovering their own faces there.

---

28. Pickstock, *After Writing*, 181.

29. Ibid.

30. Cavanaugh, *Torture and Eucharist*, 14.

Bibliography

Cavanaugh, William. *Torture and Eucharist: Theology, Politics and the Body of Christ*. Malden, MA: Wiley-Blackwell, 1998.

Chauvet, Louis-Marie. *Symbol and Sacrament: A Sacramental Reinterpretation of Christian Existence*. Translated by Patrick Madigan and Madeleine Beaumont. Collegeville, MN: Liturgical, 1995.

Clapp, Rodney, and Robert Webber. *People of the Truth: The Power of the Worshiping Community in the Modern World*. Eugene, OR: Wipf & Stock, 2001.

Dawn, Marva. *A Royal "Waste" of Time: The Splendor of Worshiping God and Being Church for the World*. Grand Rapids: Eerdmans, 1999.

Guardini, Romano. *The Church and the Catholic, and The Spirit of the Liturgy*. Translated by Ada Lane. New York: Sheed and Ward, 1935.

———. "An Open Letter." In *Foundations in Ritual Studies: A Reader for Students of Christian Worship*, edited by Paul Bradshaw and John Melloh, 3–8. Grand Rapids: Baker Academic, 2007.

Hauerwas, Stanley. "The Liturgical Shape of the Christian Life: Teaching Christian Ethics as Worship." In *Essentials of Christian Community: Essays for Daniel W. Hardy*, edited by D. Ford et al., 35–48. Edinburgh: T & T Clark, 1996.

Hoon, Paul Waitman. *The Integrity of Worship*. Nashville: Abingdon, 1979.

Jourjon, Maurice. "Justin." In *The Eucharist of the Early Christians*, edited by Raymond Johanny and Willy Rordorf, 71–85. Collegeville, MN: Pueblo, 1976.

Lathrop, Gordon. *Holy People: A Liturgical Ecclesiology*. Minneapolis: Fortress, 1999.

———. *Holy Things: A Liturgical Theology*. Minneapolis: Fortress, 1993.

———. "O Taste and See:" The Geography of Liturgical Ethics." In *Liturgy and the Moral Self: Humanity at Full Stretch before God*, edited by E. Byron Anderson and Bruce T. Morrill, 41–53. Collegeville, MN: Liturgical, 1998.

Micks, Marianne. *The Future Presence: The Phenomenon of Christian Worship*. New York: Seabury, 1970.

Mitchell, Nathan D. *Meeting Mystery: Liturgy, Worship, Sacraments*. Maryknoll, NY: Orbis, 2006.

Pickstock, Catherine. *After Writing: On the Liturgical Consummation of Philosophy*. Oxford: Blackwell, 1998.

Saliers, Don. "Liturgy and Ethics: Some New Beginnings." In *Liturgy and the Moral Self: Humanity at Full Stretch before God*, edited by E. Byron Anderson and Bruce T. Morrill, 15–35. Collegeville, MN: Liturgical, 1998.

Schmemann, Alexander. *For the Life of the World*. Crestwood, NY: St. Vladimir's Seminary Press, 1988.

Smith, Harmon. *Where Two or Three Are Gathered*. Cleveland: Pilgrim, 1995.

Wadell, Paul J. *Becoming Friends: Worship, Justice, and the Practice of Christian Friendship*. Grand Rapids: Brazos, 2002.

Willimon, William. *The Bible: A Sustaining Presence in Worship*. Valley Forge, PA: Judson, 1981.

———. *The Service of God*. Nashville: Abingdon, 1983.

Strains in the Voice of the Church Made Strange

Cheryl Pauls

1. His arms move differently than hers. He learned musicality through jazz standards, she through masterworks from Bach to Bartók. Her arms expand with the breath of each phrase, holding fragile musical lines taut in order to embrace and resist already known musical expressions. His arms dangle by his side, fingers darting out for only the this and the that of absolute necessity. He would never get lost in a sixteen-bar frame, for metric presence is the lifeblood of his practice. Sometimes she could, when the imperative to transcend the perfunctory exceeds its call and crosses into a strangely disembodied musicianship.

But when she plays Ligeti, Berio, Saariaho, or Reich, her arms resemble his in their circular breathing, as musical rhymes waft past her and collect shape in those expanses of time to which only the more distant audience is privy. She is immersed in making music; yet her presence within it harbors less an artist's vision than a competent switchboard operator's navigations amidst streams of networks. Her attunement is to music's materiality, the timbres and timing of sound production and release. Still, a tritone sounds more delicate, more compelling, and more wondrously nuanced when released from her hands than does a perfect fifth from players who speak with assurance through musical form.[1]

2. I sat through the concert with my head down, nearly imploding from the urge to scream, "Stop the show, I can't take the violence." His fingers failed to find the spring in the sound, the musical resilience residing in the key's felt as much as in the give of the digits themselves. I yearned for something compelling in sounds and silences that would call out a listener, with newly created resonances brushing against residues of well-formed habits. Instead, tones were marked by a piercing thinness, their onsets punched as if there were no before and after of musical implication. He named a compositional fault, an amnesia flaunting the end of history, memory, and time.[2] *Perhaps, if the measure of musicality rested in what could be*

---

1. Traditional qualifying labels of the lowest intervals in the harmonic series are sometimes linked to Trinitarian symbolism, with the perfect octave, perfect fifth, and perfect fourth that resonate with the unison symbolizing the perfection of the three-in-one.

2. Jeremy Begbie's theological reflections harshly critique processes of aleatoricism and integral serialism (rigorous orders) in 1950s aesthetics. I find his case overstated, failing to address factors that temper projections of a purged memory, such as the daily practice of players and analyses of texture and accent. See his *Resounding Truth*, 246–48.

read off the page, scarcely touched by the hands and contingencies of musical beings. But since when is immediacy of perception a virtue in the practice of musical time?

3. Strain. Strain. Strain. Strain. Strain. Strain. Strain. How many times can you repeat a word before it ceases to effect a statement, an imperative, or even a doubt, and is unleashed from linguistic particularity and imperative? When does human utterance reassert itself as play in consort with the earth's sounds, without abstractable content? Sometimes those who meet God through "praise and worship" music understand this better than renowned classical performers, whose overdetermined loops of Glass-like minimalism make an artifice of musical expression. Yet the former are accused of liturgically reprehensible individualism by those who can't imagine how God calls a church, a people, a humanity into being without grasping and communicating verbal detail through eyes, hands, and tone. It's relevant, though, that metaphors of conversation, such as antecedent and consequent phrases or polyphonic voices in preserved registral spaces, seldom appear in close readings of newer musics.[3] Entwined within ecologies of sonic matter, these readings place little accent on music's kinship with humankind's most significant difference from the non-human world—verbal language. Might we then ask if closing one's eyes when gathered in congregational song acts less to assert an individualized spirituality than to embody a release of the rationalism of enlightened persuasion, thereby reconciling us and the rest of creation as one in deference to God?

4. Currently a particular strain can be heard in the strains of the congregational voice in the "One-Third World" as it seeks to intone that stigmas of class and race have been overcome. At its best this voice provides the most persuasive prefiguring of messianic community on earth as it is in heaven;[4] at its worst it sources the bitterest of ecclesial separations. Better attention to liturgical form promotes movement beyond musical matters caught in distractions and dysfunctions of personal taste,[5] permitting but not privileging the kind of good singing that draws breath from the depths of the body and from faith long believed in a corporate body. Yet do not the gifts of music's contingent nature and precarious expression ask that communion in Christ be practiced through listening to our muttering voices and attuning our singing to them? For if in our cry we would hear the church made strange, we might also hear a comingling of lament and hope calling us forward, although less clearly in the texts

---

3. Counterpointing linear narratives of melodic continuity in immediate and large-scale dimensions—the legacy of Western culture's classical forms—often are notably absent, as are identitarian idioms like motivic figures, chords of given consonance, and cadentially ordered progressions. Instead, features such as musical streams and harmonic fields address periodicities—musical rhymes and resonances—in musics whose variegated surface features are incoherent through relations of identity. See Roeder, "Interacting Pulse Streams," 231–34.

4. Graham Hughes's scholarly consideration of liturgy through Piercean semiotics veers closest to sentimentalism when he suggests that in congregational singing, "the impression is nearly impossible to resist that God's self is present." See *Worship as Meaning*, 296.

5. Robert Webber has popularized "blended worship" to bring old and new traditions, and by extension practices of differing heritage, into collective coherence within the logic and order of liturgy. See *Planning Blended Worship*. Marva Dawn and Gordon Lathrop contribute further to a liturgical measuring of musical meaning and merit within worship. I endorse their explicit critique of musical self-interests, yet find that their alternative to and negation of "musical interests" relies on indefensible immediacies of sonic signification. See Dawn, *How Shall We Worship?* 14–15, and Lathrop, *Holy Things*, 112.

of our choosing than through distant rhymes in the Babel of tones of our wildly extravagant, burdened cultural tongues.

THESE ACCOUNTS LOCATE STRAINS IN THE CHURCH'S ACT OF CONGREGATIONAL SONG within a particular condition of contemporary music-making: a seeming disjunction in how the musical being—singular and corporate—relates to music's most striking and distinctive feature, repetition.[6] On the one hand, repetitive features provide an ease of engagement with musical form; on the other hand, repeated elements often feel too easy and pervasive, except when they seem not to be present at all. Building on a twofold definition of *strain*, signifying overexertion and distress as well as the distinctive characteristics of regular recurrence, the refrains introduced below attend to the congregational voice as it negotiates the concerted agency of intensified repetitive functioning in the blends of musical expression experienced in the church today. While liturgical musical practices provide the primary focus in these refrains, musical expression as a disciplinary and everyday pursuit informs how musical practices and metaphors are credible theologically. In recent writings, Harry Huebner has adopted the phrase "echoes of the Word" to describe the witness of the church to God's incarnational activity, a witness heard as "strange" when the world comprehends itself apart from God.[7] In considering echoes to be features of sound and akin to formal properties of musical repetition, the refrains that form this essay engage Huebner's metaphor and extend it to a congregational voice that perceives itself as strange because of disjunctions in how it engages musical repetition. These refrains are cast in a subjunctive mood, as if the church were hearing echoes of the indictment of Amos 5 and struggling to listen for a ring of righteousness amidst its conflicted noise.

> Take away from me the noise of your songs;
> I will not listen to the melody of your harps.
> But let justice roll down like waters,
> and righteousness like an ever-flowing stream. Amos 5:23–24 (NRSV)

Before entering these refrains, I want to consider certain features of contemporary musical expression.[8] Noted in both a saturation and a dearth of repetitive relationships, the disjunction stems from an unleashing of many of the givens through which periodicities and pulses commonly link sense and sound to construct elements of melody, meter, motive, timbre, and harmony. When released from supporting these identity-forming musical elements, repetition itself factors more as an optional idiom of expression than a condition of order, presence, and communication. Following Debussy's release of the "tyranny of the barline" and Schoenberg's "emancipation of dissonance,"[9] a reading of this condition might easily be applied to the edge of the Western avant-garde in the mid-twen-

---

6. Heinrich Schenker, quoted in Kivy, *Fine Art of Repetition*, 327.

7. See Huebner *Echoes of the Word*, 1, for reference to the book's title, and the chapter "The Church Made Strange for the Nations," 84–106, for the "strange" accounting of the church.

8 The term *musical expression* gives agency to any engagement with music, be it as a performer, listener, composer, or theorist. The term *musicking* has come to represent the range of these fields of activity. See Small, *Musicking*.

9. These phrases are widely adopted as symbols that the loudest, most easily perceptible acoustic relations need not predetermine musical concession and consonance. See Schoenberg, *Style and Idea*, 216.

tieth century; my intention is to describe a more general phenomenon that is pervasive today. Indeed, the required competence to switch the accent and style of musical gesture on a whim is currently required more in the musical sampling of casual listeners than in the construction of rigorously ordered or pastiche works. Similarly, competence is required to dwell in saturated repetition. Intensified currents of repetition contribute to musical experience engaged more through an immersion in sound than through contemplating form, communicating content, or listening structurally, to name the aesthetic priorities of the period from roughly 1850 to 1950. Further, attention to sonic or timbral characteristics (such as associating a particular band with its "sound") and rhythmic properties now tends to eclipse interest in those musical dimensions that have the strongest affinities with linguistic analogy, melody, and harmony, accenting disinclinations toward musical tones that "speak" and forms that narrate linear arguments. Certainly musicians still rely on correspondences of frequency to blend tone, time span to order breath, and analogical motive to embody relevance. However, many compelling accounts of musical flow now feature micro- and macro-dimensions that form at some distance from what is articulated through human gesture, while the "content" of musical textures and soundscapes is regarded as nonmemorable (though not in a pejorative sense). Hence the nebulous accent of repetition in contemporary music—more a way of approaching practice than a particular style—forefronts music's arbitrary, provisional means of expression.

Refrain One: A Sonic Immersion, a Declarative Rescission

Current forms of the congregational voice can be epitomized rather starkly: repetitive figures abound amidst an abundance of stylistic diversity. The narrative content of verbal texts and musical forms alike diminishes significantly as dialogical sense-making loses reasonability.[10] Thus repetitive musics known within "praise and worship," Taizé, and Eastern Orthodox traditions[11] can all be differentiated from the relatively prosaic poetry, melodic contours, and harmonic narratives of most hymns, whose texts correspond more closely to those of verbal speech. The incorporation of repetitive forms to apprehend "wonder and mystery" is not new for the congregational voice but correlates to its longstanding use of musical canons[12] and polyphony to destabilize assertions of centered individuals.

---

10. Gerald Hobbs notes this diminished role in reference to Taizé music. See "Christianity and Music," 84. Anecdotally, a music minister once indicated to me that the twenty-something generation wouldn't sing a particular hymn text by Thomas Troeger because of "too many words," even though they would greatly appreciate its theological content were it to figure elsewhere than within music. Note that a diminished role of linguistic utterance within music could also be pursued through cultural shifts favoring poetry over proclamation, and figural over discursive, conceptual uses of language, as Tex Sample does. See *Powerful Persuasion*, 142.

11. The latter are heard in both short, anonymous "Alleluias" and sacred concert works of Arvo Pärt, Giya Kancheli, Henryk Gorecki, John Tavener, and other recent composers.

12. By *canon* I mean round songs and other strict forms of musical imitation, not privileged texts! Leo Spitzer explores the Christian heritage of polyphony and rhyme, and notes the tension throughout the centuries between musical expressions that decenter selfhood and those inviting declarative clarity in gospel witness. See *Classical and Christian Ideas of World Harmony*, 46. This tension is evinced today when pianists and drummers limp along during congregational song in efforts to "get out of the way of the words," instead of supplying springing-off impulses for styles in which text and singing need form in response to a sounding beat.

Further, the release of identitarian givens located in music-making today, involving low levels of commensurability between the ordering of recurrent elements and some factor of reasonable constancy in performative engagement, provides impetus to theological imaginings of internally indeterminate, limitlessly multiple resonances of the "disorientating reorientation" of worship.[13] Yet the metaphorical agency of such expression in worship today flirts with a radical edge of chaos when confronted in the music of worship, where it is more tempered than heeded.

Let us consider the diminishing functionality of words and narrative content in musical practice to convey neither noise nor silence, but a sonic immersion marking a declarative rescission. In divesting itself of some measure of conceptual argument and control, the congregation's strain takes up two strands of Huebner's theological echoes: the release from the persuasion of human rationality at the center of truth formation,[14] and the practice of lament as a faithful and hopeful response to conflict.[15] Indeed, Huebner presents lament as "an alternative to human acts of unweaving and re-sewing the layers of history and practice . . . traced in any conflict, a critical act of embodying and confessing a release of control . . . an important stance in a world that is not as it should be . . . [A] sign that we wish it were not so, [a belief] in the possibility of its redemption . . . [and a confession that] we are unable to bring it about."[16] Further, a declarative rescission in the congregation's strain can be heard to confess human creatureliness, thereby lamenting exploitative ways of acting above the rest of creation and finding hope toward a restored ecology. Indeed, in releasing the persuasion of "mind over matter" and practicing more as ecologically responsible artisans than as artists, the congregation's musical embodiment might permit the analogues in the Amos refrain literally to become ever-flowing streams of water. This comingling of lament and hope in transformative processes corresponds to Huebner's understanding of biblical lament as an act practiced regularly and not merely when rationality is caught in quagmires of despair. By connecting lament with theologically credible approaches to all of knowledge, life, and truth, Huebner distinguishes Christian from worldly hope. He calls for hope through "practices and strategies of dispossession"[17]

---

13. Endorsing worship's meanings not as "the words we bring to it but those it gives to us," Nathan Mitchell draws on this understanding, inspired by Deleuze and Guattari, of repetition and difference with a score by Sylvano Bussotti to define Christian ritual as rhizomal, nomadic, and endlessly deferred. See *Meeting Mystery*, 38, 219. John Milbank comes close to approaching theology through the sonic imagery of Pierre Boulez' integral serialism in describing the analogous relationality of creation and a theological imagination, but ultimately rejects this music as nihilistic. See *Theology and Social Theory*, 5, 422, 434–38.

14. Huebner, *Echoes of the Word*, 6, 11, 25, 36–37.

15. Naming a disjunction in repetition as lament draws on Theodor Adorno's mid-twentieth-century hope of disarming convention and projecting a different future for Europe and beyond through heightened attunement to rigorously ordered musics that were out of step with rhythms of traditions. Adorno considered the "autodidactic reinforcement of honed [musical] patterns of response as a draining away of the capacity for the listener's discernment of difference and horrific reified untruths," and thus advocated the permutations of integral serialism. See DeNora, *After Adorno*, 153. My extension of such mitigation from a dearth to an extreme saturation of repetitive identity takes into account both Adorno's focus on destabilizing givens within musical relations, and the reassessment of his berating of jazz and popular styles as viewed as less a concern of style than of the commodification of musical material.

16. Huebner, *Echoes of the Word*, 5–6, 189.

17. Ibid., 159.

and in the "relinquishing of all strategy in the cross,"[18] thus not limiting hope "to the possibilities that emanate from our own projections . . . [but resting] in the non-strategic path opened up for us by resurrecting God."[19]

Huebner stresses that theological imagination takes material form through a transcendent relationship with God that is embodied in prayer and praise, and learned by heeding "lives . . . open . . . to the transforming power of God . . . [who has] spoken in the authoritative texts of the church, in Christ, and to the community which gathers regularly in worship."[20] Nathan Mitchell further invites a correlation between a release of human rationality and relationship with God in describing worship as a place where we face "the sober recognition that we don't know what we're doing . . . and are deprived of our desire for power, mastery and control,"[21] "for liturgy's goal isn't to produce meanings but meeting . . . in the dynamic, hospitable, yet perilous space of God's own life."[22] In this perilous space, the congregation's straining voice serves doubly: it laments a fissure between humankind and God in contemporary life, and it remembers communion with God.

Christine Longhurst points out that worship services today need to provide more opportunities for worshippers to encounter God, necessitating a shift away from an excess of thematic, conceptually based forums about God. She also urges more attention to the flow of songs in terms of words that address God directly and those through which worshippers speak to one another about God.[23] Longhurst locates encounters, or "dialogues," with God in the totality of a worship service's interactions of biblical text, preaching, offering, words of confession, and singing together, not exclusively in the relatively lengthy music sets that open many worship gatherings.[24] Nevertheless, she notes that extended times of singing primarily repetitive strains contribute significantly to leading worshippers deeper into the experience of God, and that in repetitive musics "something else is going on" beyond what is apparent at the level of immediate utterance, something that can't be dismissed as merely the manipulative power of tingling spines and "feel-good" experiences. To address this "something," we might wish that an immersion in sound would attune us to that which is sound: whole, trustworthy, and a source of renewing and reconciling waters for all. Perhaps it does, although not in a form we grasp but in the aporia at play in sound's double meaning, a nonidentity of reciprocity in a non-synthesizing reconciliation. To approach this gap in one instance of the congregation's strain, wherein verbal texts cannot be reconciled on a directly comparable plane of musical gesture, I recall a conversation.

From time to time, Huebner has suggested that the church remembers the Trinity more through congregational song than through preaching. While this suggestion is ex-

18. Ibid., 6.
19. Ibid., 198.
20. Ibid., 46.
21. Mitchell, *Meeting Mystery,* xv.
22. Mitchell draws on Phil 2:6–7 for an image of God's kenotic interpersonal life. See ibid., 59.
23. Longhurst, "Encountering God in Worship," 4–6.
24. "Encounters through immersion" is an apt descriptor, too, for services informed by Iona and Taizé communities, all of which are comprised of music, Scripture readings, and prayer. In these, though, the intended interaction amongst the elements of worship is forefronted.

pressed in a tone of respectful gratitude for the habits of the corporate voice, it carries an edge, as music's virtue seems to render irrelevant its disciplinary practice. By extolling not how the Trinity has been spun musically but merely that we have continued to sing of it, Huebner bypasses the intertextuality of those elements that are not properly text and awards confessional merit to what is known verbally. But how can the Body effectively recollect the Trinity without noticing theological confessions carried and constructed in sonic vehicles? For in "Old Hundredth,"[25] grand cumulating lines consent to closure, while the upward melodic surges of the threefold laud to the Three-in-One in "Dedication Anthem" soar playfully and concede to the tonic's gravitational pull only as a springing-off point for the Hallelujah refrain.[26] The comforting rub and drone of the phrygian E in "Mothering God" infuses the three persons in a verse-by-verse articulation without using a gathering gesture to assert "as one,"[27] while the jumbled order of Son, Father, and Spirit in "Even So Lord Jesus Come"[28] presents a Christological accent in a verbal text that contrasts with a musical hierarchy ever in flux, as phrase fragments float about a dislocated constancy of hyperspace.

Yet I need not posture defensively. Huebner's lack of attention to these differences merely echoes an inattention to song by previous generations, for surely in noting these correspondences, the gap between songs and preaching would have precipitated an adjustment to one or the other. More importantly, the mere repetition of words—an inclination common to musical practices—is where Huebner locates the remembering of what has been regrettably neglected in expository practice, thereby attesting to his belief in the limits of the discipline he practices. Indeed, while he writes that "[i]t is difficult to overestimate the importance of language for doing theology [as it] seeks to disentangle the grammar of religious practices," he refrains from giving theological work absolute importance, confessing rather its ultimate submission to letting "the Word be heard over and over in whatever form its reverberations come."[29] And perhaps in an era of heightened repetitive expression these reverberations come more as accumulated masses of resilient residue than as content approached through music's precarious analogical kinship to the communicative particularity of language.

Now, it is with reservations that I limit the notion of musical content; music is not exempt from contingencies of meaning and therefore we need to cull our repertoire. Moreover, a hearing of repetition as metaphoric residue differs starkly from that of "harmonious difference" to which Huebner appeals when invoking limitless resonance and differentiation in the incarnations of God's Word.[30] Yet the strained blends in the

---

25. *Hymnal: A Worship Book*, no. 119, and *Worship Together*, no. 92.

26. *Hymnal: A Worship Book*, no. 118; *Worship Together*, no. 93.

27. *Hymnal: A Worship Book*, no. 482.

28. In S. Bell, *Music of Steve Bell*, 83–86. Agogic accents (longer durations) on downbeats herein are ineffective when held through but released in units that project neither a singular line nor closure in a given point. Those of us inexperienced in popular music styles often fail to realize this.

29. Huebner, *Echoes of the Word*, 2.

30. Huebner draws on music's capacity for infinite relation and differentiation as proposed by John Milbank, Catherine Pickstock, and Graham Ward in their assertion of Christianity as a "best story." See

congregational voice need to grapple with the range of musical practices for which the phenomenon of the copy, not perceptible differentiation, is most aptly descriptive, and likewise conflicted difference, not resonance. To address these practices, let us consider the challenge of blending the more repetitive expressions of "praise and worship" forms and the more prosaic communication of hymns. This requires listening at more than one pace, a suggestion conjuring the clichéd sonic imagery of eternal timelines through which repetitive dimensions exceeding reasonability in truth-telling all but usher us directly into the presence of God's time.[31] Such imagery might helpfully slow us down; otherwise, its truth-value needs be constrained. Instead, I ask that we listen quite tangibly for a paradoxical truth in order to reconcile more immediate and more distant levels of accent and perception in the strain.

Differences between these levels are not necessarily mutually constructive, as evinced in the duplicity perceptible through minimalist repeated gestures in the movie *Koyaanisqatsi* (Life out of Balance). Without the use of foley to create sensations of realism or empathy in the listener, the few source sounds in Philip Glass's soundtrack emulate the music's relentless repetitive patterns. Engulfed in sameness through music and image, the movie calls out a viewer who laments the (dis)ease of the world's ecology and urban pace and yearns for a restored creation. Yet hopes of realignment are obscured as the movie projects healthy cycles of life entangled within swirling, lifeless currents of the copy, portending the viewer's capacity to effect change only as a surface fantasy. A sameness of statistical abstraction lurks at the macro-dimensions of perception. Still, the apocalyptic doom of the movie's ending dates its 1970s construction; this humors today's viewer and exposes the limits of what a single film can project—or prophesy.

Besides, it is not within the purview of the congregational voice to speak to notions of humankind as mere mechanic pawns of genetic reproduction.[32] Consider then a second example of how the congregational voice might negotiate discrepancies between its immediate utterances and larger dimensions. On the immediate level, the statements of Gavin Bryars's composition "Jesus' Blood Never Failed Me Yet" make an artifice, not an affirmation, of Christian witness. These statements are produced from an artefact of an unnamed singer, and sound as looped bits of mere habitual puppetry that signal the failure of society and soteriology. The truth of the piece lies elsewhere, in a lamenting beauty that accumulates resonance over time through the blend of performance-space acoustics and added orchestration with the artefact's crackling timbral grains and limping rhythms.

Radical Orthodoxy, 1–2. Note also that Huebner denounces "mere rote repetition," an expression corresponding well to the "copy." See Huebner, *Echoes of the Word*, 8, 89.

31. Here I affirm Begbie's critique of John Tavener's claims to "tap into the divine" with extremely slow, repetitive music as problematically overstated. See *Theology, Music, and Time*, 144–46. Note that I resist the "imagined depths . . . beyond words" of Romantic sensibilities; musicians have become well enough aware that the less closely aligned our music-making is to common speech and programmatic imagery, the more words we use to describe music's "wordless" qualities. See Cook, *Music*, 38.

32. Cook employs Richard Dawkins's river of genes metaphor to reframe musicological narratives with a diminished agency of the individual genius composer or masterwork, but to my knowledge, musicology does not address the interface of biology and anthropology with any disciplinary rigor. See ibid., 72.

Through these models of double articulation, where two levels of accentual focus demonstrate some incommensurability and the more immediate level speaks less compellingly, let us now attend to a rift in the congregational voice. Heard on a single plane, this rift tends to divide those who espouse a theology of church as a vanguard of an alternative culture from those who seek kinship with the dominant popular culture as a means of breaking down parochialism and insularity. The text of the hymn discussed below corresponds reasonably to the pacings of coherent verbal articulation, while the "praise and worship" song speaks more compellingly through accumulated repetitions rather than immediate statements. To be sure, immediate "praise and worship," and similarly Taizé utterances, are confessionally direct. Yet their repetitive dimensions produce meanings more akin to labyrinthine than linguistic experience.[33] Indeed, "praise and worship" timbres tend to be remarkably complex, carrying both immediate personal accents and macro-level impersonal ones. The former carry traces of late eighteenth-century piety, with dynamically variegated tones conveying personal devotion and resistance to intellectualized rationalities.[34] The latter correspond to postmodern leanings toward extreme repetition, and thus a dearth of personal presence in articulated content.[35]

"We" and "I" language in congregational song is often opposed through identification with community and individualized subjectivities, respectively. This reading is not musically stable, for "we" tends to be heard most compellingly at immediate levels of utterance and subject formation, and "I" in repeated dimensions that encourage dissolutions of individualized articulation and presence. For instance, the accentual properties of "we" in the sixteenth-century hymn "We Are People of God's Peace"[36] work differently from those of "I" in the contemporary song "Here I Am to Worship."[37] "We" in the hymn appears infrequently and coincides with a simultaneous metric accent at four levels of time-span articulation,[38] providing focus for the text and for the "we" that already has formed as a body to worship. Conversely, in the contemporary song, "I" sounds in the midst of an upbeat and is repeated so often—and the song itself repeated so often—that "I"

---

33. Begbie's theological engagement with God's time and Eucharist through musical analogue in multiple accent schemes and waves of metric relation beyond our common hearing is approached similarly, except that it draws primarily from eighteenth- and nineteenth-century aesthetics that assume a musical work as a multilayered but balanced whole. See Begbie, *Theology, Music, and Time,* chaps. 2 and 6.

34. In his classic social history through the piano, Arthur Loesser attributes the rise of the piano's popularity to the congruence of a personalized individual expression in the pianoforte's limitless dynamic gradations of softs and louds and the expressive piety of Christian faith of the time. See *Men, Women and Pianos,* 17–23. The frequency of the qualifiers "just" and "really" in the prayers and songs of this tradition also contribute to a confessed simplicity of truth-telling.

35. The quest for the impersonal in musical expression by composer, performer, and audient listener in the past century is traced through Igor Stravinsky, John Cage, Steve Reich, and many others, first as radical remarks by renegade composers and later as musically normative. See Reich, *Writings on Music,* 54.

36. *Hymnal: A Worship Book,* no. 204; *Worship Together,* no. 677. Differing musical settings in each of these hymnbooks are attributed to Johann Horn, 1544, although accentual properties as discussed above are highly similar. For reasons of familiarity my analysis follows the metric setting of *Worship Together* rather than the less square, Renaissance-like metric format of *Hymnal: A Worship Book.*

37. Hughes, "Here I Am to Worship."

38. These are the measure, 2-measure hyper-meter, 4-measure phrase, and verse.

does not focus larger-scale concepts or identitarian assertions, but flows into a body that is being formed at some yet unforeseen time.[39] Further, although "me" at the end of the second line of "Here I Am to Worship" receives an agogic (durational) accent, the lack of a rhyming counterpart in the phrase's antecedent and the avoidance of harmonic closure in the reversed plagal idiom (a backwards "Amen") contribute to a suppressed, deliberately underemphasized performance gesture.[40] In this way "I" is performed in flow-through gestures that release human presence and identity into resonances that are less directly ordered; whereas "we" in "We Are People of God's Peace" is performed as an affirmation of the Body that already has formed and figures in the confession of reasonably direct statements. "We" and "I" thus both resist individualistic expression, although differently. Their theological compatibility is heard, paradoxically, with the recognition of the incompatibility of their utterances within a single plane of verbal articulation. This paradox significantly complicates the flow and the experience of "noise" in blended worship; it also offers reconciling hope toward justice in the muttering tones of a burdened cultural tongue.

Refrain Two: Hope in the Burdened Cultural Tongue

Around 1970, the radical edge of the Western musical avant-garde began to fray, as giving ear and voice to global others assumed the forefront of musical interests. Since then, ethical and political dimensions in music-making have become foregrounded in narratives of musical activity. Also, engagement with world musics[41] now provides easily referenced commonalities for adherents of both "classical" and "popular," or "hymn" and "praise and worship" musical streams and often effectively blurs distinctions between them. However, the notion of easy reference evinces the superficial ease of honoring justice amid the indeterminate plurality of networks and exchanges in the world's musics, which often are too strange to each other for frictions of misunderstanding. The congregational voice hears calls to righteousness as it learns to pray and worship "globally."[42] Yet its urgings "beyond musical interests" do not proffer an alternative to the secular world, which also heeds musical contributions to pain, joy, and "a future with hope."[43] Thus variously centered imaginations converge on a question of performance expression: what are we listening for as we seek musicality—an attunement responsible to what music has been as much as to

---

39. The logic here resembles a longstanding musical paradox that if you repeat a tonic chord often enough it acquires the resonance of a dominant function, releasing its presentation of closure in a requirement for resolution or movement elsewhere, which attends to macro- dimensions. In "Clashing Aesthetics" William Buis forefronts micro-dimensions in demonstrating how African-derived rhythmic sensibilities are more significant in contemporary Christian music today than common features of meter in Western tradition.

40. This analysis demonstrates why "I" cannot simply be replaced with "we." Note that the comparison of such divergent styles fails to problematize its ease, even if I can attest that similar differences are remarkably consistent, in analyses that go beyond the scope of this essay.

41. Simon Frith notes that the label "world music" emerged as a commodity of the recording industry in 1987. See "Discourse of World Music," 305.

42. Mitchell references Rev 21:24–26 as a global ingathering when the glory and honor of the nations will be brought into God's presence. See *Meeting Mystery*, 71.

43. The biblical reference is Jer 29:11. A secular engagement "beyond music" is evinced in the largely Marxist-influenced essays of Krims, *Music/Ideology: Resisting the Aesthetic*.

what it is becoming—in the blended future of deconstructed hierarchies and pluralized forms? With refrain two we now listen to a burden in the tongue of the Western world as it strives to honor the cross-cultural coalition that is the source for much of our reawakened love of repetitive, cyclic, and rhythmic dimensions, and hears hope in who we—the church, humanity, all of creation—are becoming as our singing echoes the polyrhythms of Aka Pygmies, the *tālas* of Hindustani tabla drumming, the *kotèkan* of the Balinese gamelan, and the canonic chanting of Eastern Christianity, some of which are labeled orthodox, others New Age appropriations.

Although performative lament is rarely practiced in ritual forms, traces are carried in rhetorics of difference and alternative epistemologies of secular engagement; these strive toward a sustainable plurality of musics. In seeking to resist a ruthless reducing of all the world's musics to much the same sound,[44] the discourse around "worldbeat" (a fusion of folk music traditions with Western rock and pop) locates risks of commodification, as ostensibly celebrated voices of the global margins serve as cultural icons, sound bites, and a set of accents merely exchanged for those of nuanced styles.[45] Further, scholarly communities demonstrate that musical credibility needs to attend to relationships among people and peoples. For instance, the tones of silence following a timely, politically motivated plenary conference session on "Classical Music in Iraq"[46] conveyed an acknowledgment of a world "not as it ought" more than a scholarly ignorance. This response to cultural negotiations presently incomprehensible yet required within a burdened global crisis of imagination evinces the secular academy recalling some measure of what Huebner articulates as the beginning of Christian lament, the recognition of hopelessness and the releasing of human strategy.[47]

The complexity of the cultural work in the lament of "worldbeat" hints further at a Christian imagination: it recognizes that no one has access to positions from which righteousness can be unequivocally grasped, or where acts of sharing can be distinguished definitively from imperializing imposition and those of receiving from appropriating consumption. Further, the coincidence of destabilizing the metaphor of "universal language" within musical engagement and adopting a non-totalitarian globalized musical imagination that aims to sustain cultural plurality suggests a world with more plausible cultural transfers, and greater insufficiencies of cultural exchange. How we practice whatever it is we are listening for in perceived periodicities and irregular pulses of world musics thus is necessarily urgent yet halted, celebrative yet grieving, hopeful yet lamenting.

---

44. Philip Bohlman notes how national anthems tend toward homogeneity. See *World Music*, 100. John Mowitt notes how the category of "worldbeat" risks reducing difference to diversity in a common frame; *Percussion*, 115

45. Robert Fink defines the instability of postmodern expression as the awareness that no matter how well behaved (accords to expectations of a given style) a musical surface, the possibility of sudden change lurks in every moment, making it impossible to be present to nuances of a particular style. See "Going Flat," 131. Note that the destabilizing of repetition carries both an anti-academic and an ultra-intellectual edge.

46. Danielson, "Classical Music in Iraq."

47. Huebner, *Echoes of the Word*, 6.

The complexity of lament's liturgical work is evident in the Iona Community, an important agent in the distribution of a worldwide repertoire of congregational song.[48] Oneness as the gift of adoption and reconciliation in Christ motivates Iona's practices of embodying songs that have been shared by persons and congregations globally. Iona's distribution practices go beyond legal requirements in attending to disparities of economic and cultural privilege. Thus, in remembering and honoring the culturally divergent others with whom it shares the "curious legacy of a post-Christian west and a post-Western Christianity,"[49] this community encourages the Christian church to sing who it is becoming through a political theology of both kinship and difference.

The strangeness in the congregational voice accents music's strong capacity for recollection, its few representational links to words and images, its highly fluid and transferable relational networks, and its considerable capacity for disjunction of time and place in empowering deep memory. These factors bring further complexity to the congregation's voice when it sings with communities extending from Lebanon, Japan, and Zambia to native North America. The heart of the Christian gospel may transcend privilege and particularity of cultural tradition, but the echoes in the voice of Christian liturgy now involve not only a cross-cultural plurality but an inter-religious polyphony. For as we approach the unity of today's church through the diversity of its peoples and cultural styles, we also bring together the musics of today's world through the diversity of its peoples and religious accents.[50] Indeed, as Western music increasingly is viewed as one of the world's musics, secular scholarship attends to religious confession as entwined within and vital to musical expression in Western culture as in any other. The congregational voice thus hears its echoes through overlapping but non-coinciding synoptic accounts of faith and cultural traditions. These are comprised of highly congruent resonating factors, with religious and cultural elements neither indelibly distinguishable nor bound together.

Recently Huebner has become involved in the developing practice of inter-religious dialogues, particularly between Iranian Muslims and North American Mennonites. In these he draws on Alasdair MacIntyre for a hopeful alternative to both universalist conceptions of truth and the chaos of relativism. Huebner thus confesses to Christian truth within a logic of traditions: networks of relationship providing coherence, interaction, and ongoing renegotiation without overarching frameworks.[51] Huebner speaks of a sense of calling to these conversations, but acknowledges that a theology of interfaith exchange has not been developed and that he has no sense of what the outcome may be.[52] Questions of musicality, of what we are listening for in the mingling of echoes in the congregational

---

48. The title of the following songbook exemplifies this focus: J. Bell, *One Is the Body: Songs of Unity and Diversity*. The Iona Community exceeds legal requirements in its published attributions of song sources and royalties, as a symbol of commitment toward the redistribution of global capital.

49. Walls, "Ephesians Moment," 36.

50. The similarities between Farhadian, *Christian Worship Worldwide*—a collection of essays pursuing the church through cultural diversity—and Beck, *Sacred Sound*—pursuing music through religious diversity—attest to this.

51. Huebner, *Echoes of the Word*, chap. 2, "Imagination/Tradition: Disjunction or Conjunction."

52. Comments made by Huebner at presentations to Canadian Mennonite University faculty, October 2008 and June 2009. Gordon Zerbe identified purposes of understanding, exchange, friendship, and peace.

voice, urge these conversations forward, for its multi-voiced traditions do not form coherent alternatives to universal or relativistic forms of reason. Let us now begin an engagement with one mediating stream. It flows through secular conversations and draws on Christian hope.

Within the past decade, musicological discourse has become less sharply critical of the church's impulse to sing together worldwide, as rhetorics of difference have become increasingly less persuasive. Music theorist Kofi Agawu notes how historicist-preservationist models of identity contribute to simplistic reductionism and further imperializing by "clinging to what Africa is—including its ostensible difference from the West—rather than what Africa could be if global resources were differently distributed."[53] Agawu proposes future-oriented frames of engagement that might pave the way for political and musical empowerment,[54] and urges that persons and cultures worldwide "recover our commonality" with a "carefully defined sameness"[55] that is not a method or identity but an attitude that looks beyond the immediate material level.

Musicologist David Clarke recently has proposed a radical dialecticism, inspired by Agawu, Theodor Adorno, and Slavoj Žižek, in a call to move beyond relativism's relatively discrete musical traditions—represented, for example, by the mainstream popularity of Elvis and the avant-garde projects of Darmstadt—and toward negotiations through which musical difference can be sustained without the indifference of tolerant liberalism.[56] Clarke asserts Žižek's critique of ideology, wherein antagonisms—assumed incompatibilities of interaction, or active opposition and hostility—provide a means to experience the position of an other, to find common ground in a shared realization of the absence of common factors of identity, and to attend to entities of collective agency that accumulate in spite of the impossibility of concerted practice.[57] He does not advocate that antagonisms be resolved in universally coherent wholes, but that we recognize the "not all" in the located spaces within which we always necessarily hear. Clarke further urges us to listen for antagonisms transformed to agonisms, reconciliations amidst irreducible differences. While referencing a vision that is far from realized, he daringly projects "a future moment . . . of what—'if speculation on the state of reconciliation were permitted'—might resemble peace among human beings."[58]

Žižek has been of recent interest not only to musicologists but also to theologians. He is one of several post-Marxist philosophers who connect Christian messianic thought with revolutionary process,[59] drawing on a strand of Pauline prolepsis that encourages a future

---

53. Agawu, "Contesting Difference," 171. Interestingly, Agawu nearly rises to Christianity's defense in critiquing the hardly disguised impatience of ethnographers toward the influence of "Christianity, classical music, or electric guitars."

54. Ibid., 170.

55. Ibid., 169

56. Clarke, "Elvis and Darmstadt," 3.

57. Ibid., 25. References to Žižek are drawn primarily from *Sublime Object of Ideology* and "Spectre of Ideology," in *Mapping Ideology*.

58. Clarke, "Elvis and Darmstadt," 41. The conditional phrase Clarke cites is Theodor Adorno's.

59. Zerbe, "On the Exigency of a Messianic Ecclesia." Works by Žižek referenced by Zerbe, such as *Puppet and the Dwarf*, predate those cited by Clarke.

reconciliation between the community of the Messiah and the remainder of humanity within the scope of the reign of God. Identity and reality thus are not formed in a preserved past, but in a "not yet" of what the church is becoming, a whole it is unable to grasp or deduce from the part in which it already participates, as Gordon Zerbe demonstrates.[60] While not endorsing inferences that Christian institutions must die to save their treasure, Zerbe encourages the church to attend how these philosophers position Christian hope precariously rather than by "basking in the security of mystical or individualist subjectivity, retreating into identitarian communical havens . . . or acquiescing to the niceties and comforts of liberalism and global capital."[61]

A precarious straddling of these alternatives picks up the strains of the congregational voice's non-corresponding tripartite antagonisms, from the opposition of repetitive utterances and "I" language with more reasonably verbally coherent "we" formations, and from these in tandem to burdened hope when embodying "worldbeats." Might it be possible for us to listen to this blend with a carefully defined sameness, not of expressive identity or musical grace, but in reconciling ways of listening to irreducible differences amongst the musics gathered in liturgical flow? The friction and oft-disregarded incongruencies in how language works when singing "we" and singing "I"—confusing because seemingly so directly opposed—would then become an agonism, as the congregational voice would hear not a people of God over against a personalized relation with God, but an instability of subject formation within the Western church as it continues to release the inherited power of individualized human reason and as it becomes as one but not all with a worldwide Body. This instability would serve the church's hope, the reconciliation of all things in Christ, as it concurrently but dissimilarly participates in dissolving provisional, interim remnants of gravitations toward self, culture, and even its own voice in what it is becoming. May the congregation's voice thus ever attune to the strange sounds of its noise so that justice might roll down like waters and righteousness like an ever-flowing stream.

---

60. Zerbe, "Relevance of Paul's Eschatological Ecclesiology," and "On the Exigency of a Messianic Ecclesia."
61. Zerbe, "On the Exigency of a Messianic Ecclesia," 281.

Bibliography

Books and Articles

Agawu, Kofi. "Contesting Difference." In *Representing African Music: Postcolonial Notes, Queries, Positions*, 151–72. New York: Routledge, 2003.

Beck, Guy L., editor. *Sacred Sound: Experiencing Music in World Religions*. Waterloo, ON: Wilfrid Laurier University Press, 2006.

Begbie, Jeremy. *Resounding Truth*. Grand Rapids: Baker Academic, 2007.

———. *Theology, Music, and Time*. Cambridge: Cambridge University Press, 2000

Bohlman, Philip V. *World Music: A Very Short Introduction*. Oxford: Oxford University Press, 2002.

Buis, William. "Clashing Aesthetics: Understanding African-Derived Sensibilities in Contemporary Christian Music in America." Paper presented at the annual meeting of the Forum on Music and Christian Scholarship, Baylor University, 2008.

Clarke, David. "Elvis and Darmstadt, or: Twentieth-Century Music and the Politics of Cultural Pluralism." *Journal of Twentieth-Century Music* 4 (2007) 1–33.

Cook, Nicholas. *Music: A Very Short Introduction*. Oxford: Oxford University Press, 1998.

Danielson, Virginia. "Classical Music in Iraq." Plenary address presented at the annual meeting of the Canadian University Music Society, Dalhousie University, Halifax, NS, 2003.

Dawn, Marva. *How Shall We Worship? Biblical Guidelines for the Worship Wars*. Wheaton, IL: Tyndale House, 2003.

DeNora, Tia. *After Adorno: Rethinking Music Sociology*. Cambridge: Cambridge University Press, 2003.

Farhadian, Charles E., editor. *Christian Worship Worldwide: Expanding Horizons, Deepening Practices*. Grand Rapids: Eerdmans, 2007.

Fink, Robert. "Going Flat: Post-Hierarchical Music Theory and the Musical Surface." In *Rethinking Music*, edited by Nicholas Cook and Mark Everist, 102–37. Oxford: Oxford University Press, 1999.

Frith, Simon. "The Discourse of World Music." In *Western Music and Its Others*, edited by Georgina Born and David Hesmondhalgh, 305–22. Berkeley: University of California Press, 2000.

Huebner, Harry. *Echoes of the Word: Theological Ethics as Rhetorical Practice*. Kitchener, ON: Pandora, 2005.

Hobbs, Gerald. "Christianity and Music." In *Sacred Sound: Experiencing Music in World Religions*, edited by Guy L. Beck, 61–88. Waterloo, ON: Wilfrid Laurier University Press, 2006.

Hughes, Graham. *Worship as Meaning: A Liturgical Theology for Late Modernity*. Cambridge: Cambridge University Press, 2003

Kivy, Peter. *The Fine Art of Repetition*. Cambridge: Cambridge University Press. 1993.

Krims, Adam, editor. *Music/Ideology: Resisting the Aesthetic: Essays*. Amsterdam: G + B Arts International, 1998.

Lathrop, Gordon. *Holy Things: A Liturgical Theology*. Minneapolis: Fortress, 1993.

Loesser, Arthur. *Men, Women and Pianos: A Social History*. New York: Simon and Schuster, 1954.

Longhurst, Christine. "Corporate Prayer." Workshops at River East Mennonite Brethren Church, Winnipeg, May, 2007.

———. "Encountering God in Worship." *The Messenger* 47 (2009) 4–6.

Milbank, John. *Theology and Social Theory: Beyond Secular Reason*. **2nd ed.** Oxford: Blackwell, 2006.

Milbank, John, Catherine Pickstock, and Graham Ward, editors. *Radical Orthodoxy*. London: Routledge, 1999.

Mitchell, Nathan. *Meeting Mystery: Liturgy, Worship, Sacraments*. Maryknoll, NY: Orbis, 2006.

Mowitt, John. *Percussion: Drumming, Beating, Striking*. Durham, NC: Duke University Press, 2002.

Reich, Steve. *Writings on Music: 1965–2000*. Oxford: Oxford University Press, 2002.

Roeder, John. "Interacting Pulse Streams in Schoenberg's Atonal Polyphony." *Music Theory Spectrum* 16 (1994) 231–49.

Sample, Tex. *Powerful Persuasion: Multimedia Witness in Christian Worship*. Nashville: Abingdon, 2005.

Schoenberg, Arnold. *Style and Idea: Selected Writings*. Edited by Leonard Stein. Berkeley: University of California Press, 1984.

Small, Christopher. *Musicking: The Meanings of Performing and Listening.* Hanover, NH: University Press of New England, 1998.

Spitzer, Leo. *Classical and Christian Ideas of World Harmony.* Baltimore: Johns Hopkins Press, 1963.

Walls, Andrew. "The Ephesians Moment in Worldwide Worship." In *Christian Worship Worldwide: Expanding Horizons, Deepening Practices,* edited by Charles E. Farhadian, 27–38. Grand Rapids: Eerdmans, 2007.

Webber, Robert. *Planning Blended Worship: The Creative Mixture of Old and New.* Nashville: Abingdon, 1998.

Zerbe, Gordon. "On the Exigency of a Messianic Ecclesia: An Engagement with Philosophical Readers of Paul." In *Paul, Philosophy, and the Theopolitical Vision: Critical Engagements with Agamben, Badiou, Žižek, and Others,* edited by Doug Harink, 254–81. Eugene, OR: Cascade, 2010.

———. "The Relevance of Paul's Eschatological Ecclesiology for Approaching Ecumenicity in a Believers Church Perspective." In *New Perspectives in Believers Church Ecclesiology,* edited by A. Dueck, H. Harder, K. Koop, 30–47. Winnipeg: CMU Press, 2010.

Žižek, Slavoj, editor. *Mapping Ideology.* New York: Verso, 1994.

———. *The Puppet and the Dwarf: The Perverse Core of Christianity.* Cambridge, MA: MIT Press, 2003.

———. *The Sublime Object of Ideology.* New York: Verso, 1989.

Musical Scores, Recordings, and Film

Bell, John L., editor. *One Is the Body: Songs of Unity and Diversity.* Chicago: GIA, 2002.

Bell, Steve. "Even So Lord Jesus Come." In *The Music of Steve Bell: A Songbook, 1989–1995,* arr. Linda Schwartz and Lisa Ilchyshyn, 83–86. Winnipeg: Signpost, 1998.

Bryars, Gavin. *Jesus' Blood Never Failed Me Yet.* Produced by Michael Riesman, 1971. CD, New York: Point Music, 1993.

Hughes, Tim. "Here I Am to Worship." Kingsway's Thankyou Music, EMI Christian Music Publishing, 2000.

Hymnal: A Worship Book. "Praise God from Whom All Blessings Flow" (DEDICATION ANTHEM), no. 118; "Praise God from Whom All Blessings Flow" (OLD HUNDREDTH), no. 119; "We Are People of God's Peace" (AVE VIRGO VIRGINUM), no. 407; "Mothering God, You Gave Me Birth" (MOTHERING GOD), no. 482. Scottdale, PA: Mennonite Publishing House, 1992.

Koyaanisqatsi. Directed by Godfrey Reggio, music by Philip Glass, 1975–82. DVD, Santa Fe: Institute for Regional Education, 2002.

Worship Together. "Doxology" (OLD HUNDREDTH), no. 92; "Praise God from Whom All Blessings Flow" (DEDICATION ANTHEM), no. 93; "We Are People of God's Peace" (AVE VIRGO VIRGINUM), no. 677. Winnipeg: The Christian Press, 1995.

He Who Brings Light to Dark Places
Christ and the Redemption of Memory

Jane Barter Moulaison

BIBLICAL FAITH UNDERMINES ORDINARY ASSUMPTIONS ABOUT TIME—ABOUT THE sequential and cumulative character of past, present, and future. For Christians, as for Jews, the past must not be overcome; it must in some sense be *lived*. Within the last century, we have learned of the abiding significance of the past from Jewish thinkers who seek to live faithfully the memory of those killed in the Shoah. Writers such as Emil Fackenheim[1] and Elie Wiesel[2] have sought to keep faith with those killed by not permitting the world to forget. Likewise, Christian theologians have attempted to heed the call to remember, keeping ever mindful of the atrocities that humans have committed within the past century and the church's complicity within them.[3] Any theology that forsakes the task of remembering the failure of humanity, and particularly of the churches, in the

---

1. In his famous "614th commandment," Emil Fackenheim urges Jews not to hand Hitler a posthumous victory. "We are, first, commanded to survive as Jews, lest the Jewish people perish. We are commanded, secondly, to remember in our very guts and bones the martyrs of the Holocaust, lest their memory perish. We are forbidden, thirdly, to deny or despair of God, however much we may have to contend with him or with belief in him, lest Judaism perish. We are forbidden, finally, to despair of the world as the place which is to become the kingdom of God, lest we help make it a meaningless place in which God is dead or irrelevant and everything is permitted. To abandon any of these imperatives, in response to Hitler's victory at Auschwitz, would be to hand him yet other, posthumous victories." Fackenheim, *To Mend the World*, 213.

2. See also Elie Wiesel's Nobel Lecture: "Remembering is a noble and necessary act. The call of memory, the call *to* memory, reaches us from the very dawn of history. No commandment figures so frequently, so insistently, in the Bible. It is incumbent upon us to remember the good we have received, and the evil we have suffered. New Year's Day, *Rosh Hashana*, is also called *Yom Hazikaron*, the day of memory. On that day, the day of universal judgment, man appeals to God to remember: our salvation depends on it. If God wishes to remember our suffering, all will be well; if He refuses, all will be lost. Thus, the rejection of memory becomes a divine curse, one that would doom us to repeat past disasters, past wars." Wiesel, "Hope, Despair and Memory."

3. See, for example, "We Remember: A Reflection on the Shoah," a document of the Vatican's Commission for Religious Relations with the Jews. "Before this horrible genocide, which the leaders of nations and Jewish communities themselves found hard to believe at the very moment when it was being mercilessly put into effect, no one can remain indifferent, least of all the Church, by reason of her very close bonds of spiritual kinship with the Jewish people and her remembrance of the injustices of the past. The Church's relationship to the Jewish people is unlike the one she shares with any other religion. However, it is not only a question of recalling the past. The common future of Jews and Christians demands that we remember, for 'there is no future without memory'. History itself is *memoria futuri*."

wake of massive human suffering is to be regarded as woefully irresponsible. A recent book by Miroslav Volf, however, has challenged several of these commonplaces. In *The End of Memory: Remembering Rightly in a Violent World*, Volf argues forcefully that it is not to remembering, but to remembering rightly that we are enjoined. According to Volf, remembering can often perpetuate rather than put an end to violence. Hence, in the most controversial argument of this book, Volf asserts that at times remembering rightly includes *forgetting* violence and suffering.

In this essay, I wish to consider what it means to "remember rightly in a violent world," a theme that is also clearly of central importance to the theologian of peace being honored in this Festschrift.[4] In so doing, I will engage Volf as my main conversation partner, but my own argument will be informed by drawing on another theologian of memory, Augustine of Hippo. Saint Augustine offers considerable theological challenge to Volf's proposals. For Augustine would argue that right remembering can only be achieved through the rectification of memory by way of justice. It is justice that does not permit past atrocities to be forgotten, but such a justice is of a particular kind. It is a justice that has everything to do with the redemption of memory and of history that is achieved in Jesus Christ.

Types of Remembering

Whereas prophets of memory such as Elie Wiesel argue that "salvation, like redemption, can be found only in memory,"[5] Volf issues a cautionary note, asserting that memory in itself is not a form of salvation, since all political and social goals seek to justify themselves in a particular kind of remembering. Therefore the injunction to remember is vapid at best and lethal at worst, as our memories can be self-serving, ideological, or even vengeful. As Volf puts it: "As victims seek to protect themselves they are not immune to becoming perpetrators . . . The memory of their own persecution makes them see dangers lurking even where there are none; it leads them to exaggerate dangers that do exist and overreact with excessive violence or inappropriate preventative measures so as to ensure their own safety. Victims will often *become* perpetrators precisely *on account of* their own memories. It is because they remember past violence that they feel justified in committing present violence."[6] Memory of past wrongs can inure victims to their own complicity and responsibility; further, it can goad them to violence in order to ensure that they will not be victims again. Christians enjoined to forgiveness are therefore to be cautious with memory; memory must give way to a higher end, which is not righteous anger or exclusion, but enemy-love, or embrace.

This moral injunction is no mere platitude for Volf—he knows full well the difficulty of practicing costly forgiveness. Woven throughout *The End of Memory* are his own efforts

---

4. Harry Huebner has written some in-depth essays on the nature of memory in his political and personal essays. Huebner's insights, as I read them, are in keeping with (if not drawing on directly) Augustine's theology of memory. See "Politics of Memory and Hope" and "On Being Stuck with Our Parents: Learning to Die in Christ," in Huebner, *Echoes of the Word*, 153–66; 167–75.

5. Wiesel, *From the Kingdom of Memory*, 201, quoted in Volf, *End of Memory*, 19.

6. Volf, *End of Memory*, 33.

to remember his past rightly, a past that involves real enemies—in particular Captain G., a military officer who subjected Volf to intense and constant scrutiny and interrogation during his mandatory year of military service within the then-communist army of Yugoslavia. Writes Volf: "What would it mean for me to remember Captain G. and his wrongdoing in the way I prayed to God to remember me and my wrongdoing? How should the one who *loves* remember the wrongdoer and the wrongdoing?"[7] Thus, the end of memory is to so remember the wrongdoer that love for him is not impeded or restrained. Justice must always be predicated by its higher end, which is enemy-love.

How Long Should We Remember?

According to Volf, the command to love necessitates a limitation of memory of past wrongs in order to open a way for reconciliation. In the concluding section of the book, Volf argues that we should, under certain conditions, aim to *let go* of our memories of wrong suffered because such letting go is the appropriate response to the very giftedness of the world God has created. Letting go is a thankful acknowledgment of God's "creation of the world of love."[8]

Love, the power at creation's center, seeks out the healing of perpetrator and victim alike, both of whom are trapped inside the cyclical and violent demands of setting accounts right. Thus remembering not only impedes the victim's ability to love the enemy but also threatens to diminish her identity, offering her only a limited view of herself and her biography. Contrary to popular psychology, healing from past trauma ideally involves forgetting, or non-remembrance of past wrongs. This non-remembrance is not erasure but a lack of presence of memory, as memories "fail to surface"[9] persistently in the consciousness of the wounded. As Volf writes: "Only non-remembering can end the lament over suffering which no thought can think away and no action can undo."[10]

This is not to say that Volf believes that forgetting can be achieved solely by an act of will. Forgetting in itself is not an ideal to be pursued as an independent project or therapy on the part of the victim; much less ought it to be a prescription offered to those who have suffered.[11] Instead, what Volf prefers to call the "not coming to mind" of past wrongs is an eschatological promise, the consequence of our restored relations in Jesus Christ, and can only be fully realized in the world to come. In the world to come, the victim and the perpetrator (imprecise as those words often are) will be reconciled to one another before non-remembrance is enacted. In the present world, such reconciliation can only be anticipated, for justice demands exposure of past sins. Hence forgetting can only be gestured toward, but in that gesturing there exists the real hope for memory's "own superfluity."[12] Thus the hope of the world to come, a hope in which the not coming to mind is the final moment

---

7. Ibid., 9.
8. Ibid., 147.
9. Ibid., 145.
10. Volf, *Exclusion and Embrace*, 135.
11. Volf, *End of Memory*, 146.
12. Ibid., 150.

in the reconciliation of enemies, can only be undertaken "partially and provisionally."[13] Yet positively, this deferred hope also offers a great deal to those currently suffering from the wound of memory. For one, belief in erasure of past wrongs in the world to come prohibits any efforts to explain away suffering of the past or to attempt to uncover its meaning. For Volf, past suffering, especially memory of violence, will not be revealed as God's will but will be set right in the world to come in God's judgment of perpetrators, honoring and healing of victims, and release of memories of suffering. Memories of wrong will "wither away like plants without water," because our minds will be rapt in the goodness of God.[14]

Because we await this final reconciliation, Christians need not be overly concerned with creating meaning from personal suffering. Memory of past wrongs will not be elucidated in the world to come, much less in this world, by a neat theodicy; rather, the meaning of our lives will be rendered secure through the interpolation of another story, another memory that offers meaning—the memory of Christ's reconciling act of love. Thus to remember rightly is to remember our life stories as "displaced," as "living outside the self" and God.[15] To remember rightly is to remember the triumph over evil that is offered in Christ's redemption of humankind. Drawing on Martin Luther's *The Freedom of a Christian*, Volf argues that redemption involves a "wonderful exchange" between the believer and Christ, the bride and the bridegroom. In this exchange, the groom gratuitously takes on all the sin and infirmity of the bride through his "wedding ring of faith."[16] Through this union, the sins of the bride, even the scourge of death and hell, are "swallowed up"[17] by Christ, and she comes to take on a new identity of "eternal righteousness, life and salvation."[18] To Volf, such a promise is profoundly hopeful for those who have been trapped in their memories.

Meaning, therefore, is not to be found in the suffering of humans but in the specific suffering of Jesus Christ, who takes on our sins once and for all. Volf is thus careful to distinguish between the efficacy of Christ's sacrificial death and the sacrifice of victims. Only Christ's death has the power to free us from sin, and as such, Jesus's sacrifice, not that of others, is the means through which a new relationship between God and humans and among humans is attained. In this sacrifice, Christ sets us free from the power of sin and death, and by extension, from the tyranny of past suffering. We are not justified by our memories, but by grace alone. It is grace that wipes away the suffering of the past and points us in the direction of a new future. Thus Volf asserts that "being in God frees our lives from the tyranny the unalterable past exercises with the iron fist of time's irreversibility."[19]

This orientation toward the future is true also of Christ's own suffering. The cross is thus viewed as "a stage on the road to resurrection and exaltation"—and as such, it is "a

13. Ibid., 151.
14. Ibid., 214.
15. Ibid., 198.
16. Ibid., 187.
17. Ibid., 188.
18. Ibid.
19. Ibid., 201.

stage that can be left in the past even if its effects last for eternity."[20] Because enmity has been overcome at the cross, the cross can fade into oblivion.[21] As Volf challenges, "If Christ was not the Crucified One before creation, why would he have to be the 'Crucified One' after redemption has been completely and unassailably secured in the world to come?"[22] The cross effects its own withdrawal from the world and becomes redundant in its very efficacy.

Throughout his account, Volf unfortunately presents a soteriology that is cast temporally in distinct and exclusive occasions. He first addresses suffering and enmity, then memory, then sin's defeat at the cross, then judgment, next reconciliation, and finally forgetting. Moreover, these stages of salvation are also rather neatly divided between the historical (sin, memory, the cross) and the eschatological (judgment, healing, reconciliation, and forgetting). Finally, there is a deep fissure between justice (judgment) and love (healing, reconciliation, forgetting), with love always surpassing justice as the future goal of history and the character of the world to come. What is lost in such a construal of time is the manner in which the kingdom of God is inflected throughout the grammar of historical time and memory—past, present, and future—and that God's time disrupts all notions of linear progress. What is also lost is the manner in which, in both this world and the world to come, love and justice are inexorably linked; they are bound together on earth as in heaven. As Augustine shows, God's abiding presence is to be known not in a flight from memory or time but in memory's recapitulation in Christ, through memory's just ordering. A return to Augustine on memory, I believe, offers a way forward for the very important problems that Volf presents.

Memory in Augustine

In his *Confessions*, Augustine writes a narrative that also places memory at the center of his theological reflection. It is *theological* reflection because, as Augustine shows, one's life, even one's life as it is caught up in sin, reflects the story of God's love and mercy. Even through the messy and recalcitrant matter that is our lives, God is at work. Thus *confession* takes on a double meaning: it is a confession of Augustine's life of waywardness and homecoming, while also the confession of the Christian in the recounting of the story of salvation in Jesus Christ.

To come into the mind's presence is to possess an awareness of the self not in the past, but in the present. Thus Augustine celebrates the power of memory,[23] even at its

---

20. Ibid., 191.
21. Ibid., 190.
22. Ibid.
23. See Augustine, *Confessions*, 10.17 (Sheed, 186): "Great is the power of memory, a thing, O my God, to be in awe of, a profound and immeasurable multiplicity; and this thing is my mind, this thing am I. What then am I, O my God? What nature am I? A life powerfully various and manifold and immeasurable. In the innumerable kinds of things, present either by their images, as are all bodies, or in themselves as our mental capacities, or by certain notions or awarenesses, like the affections of the mind—for even when the mind is not experiencing them, although whatever is in the memory is in the mind too—in and through all these does my mind range, and I move swiftly from one to another and I penetrate them deeply as I can, but find no end. So great is the force of memory, so great the force of life even when man lives under the sentence of death here."

natural, material level, such as the sensible images carried in the mind, a faculty that even the beasts share with humans. Memory also has the capacity to grasp and retain objects of knowledge.[24] Further, human memory is able to contemplate the abstract, such as emotions that were once suffered but that are now recollected in tranquility. Finally, memory retains vestiges of joy, as it endlessly seeks out the soul's happiness. It is here that the power of human memory or the human mind falls short, for while the mind seeks out joy, it cannot attain it, and without the grace of God the soul is likely to fall into error as it seeks out those things that are finite as the objects of its love.

In spite of its fallen nature, memory is a gift from God through and through. It is a source of wisdom while also offering the soul an awareness of its own finitude. Like the knowledge derived from the philosophers, memory can only lead Augustine to an awareness of the finitude of the mind, but this awareness also is the occasion for the recognition that there exists beyond the mind that which is infinite. Augustine realizes this in contemplating forgetting. The phenomenon of forgetting actually displays the power of memory, for forgetting is not the absence of memory but its faultiness, for we are not by nature compelled to forget but to remember, as evidenced by the nagging persistence with which the mind seeks out that which it has forgotten. Such seeking for something that is lost is a purposive activity of memory, and it is an activity that is especially significant in humans as they seek joy. Memory of joy is retained in the mind, even among those who have not experienced joy. And yet joy is not fully known in the mind, nor in the human grasping to attain those images; such joy is only known as it is received. Such joy is only received in the eternal and excessive gift that is grace. However great the power of human memory, it alone is insufficient to contemplate the eternal things for which it yearns, for God transcends not only what is to be known but also the mind itself.

Thus Augustine concludes that while God dwells in the memory, God also exceeds the memory. God is "Lord God of the mind"[25] and seeks out the pilgrim even within memory, and thus works on the mind/memory to transform her desires into God's own. Here we have the first and most fundamental difference between Volf and Augustine. For Augustine, memory, although fallen and often given over to partial ends, is not to be subordinated or overcome; for it is the home of God's very self-communication. This is so because the minds of humans have been healed in the incarnation, as Jesus the Physician[26] reconciles us to God even in our wounded knowledge. Thus our memory is a place of tremendous possibility, for it is in the memory that God draws near and takes up our memory into his own telling. Like the thief crucified next to Jesus, we are remembered as we remember God (Luke 23:42). We remember rightly, according to Augustine, through God's self-communication in the Son who redeems and restores memory, as he redeems and restores time. God's redemption of the world does not impose a kind of docetic eternity, but, as the *Confessions* amply displays, works through the reconciliation of fallen time, and hence of fallen memory.

24. Ibid., 10.12 (Sheed, 182).
25. Ibid., 10.25 (Sheed, 192).
26. Ibid., 10.28 (Sheed, 193).

The Tutelage of Memory

Thus the linear relationship of God's salvation—of the distinct moments of past, present, and future—is disrupted profoundly in memory. Remembering is not simply the recollection of past events in one's own biography; it is properly the present awareness of the self's home, which is found in a God who is, as Augustine describes, "not far from every one of us."[27] Remembering is also inexorably linked to and contingent upon a future destination, as our narrative gains its meaning and purpose in the eternal purposes of God. As Rowan Williams writes, "What we do not and cannot know about our past, present, and future is given over to God, who will draw out of us cries and aspirations that more and more clearly give voice to what is hidden in us, knowing that all this elusive human agenda unrecognized within us is embraced in the incarnation and may be employed by Christ in his work."[28]

There is a heuristic structure to memory. Augustine is no less concerned than Volf with remembering rightly, but for Augustine, right remembering will follow a very different pattern of redemption. The human narrative is not to be overcome or displaced, for it is itself an outworking of the logic of grace, although that grace remains largely hidden. Thus all of the human being, all of our "elusive human agenda," is given over to God for God's eternal purposes.

Here we see a related difference between Volf's account of memory and Augustine's: for Augustine, grace involves not merely the displacement of the self but a *coming to the self*, which is now seen as the theater of divine purposive activity. And yet grace awakens not only the knowledge that the self has been addressed and arrested by God, but that grace has, for Augustine, always been at work upon his personal narrative even when he was unaware. Thus the story of the soul's redemption as set forth in the *Confessions* is, in fact, a parable of the redemption of the entire created order. It is a recollection of the fragmented and wayward creature and an invitation to participate in God's redemptive purposes. This divine remembering does not abjure suffering and sin but works through these in its giving, forgiving, and fore-giving. As Augustine writes most beautifully,

> Late have I loved you, beauty so old and so new: late have I loved you. And see, you were within and I was in the external world and sought you there, and in my unlovely state I plunged into those lovely things which you made. You were with me, and I was not with you. The lovely things kept me far from you, though if they did not have their existence in you, they had no existence at all. You called and cried and shattered my deafness. You were radiant and resplendent, you put to flight my blindness. You were fragrant, and I drew in my breath and now pant after you. I tasted you, and I feel but hunger and thirst for you. You touched me, and I am set on fire to attain the peace which is yours.[29]

What role, then, does memory of sin and suffering have in the course of redemption? Is it the case that Augustine concurs, as Volf claims, that the forgetting of past sin is

---

27. Ibid., 10.25, p. 192.
28. Williams, "*Augustine* and the *Psalms*," 19.
29. Augustine, *Confessions* (Chadwick, 201).

intrinsic to remembering rightly?[30] Augustine would argue that the memory of oneself as a sinner is essential to redemption, not only of the individual soul but also of the properly ordered city, as the political virtue most to be desired in the earthly city is humility.[31] Humility is the highest political virtue because it enables people to live together truthfully and therefore justly. The political agent who is informed by the Christian virtue of humility is one who is able to recognize Christ's prevenient and persistent work in the healing of the soul and city, bringing order out of nothingness, bringing fruit out of barrenness.[32] Such creative activity of God is analogously related to the illumination of the heart as it remembers its darkness:

> What fruit therefore had I (in my vileness) in those things of which I am now ashamed? Especially in that piece of thieving, in which I loved nothing except the thievery—though that in itself was no thing and I only the more wretched for it. Now—as I think back on the state of my mind then—I am altogether certain that I would not have done it alone. Perhaps then what I really loved was companionship of those with whom I did it. If so, can I still say that I loved nothing over and above the thievery? Surely I can; that companionship was nothing over and above, because it was nothing. What is the truth of it? *Who shall show me, unless He that illumines my heart and brings light into its dark places?*[33] (italics mine)

In this sense the remembering of the past sins of Augustine and his companions is requisite to understanding his need for the grace of illumination. More than merely instrumental to illumination, the confession of sin for Augustine is simultaneous with the redemption of memory.

The soul's redemption takes place in the mustard seed of confession, repentance, and forgiveness through the mediating activity of Christ persistently upon the pilgrim. Such a mediating activity is not merely a stepping in of Christ on behalf of sinners so much as it is a restoration of their wills through the power of the crucifixion and resurrection as sinners themselves participate in the economy of salvation—they die with Christ and rise again with him to a restoration of relations. Divine forgiveness involves not merely an overcoming of past sin through the power of the cross but a setting right of the past. It is a

---

30. See Volf's treatment of Augustine as a defender of forgetting in Volf, *End of Memory*, 22–24, and 133.

31. See my essay "Lord of Two Cities."

32. Of all the political philosophers, Hannah Arendt probably saw this implication of Augustine's thought most clearly. Arendt's notion of "new beginnings" or "natality" draws heavily upon Augustine. And like Augustine, Arendt sees political natality not as the eradication of the past, and certainly not as its perpetuation, but as a revolutionary birthing of possibility beyond tragedy and revenge. "But there also remains the truth that every end in history necessarily contains a new beginning; this beginning is the promise, the only 'message' that the end can ever produce. Beginning, before it becomes a historical event, is the supreme capacity of man; politically it is identical with man's freedom. *Initium ut esset, homo creatus est*, 'that a beginning be made, man was created,' said Augustine. This beginning is guaranteed by each new birth; it is indeed every man." Arendt, *The Origins of Totalitarianism*, 479. While surely this analysis is overdrawn, perhaps on account of Heidegger's abiding influence upon Arendt, it would be safe to say that Arendt is right in recognizing a profoundly creative possibility that inheres in Augustine's theology. The creation of the world from nothingness is echoed in human minds in the shedding of light upon the darkness of sin, through the power of memory. This is not a human capacity so much as it is a gift accommodated to our minds.

33. Augustine, *Confessions*, 2.8 (Sheed, 30).

setting right of the past because in God's time, the past, even the past marred by sin, is not exhausted of possibility. This does not mean that the past can be revised through a historical sleight of hand, but it does mean that it can be corrected through its public renunciation, through its confession, and through its referral to a new trajectory of hope. There still exists, within God's purposes and time, the possibility of the redemption of memory, not through its annulment but through its *metanoia*. Confession provides the occasion for the soul to acknowledge its own need of God, precisely through the acknowledgment of past sins. Without such acknowledgment, the soul remains cut off from grace's future working upon it. While Volf does not wish to deny the importance of repentance, its capacity to restore past relations is understated. That is to say, the soul's turning away from sin involves a changed relationship to the past, in which the past sin becomes in a sense open to new possibility. Thus the past can itself be visited upon by transfiguring grace, and as such, its memory ought never be squandered. John Milbank puts it well when he says, "[I]t is not that forgiveness nihilistically pretends to obliterate past evidence, but rather that this past existence is itself preserved, developed and altered through re-narration. In this re-narration one comes to understand why oneself or others made errors, in terms of the delusions that arise through mistaking lesser goods for the greater."[34]

So while memory is not squandered, it also does not remain stable in its redemption. Augustine therefore makes a stark distinction between memory and the affections that accompany it. He would disagree strongly with Volf's assertion that memory is authentic insofar as it is preserves its original "sensibilities."[35] As Volf argues, "Memories of suffering unaccompanied by corresponding feelings of pain inevitably involve forgetting."[36] For Augustine, the transfiguration of memory through charity involves not forgetting the sensibilities but disciplining them through properly ordered desire. Contemplation of memory through love of Christ permits a transfiguration of memory from passion to continence. Christ's tutelage of memory, a tutelage that involves prayer and the mediation of the church, evokes charity, which dissolves not memory but transforms passions that accompany trauma, prominently anger, the desire for revenge, and the sense of futility or hopelessness.

What then of memory of evil? As Volf rightly argues, evil is deprived of permanency—it will fade into oblivion. While evil has no final permanency, memory of loss, of the homelessness of the soul, remains characteristic of knowledge of God itself.[37] Understanding of oneself as being visited upon and endowed with grace involves an awareness of the corrupting power of sin. Thus the human sojourner finds herself, by grace, capable of reading her own narrative as the story of God's purposive activity. Such a re-narration of her story does not involve a blotting out of memory of personal transgression, or of transgressions against her, but rather an acute awareness of them. Further, this is not simply an awareness of Christ's redemption overcoming all the instances of sin and waywardness in one divine fiat; instead, for Augustine, such memory of one's own propensity to sin involves a

---

34. Milbank, *Being Reconciled*, 53.
35. Volf, *End of Memory*, 23.
36. Ibid.
37. See Augustine, *City of God*, 22.30 (Dodds, 510–11).

steady and patient vigilance, both within the psyche and within the city. This is not to say that Augustine envisages no restoration of the soul, but that restoration takes place over time, in the patient and durable practice of confession and supplicant prayer—practices of humility that give rise to the soul's and the city's proper ordering. This proper ordering, this tutelage of memory, is what Augustine calls justice. Justice, or the proper ordering of the soul (and city), has everything to do with the kind of redemption we have received in Christ.

Why Should the Cross Be Remembered?

As we have seen, for Volf, the cross can fade away even though its effects are eternal; for Augustine, on the other hand, the cross is to be remembered not as a surd, not as an interruption of the story of salvation, but as the extension of the divine gift even at the farthest reaches of human agony and desolation. This gift is not only given on the cross, it is a re-narration of an original gift—given in the foundations of the world, in the outpouring of the Father's love for the Son and the Son's love for the Father. And yet this gift is in no way withheld or denied upon the cross. The cross provides a crack through which the light shines amidst the darkness and death. It offers, in the midst of violence, neither retaliation nor resignation but perfect obedience, which is perfect forgiveness, perfect peace. Through the outpouring of love, even in the midst of violence, Christ reveals to be naught the supposed power of those who sentence him to death, as he reveals the hidden power of God at work. As Augustine writes,

> For He was not stripped of the flesh by obligation of any authority, but He stripped Himself. For doubtless He who was able not to die, if He would not, did die because He would; and so he made a show of the principalities and powers, openly triumphing over them and in Himself. For whereas by His death the one and most real sacrifice was offered up for us, whatever fault there was, whence principalities and powers held fast as of right to pay its penalty, He cleansed, abolished, extinguished; and by His own resurrection He also called us whom he predestinated to a new life, and whom He called, them He justified, and whom He justified, them He glorified. And so that devil, in that very death of the flesh, lost man.[38]

While Christ breaks the hold of the powers and principalities, at the same moment he calls us to a new life; he restores us. Whereas in Volf we see Christ's triumph over past sins that held us in bondage, in Augustine we see not only the loosening of bonds but also the glorification of those set free by the power of the divine and eternal gift from one "not able to die" who nevertheless "did die because he would."

This view of salvation has profound implications for human life together. The gift of divine life that is not withheld upon the cross is also the gift of forgiveness of sins—forgiveness in which the church is called to participate. It is a gift that is given in excess. It is also a gift that does not seek to domesticate evil either by explaining it away or by letting go of its memory, but it is a gift that looks at the evil of those who have sentenced Christ to die and still proclaims, "Father, forgive them, for they know not what they do" (Luke

---

38. Augustine, *On the Holy Trinity*, 4.13 (Hadden, 78).

23:34). It is a gift that remembers an entire history of human recalcitrance and malice and yet pronounces blessing. It is because of this giver of divine forgiveness—who is not the substitute for but the prototype of humanity—that human forgiveness is made possible.

Forgiveness among humans is not so much willed as it is received. It is a gift that is made possible through memory of the working of God's grace upon the one who is forgiving. The bestowal of forgiveness by the forgiver is thus an active memory, one that remembers the forgiver's own past sins, attends truthfully to perpetrator's wrongs, and beseeches God's active restoration of the past. It is for this reason that Augustine refers to Christ as Mediator: not simply because Christ overcomes a gulf between God and humans, but because he conjoins the human and divine and therefore presents the appropriate posture of human relations, which invites us to neighbor love in excess. Because Christ has interceded, we are bound to surpass the measure of distributive justice. Thus while the past cannot be simply revised, it can be re-narrated through the participation of memory in the divine gift. Such a gift does not eradicate a past of suffering, but it mediates it, and thus mitigates its hold and thwarts its replication.

Captain G.'s petty taunts and intimidations are not permanently replicated because they themselves constitute nothing—they only signal repetitive, banal, and noncreative acts, and thus cannot but dissolve into oblivion. And yet the memory of this suffering can become the occasion (although not the cause) of God's creative purposes. The work that is *The End of Memory* is itself a testimony to this possibility. The objectification of violent acts in memory, when recollected through the mediating power of Christ, becomes an instance of lament over a world that longs for God's justice and mercy; it can also, by grace, become transfigured from lament to charity. For Augustine, the work of justice does not involve remembering past sins primarily for the distribution of reward and punishment but instead involves the visitation of Christ's grace even at the farthest reaches of torment. In the justice that God commands of the church, nothing in this life can fall outside that cannot be brought back to God to be healed. There is no de facto caducity within the world that God created and redeemed.

A Different Justice

Christ appears to his disciples not as a healed and perfect body, but as a body that still bears the marks of his crucifixion, although these are no longer bleeding wounds. The resurrected Christ invites Thomas to probe those wounds, and Thomas finds in this physical memory of torture not something that is repugnant but something worthy of adoration: "Thomas says to him: 'My Lord and My God'" (John 20:28). Just so, our memories of pain and suffering (even, we might say, the very suffering we have caused, for surely Jesus's wounds are also this) also carry with them the potential to become signs through which God's glory is revealed. Here is a profoundly different kind of ordering from that of contemporary politics. Here is a profoundly different justice.[39] Justice is not to be won

---

39. Again, Harry Huebner is efficient and direct here: "The way of justice for the Christian community is rooted in the character of the justice of God. God gives the disciples life through forgiveness and peace and, as gifted people, we can do no other to those who have been caught up in the grips of injustice." Huebner, "Justice and the Biblical Imagination," 145.

through the distribution of time-specific punishment and amnesty, but in the acknowledgment and the healing of the Body's wounds. Nothing can be squandered in this justice. It must all be referred to God, who is "all in all" (1 Cor 15:28).

Perhaps the prophets of memory—Wiesel, Fackenheim, and others for whom time has not erased the memories of their people's suffering—are not far from Augustine's justice. It is a justice that refuses to yield the memories of victims to any kind of future in which they are not present, in which they are not, in some sense, restored. While it is true that the keeping of memory can become a weapon in the world of fallen time, it is no less true that forgetting can far too easily become a shield that obscures the future to which we are called, and to which their memories and their witness beckons. In the Talmud, it is written, "Attend to three things, and you will not come into the hands of transgression. Know what is above you: an eye sees, an ear hears, and all of your deeds are written in a book."[40] Augustine has shown us how this eye and ear are not only above but also within, and that the book is not only a book of judgment but also a book of life.

---

40. Avot 2:1, quoted in Fonrobert and Jaffee, *The Cambridge Companion to the Talmud and Rabbinic Literature*, 325.

Bibliography

Arendt, Hannah. *The Origins of Totalitariansm*. Orlando: Houghton, Mifflin, Harcourt, 1976.

Augustine, Saint. *City of God*. Translated by Marcus Dods. Nicene and Post-Nicene Fathers, ed. Philip Schaff, series 1, vol. 2. Peabody, MA: Hendrickson, 2004.

———. *Confessions*. Translated by Henry Chadwick. Oxford: Oxford University Press, 2008.

———. *Confessions*. Translated by F. J. Sheed. New York: Sheed and Ward, 1942.

———. *On the Holy Trinity*. Translated by Arthur West Haddan. Nicene and Post-Nicene Fathers, ed. Philip Schaff, series 1, vol. 3. Peabody, MA: Hendrickson, 2004.

Barter Moulaison, Jane. "Lord of Two Cities: Political or Christological Realism in Augustine's City of God?" In *From Logos to Christos: Essays in Honour of Joanne McWilliam*, edited by Ellen Leonard and Kate Merriman. Waterloo, ON: Wilfrid Laurier University Press, 2010.

Fackenheim, Emil. *To Mend the World: Foundations of Post-Holocaust Jewish Thought*. New York: Schocken, 1994.

Fonrobert, Charlotte Elisheva, and Martin S. Jaffee, editors. *The Cambridge Companion to the Talmud and Rabbinic Literature*. Cambridge: Cambridge University Press, 2006.

Huebner, Harry. *Echoes of the Word: Theological Ethics as Rhetorical Practice*. Kitchener, ON: Pandora, 2005.

———. "Justice and the Biblical Imagination." In *Church as Parable: Whatever Happened to Ethics?* edited by Harry Huebner and David Schroeder, 120–46. Winnipeg: CMBC Publications, 1993.

Milbank, John. *Being Reconciled: Ontology and Pardon*. London: Routledge, 2003.

Volf, Miroslav. *The End of Memory: Remembering Rightly in a Violent World*. Grand Rapids: Eerdmans, 2006.

———. *Exclusion and Embrace: A Theological Exploration of Identity, Otherness, and Reconciliation*. Nashville: Abingdon, 1996.

"We Remember: A Reflection on the Shoah." Vatican: Holy See, Commission for Religious Relations with the Jews, March 16, 1998. Online: http://www.vatican.va/roman_curia/pontifical_councils/chrstuni/documents/rc_pc_chrstuni_doc_16031998_shoah_en.html, accessed August 11, 2009.

Wiesel, Elie. *From the Kingdom of Memory: Reminiscences*. New York: Summit, 1990.

———. "Hope, Despair and Memory." Nobel Lecture, December 11, 1986. Online: http://nobelprize.org/nobel_prizes/peace/laureates/1986/wiesel-lecture.html, accessed August 11, 2009.

Williams, Rowan. "*Augustine* and the *Psalms*." *Interpretation* 58 (2004) 17–27.

———. *Resurrection: Interpreting the Easter Gospel*. Cleveland: Pilgrim, 2003.

Is a Christian University Strange Enough?

Reflections on Loving and Hating the University

Chris K. Huebner

READERS FAMILIAR WITH THE WORK OF HARRY HUEBNER WILL NO DOUBT BE AWARE OF his interest in the idea of a Christian university. Both in his written work and during his tenure as academic dean at Canadian Mennonite University, Huebner has explored what it might mean to imagine the university as something that is shaped by the body of Christ. What might it look like, he asks, to approach university education on the basis of the assumption that "ecclesiology precedes pedagogy?"[1] In his attempt to answer this question, Huebner employs another theme that can be found throughout his work—namely the strangeness, otherness, or difference of the church. Too many instances of Christian education, he argues, simply apply a "'Christian values' overlay on an otherwise standard university curriculum."[2] But he claims that such an approach is insufficiently Christian in the sense that it is not strange enough. This sort of approach does not adequately reflect the otherness of the church. As Huebner puts it, "unless learning itself is first of all made strange by gospel speech, which is something quite different than the speech of dominant culture, the likelihood of education taking place under the Lordship of Christ is not high."[3]

Although Huebner's interest in the idea of the university might be seen as a relatively recent development, the category of strangeness has been with him from the very beginning. Indeed, he describes it as a central element of his moral formation at the hands of his mother:

> An important moral category for my mother was the Low German word *aundasch*, which literally means "different." It functioned as a moral term for her because whenever she saw someone outside the community do something we should never do, she would call it *aundasch*. She seemed to know implicitly that just as their actions flowed from their historical narratives, ours had a different narrative. Because the narratives were different, so were the actions. She was not critical of their story. It just was not our story, hence could not be used to justify our actions. It made no sense for us to act on the basis of someone else's identity. She knew that acts come not in isolated and disconnected episodes but they arise out of religious and cultural

---

1. Huebner, "Learning Made Strange," 302.
2. Ibid., 282.
3. Ibid.

identities. Our story was the story of Jesus and the church. We must be the kind of people capable of "putting on" that story.[4]

A sense of Christian strangeness has always been there. And so when Huebner comes to explore the question of the Christian university, we should not be surprised to find him describing it as something strange.

This essay attempts to reflect further on the intersection of these two strands of Huebner's recent work: the strangeness of Christianity, and the idea of the Christian university. Following Huebner's lead, I am interested in exploring the question of whether the Christian university as we know it is strange enough. I shall address this question by reflecting on the theological interplay between love and hate. Put briefly, I argue that if it makes sense to speak of something called the Christian university, we should find ourselves torn between loving and hating such an entity. Christianity is, after all, founded on a form of love that calls us to hate our "fathers and mothers, wife and children, brothers and sisters . . . and even life itself" (Luke 14:26). Moreover, the Apostle Paul suggests that the love of Christ is such that it runs counter to that which we associate most closely with the university, namely knowledge (see 1 Cor 13:8–10). Anybody who claims to take Christian love seriously should at least have a healthy suspicion about the idea of a Christian university. This is at least part of the reason we might be tempted to describe such a university as strange. In this respect Christian strangeness elicits a form of desire in which love and hate are somehow bound up in a kind of ongoing dialectical interplay with one another. Or perhaps better put, the strangeness of Christianity is reflected in a continuing and rather difficult attempt to discern which of our loves and hates is real and which is somehow distorted or misdirected. Accordingly, it is possible that the strange is that which resists being loved straightforwardly, while at the same time it cannot be altogether hated. And yet my sense is that an appreciation of the significance of this tension tends largely to be missing from much of the recent discussion concerning the question of the Christian university. Indeed, too much contemporary reflection on the Christian university reflects a set of assumptions in which love and hate are understood as necessarily excluding one another.

How might this be? How are we to understand this all too schematic and perhaps rather strange set of claims? Let me begin by suggesting that such a discussion should not begin with the question of what the Christian university should look like, as if the general idea of a Christian university is a straightforward and natural one. This assumes that the existence of something we call the Christian university is a given and the only question has to do with its specific character. I want to argue that it is precisely such an assumption that needs to be subjected to greater critical scrutiny. Accordingly, I shall begin with an examination of the recent fascination with the idea of a Christian university in the first place.

On the one hand, the sheer explosion of interest in the topic of the Christian university within the last ten years or so is quite astounding. On the other hand, I am struck by how innocuous such a discussion appears to be, at least in North America, where there appears to be a relative absence of debate on the topic. We find advocates of the Christian university proceeding as if it is the most natural thing in the world to consider. To be

---

4. Huebner and Schroeder, *Church as Parable*, 173.

sure, there are all kinds of disagreements with respect to some of the details of what such a university might look like. But as for the question of the Christian university itself, one gets the impression that it is a relatively straightforward notion and an unquestionably good thing. Indeed, it is quite difficult to find genuine disagreement on the subject. What we typically find would not best be characterized as dissent, but as an attitude of utter indifference. In other words, those who do not find the idea of a Christian university compelling do not actively oppose it so much as ignore it altogether. In neither case, apparently, is the Christian university understood to be something worthy of the description "strange"—it is not something about which we find ourselves unsure of how to respond. On the contrary, it seems to be a question of all or nothing. But I want to suggest that the idea of a Christian university is one about which we Christians rightly find ourselves torn. It is something we ought simultaneously to be for and against, such that the very idea of the Christian university constantly eludes our attempts to make sense of it.

To develop this claim, I will consider the following general description of what is usually presented as the Christian university. Most recent discussions of the Christian university, it seems, trade on an identification of two incompatible wholes—the Christian and the secular—and argue for one at the cost of the other. Such a move is commonly bolstered by an attempt to turn the tables on what is called the secular university by suggesting that the Christian university is willing to entertain and subject to critical scrutiny assumptions that the secular university simply takes for granted. Some favorite targets here include notions concerning freedom, human nature, universal reason, technology, and so on. It can then be argued that the secular university is limited, provincial, and prejudiced in a way that the Christian university is not. Similarly, the Christian university is said to hold everything together in an integrative and balanced way while the secular university, by contrast, is depicted as prone to compartmentalization and internal division, if not incoherence, among its various faculties. In short, the Christian university is said to be "more comprehensive" or "integrative" than its non-Christian counterpart because it alone is capable of taking everything into consideration.[5] This alleged superiority of the Christian university is usually translated more concretely into a stated concern for something called the "whole person." This holism is also reflected in a curriculum that is said to be properly integrative, and typically emphasizes the need to subject all areas of enquiry to more significant "ethical" consideration.[6]

Of course, there is a sense in which all of these claims may be true, at least to a certain extent. But I am not interested in exploring their truth at the moment. Rather, I want to explore some ways in which these depictions of the Christian university might foster habits of blindness, or at least shortsightedness, that end up insulating those who defend the so-called Christian university from a disciplined attentiveness to its own characteristic limitations and failures. At the risk of oversimplification, these limitations might be sum-

5. Take, for example, the following claim by Richard John Neuhaus: "A Christian University will settle for nothing less than a comprehensive account of reality. Not content with the what of things, it wrestles with the why of things; not content with knowing how, it asks what for. Unlike other kinds of universities, the Christian university cannot evade the hard questions about what it all means. Therefore theology and philosophy, the sciences of meaning, are at the heart of the university." In Neuhaus, "Christian University: Eleven Theses."

6. For a further elaboration of these claims, see Hauerwas, *State of the University*, 48, 127–31.

marized in terms of the Christian university's preoccupation with holism, both in terms of its students and its curriculum.

As far as its approach to students goes, the Christian university's purported concern for the whole person often ends up being somewhat disingenuous. The concern for students is typically articulated in terms of being more sympathetic to the so-called needs of students in ways that are said to give rise to easier transitions and more friendly educational experiences. But I wonder whether this way of putting it is more characteristic of the landscape of contemporary university education and less reflective of a particularly Christian ethos. After all, every university on the hunt for a share of the market currently makes a similar claim. But more significantly, this sort of claim too easily risks obscuring the fact that the task of Christian education involves the radical transformation of our "needs" and "desires" in ways that cannot but be profoundly unsettling and often quite painful. In other words, the rhetoric of holism presents the needs of students as if they are straightforward and somehow given. In doing so, it offers students a promise of self-confirmation by telling them, in essence, that they will find themselves "at home" in a Christian university, whereas a secular university will leave them with a profound sense of alienation. But this suggests that the Christian university is a non-alienating place in a way that is theologically quite problematic. The rhetoric of Christianity reminds us that our so-called needs are, more often than not, in need of reorientation. To describe a Christian university as one that is more attentive to the needs of students than a secular university can be is thus, at the very least, in need of further clarification. But that sort of clarification is characteristically missing from the discussion.

Turning to the question of curriculum, it might be suggested that the preoccupation with curricular holism is similarly shortsighted. Typically presented as radical and revisionary, Christian curriculum often seems to involve little more than tweaking and tinkering on the surface in a way that leaves the more significant questions that the Christian university allegedly pursues unasked, or at least underappreciated. To take just one example, in a Christian university one can often find a range of professional programs—business seems to be particularly common—that require their students to take a course or two in ethics. Such a requirement is defended as a way of striving to ensure that the university produces professionals who are sufficiently equipped with so-called Christian values. But once again, it strikes me that this reflects the landscape of the contemporary university more than it does the strangeness of Christianity Huebner points to. That is because his conception of Christian strangeness has everything to do with his understanding of ethics. Huebner argues that Christian ethics, to be intelligibly Christian, cannot be reflected in so-called values that are sprinkled on top of a range of given activities and practices.[7] Rather, ethics names a different way of life that goes all the way down, so to speak. But where that way of life includes cultivating forms of poverty and patience, appending an ethics course to an otherwise fairly standard business program seems a shallow manifestation of the Christian difference.[8]

---

7. See for example Huebner, "Church Made Strange for the Nations," especially 97–101.

8. For an incisive examination of the way Christian ethics tends systematically to evade questions of poverty and stewardship by obscuring the role of beggars in the Christian life, see Johnson, *Fear of Beggars*.

In addition to these specific weaknesses, the general argument commonly advanced in favor of the Christian university is similarly flawed. That is, the above-mentioned weaknesses of the Christian university can be read as symptomatic of a more general weakness that is reflected in one of the popular ways of articulating and defending the very idea of the Christian university. It is striking that much of the rhetoric of the Christian university tends to be clothed in images and metaphors that make it sound as if it were a kind of self-contained fortress. This is in part reflected in the tendency to invoke the language of holism and integration to which I have already alluded—a tendency that is perhaps especially evident in evangelical Protestant accounts of the Christian university. At the same time, the rhetoric of the Christian university is often shot through with triumphalistic tones. This is reflected in a tendency to present the Christian university as having a better chance of succeeding in those projects where the so-called secular university has failed. In this respect, it might be suggested that the standard account of the Christian university is inherently reactive. Its language is disproportionately dedicated to the task of self-legitimation and seems to express a posture that is generally apologetic and defensive. The logic of the Christian university is dialectically overdetermined by the secular university to which it presents itself as an alternative. Or, to put it in terms of love and hate, the love of the Christian university is informed by too strong a hatred of the so-called secular university.

It is possible to assume that my use of the terms *reactive* and *self-contained* suggests that the Christian university is an essentially sectarian institution. This may well be an appropriate description. But if it is, then it is important to recognize that at the same time it reflects a Constantinian attitude that understands power in an establishmentarian sense. Among other things, this is to suggest that the distinction between sectarian withdrawal and churchly establishment is of little use when it comes to describing the character of the contemporary Christian university. In his recent book on the university, Stanley Hauerwas credits Sam Wells with the observation that "whenever 'Christian' is used as an adjective you can be confident that you are reproducing the habits of Constantinianism."[9] I think that Wells is right. To put his point somewhat differently, if the idea of a Christian university is to be intelligible in the first place, we should be able to speak of it in terms that are not essentially reactive. But just to the extent we are able to do so, we might find ourselves with little use for the adjective "Christian." That we have not been terribly successful in speaking of the Christian university in nonreactive terms can be interpreted as evidence that we continue to be at least partially implicated in a Constantinian strategy to secure power in the absence of compelling forms of witness.

Once again, these sorts of questions are at least implicit in much of Huebner's work. But at this point I want to borrow an image from Peter Dula, who borrows it from Sheldon Wolin, in an attempt to gesture toward some alternative ways of approaching this conversation. Drawing on Wolin's notion of "fugitive democracy," Dula points out that much of the more interesting work done by contemporary theologians seems to push them—although sometimes against their own stated conclusions—toward an account of the church

---

9. Hauerwas, *State of the University*, 7.

he describes as fugitive.[10] By "fugitive ecclesia," Dula means that the church is episodic and rare. Although there is continuity within the body of Christ, it is not easy to point to, whether spatially or temporally. Accordingly, the church's life is characterized by a sense of struggle as it patiently works through conflicts and tensions on a number of different levels. At the same time, it is vulnerably attentive to its own failures and dedicated to the hard work of reckoning with them, as difficult a task as that may be. Moreover, it is not a self-contained fortress, but involves a number of what we might call porous practices that collectively cultivate an openness to receive gifts from a wide range of others. One way of interpreting scholars such as Yoder and Hauerwas, not to mention Huebner, who emphasize the difference between church and world, is to see the church as a body that lives on the "edges and overlaps" of precisely that which they name as "world."[11] All of this can be taken as heightening the sense in which Christianity names something difficult and different. And this takes us to the heart of my biggest worry about the idea of a Christian university, namely, that it seems naturally drawn to rhetorical strategies that make it all look just a bit too easy. To be sure, the rhetoric makes it look easier than it really is. But that is all the more reason to be somewhat wary of too readily accepting the standard account of the Christian university.

These claims are at least implicit in the main contours of Huebner's work. And yet Huebner has also served many years as the dean of an institution that proudly describes itself as a Christian university. In this respect, it should not be surprising that we can identify a tension between Huebner the professor and academic, and the university in which he served for a number of years as academic dean. For example, anyone who has taken an ethics course with Huebner has learned—or at least should have learned—that he doesn't really believe in a discipline called "ethics." Or at least he doesn't believe that "ethics" names an autonomous field of study to be differentiated from other disciplines within the university. In particular, he is suspicious of approaches that construe ethics as a theoretical enterprise, the task of which is to guide us through making tough decisions. Rather, Huebner understands ethics to be involved in the business of crafting people. But that means there is no such thing as ethics, if by that we mean to invoke something called the "realm of the ethical." We are always already immersed in the work of ethics, just to the extent that we are always and everywhere involved in the business of character formation. Accordingly, to offer courses in ethics tempts us to develop interpretive habits that blind us to the kinds of formation that are going on in other courses or spheres of activity that are not explicitly described as ethical. So when Huebner teaches courses in ethics, a good deal of his energy is dedicated to the task of demonstrating that teaching courses in ethics is a bad idea, in that it cultivates forms of self-deception that lead us to misunderstand who we are. The upshot of this is that ethical formation is often most significant just where it is the most subtle. And the same could be said for the work of the university and the church. Huebner teaches us to see that our lives are formed in the midst of processes that

---

10. Dula, "Fugitive Ecclesia."

11. I owe the image of living on the edges and overlaps to Rom Coles, who also points our attention to Wolin. See Coles and Hauerwas, *Christianity, Democracy, and the Radical Ordinary*, 174.

we would often describe as not having anything to do with what we think of as "ethical," let alone "Christian."

And yet Huebner the academic dean has found himself involved in the development of a business program, one of the distinguishing characteristics of which is that it requires its students to take courses in ethics. In doing so, he participates in the perpetuation of one of the defining features of the contemporary Christian university in the most straightforward and, I think, unfortunate senses of the term. Huebner the dean thus finds himself playing a game that requires him to perform moves that his work suggests are highly problematic. These moves might be said to obscure what he means by speaking of the church as strange. This is not to suggest that Huebner was a bad dean. I suspect he was all too painfully aware of the extent to which his work as academic dean was in tension with his teaching and writing. Rather, I read this example as demonstrating that the Constantinian temptations implicit in the idea of the Christian university are very powerful and subtle ones. Indeed, they are powerful, in part, just because they are so subtle and easy to miss.

This last point is perhaps best dealt with by pointing to another notable feature of Huebner's work, namely, the need to cultivate postures of lament, penitence, and silence. If my characterization of the Christian university as a triumphalist project is correct, it is marked by anything but these sorts of postures. Indeed, some of the clearest examples of penitence and lament can be found within the so-called secular university, at least insofar as it has attempted to come to grips with its history of participation in strategies of domination, from sexism to colonialism. But the importance of this sort of self-critical stance is present in Huebner's work, too. By developing an account of the church that can be summarized in terms of what Dula calls the fugitive ecclesia, Huebner draws attention to the need to cultivate forms of lament that allow us to reckon with, among other things, our ongoing complicity in sovereign models of rationality and their contemporary expressions in an ethos of bureaucratic managerialism. As dean, he may have found himself forced to assume the stance of precisely the sort of bureaucratic manager that his work calls into question, not least in the sense in which he was placed in the position of a sovereign whose task it is to oversee the coherence of a curriculum. But the point is not that his deanship somehow forced him to compromise his vision for the university. I am not suggesting that it is the bane of a dean's work to violate principles that might somehow be thought of as pure. Rather, I am arguing that Huebner draws attention to the importance of cultivating pedagogical practices that might allow us to recognize the extent to which we are always already implicated in the sorts of tensions and failures he experienced while he served as dean.

So while it may be true that Huebner's work is at odds with what might be expected of a dean of the sort of Christian university he imagines, at the end of the day, such a claim is not finally all that interesting, at least if it is supposed to stand on its own. What is interesting to consider is whether he has left us with a vision of the university as a place that strives to create meaningful spaces for identifying and confronting the weaknesses that run through the very fabric of its being. I believe that is just the sort of task to which Huebner's work points. In other words, he helps us see that the university is not something whose legitimacy and coherence it is finally up to us to articulate and defend. This would surely be a strange sort of university—and perhaps even one worthy of the name Christian.

Let me be clear that I am not suggesting that those of us committed to the project of a Christian university are *necessarily* susceptible to the criticisms I have attempted to develop here. And yet we should not be too quick to convince ourselves that we are entirely innocent, either. At the very least, I think we ought to be haunted far more significantly by the possibility of these sorts of tensions than we seem to be. More broadly, I suggest that any discussion that might be tempted to consider something called a Christian university ought to be more attentive to what I have called the fugitive character of the church. Stanley Hauerwas suggests that the important question is not so much what a Christian university should look like, but rather what "difference church practices might make for the very shape of knowledges in the university."[12] To this I want to add the suggestion that the desire to place our hope in something called a Christian university is perhaps best read as a symptom of an evacuation of exactly those practices that constitute the church as church. Accordingly, I want to suggest that those of us who are unwilling to concede that God has altogether abandoned the church ought to be wary of placing our hope in something called the Christian university. Please note that I have not attempted to develop a criticism of the Christian university that would lead us to conclude that the secular university is not as bad as it seems. Rather, I have attempted to call into question the givenness of the sort of discussion that finds us assuming that the Christian university and the secular university somehow exhaust the range of alternatives whereby Christians might imagine the task of education. Put differently, I have argued the idea of a Christian university is not nearly strange enough, sometimes precisely because it is far too strange. And this is at least in part because it too easily allows us to take our loves and hates for granted.

---

12. Hauerwas, *State of the University*, 7.

Bibliography

Coles, Romand, and Stanley Hauerwas. *Christianity, Democracy, and the Radical Ordinary: Conversations between a Radical Democrat and a Christian*. Theopolitical Visions. Eugene, OR: Cascade, 2008.

Dula, Peter. "Fugitive Ecclesia." In *The Gift of Difference: Radical Orthodoxy, Radical Reformation*, edited by Chris K. Huebner and Tripp York, 103–28. Winnipeg: CMU Press, 2010.

Hauerwas, Stanley. *The State of the University: Academic Knowledges and the Knowledge of God*. Oxford: Blackwell, 2007.

Huebner, Harry J. "The Church Made Strange for the Nations." In *Echoes of the Word: Theological Ethics as Rhetorical Practice*, 84–106. Kitchener, ON: Pandora, 2005.

———. "Learning Made Strange: Can a University Be Christian?" In *God, Truth, and Witness: Engaging Stanley Hauerwas*, edited by L. Gregory Jones, Reinhard Hütter, and C. Rosalee Velloso Ewell, 280–308. Grand Rapids: Brazos, 2005.

Huebner, Harry, and David Schroeder. *Church as Parable: Whatever Happened to Ethics?* Winnipeg: CMBC Publications, 1993.

Johnson, Kelly S. *The Fear of Beggars: Stewardship and Poverty in Christian Ethics*. Grand Rapids: Eerdmans, 2007.

Neuhaus, Richard John. "The Christian University: Eleven Theses." *First Things* (January 1996). Online: http://www.firstthings.com/article.php3?id_article=3799, accessed May 22, 2008.

14

Moving the Historic Wall of Estrangement
A Reflection on the Catholic-Mennonite Dialogue (1998–2003)

Helmut Harder

The story is told of a group of soldiers who brought two fallen comrades to a French village not far from the battleground where they had recently engaged the enemy. There they sought permission from the local priest to bury their friends in the cemetery adjacent to the local church. "Are they Catholic?" asked the priest. "No," answered the soldiers. "In that case," said the priest, "you may bury your friends just outside the cemetery fence." He assured the two that the burial plots would be tended there. The soldiers did as the priest had instructed, and left. Some time later the soldiers revisited the village to check on the burial plots and pay their respects. But even though they had taken careful note of the burial site, they could not find the graves. Fearing the worst, they inquired of the parish priest as to who might have removed the bodies, and where the remains had been taken. "The bodies are still there, where you laid them," explained the priest. "After you left I spent a restless night, troubled by my instructions to you. In the morning I asked the custodian of the cemetery garden to move the fence. Your comrades now lie inside the cemetery wall."[1]

IN THE FALL OF 1998, THE CATHOLIC CHURCH'S PONTIFICAL COUNCIL FOR PROMOTING Christian Unity, together with the General Council of the Mennonite World Conference, launched a five-year Catholic-Mennonite dialogue under the theme "Toward a Healing of Memories." A representative group of fourteen persons—seven Catholics and seven Mennonites—was entrusted by their churches with the weighty task of repairing relationships so unceremoniously broken off in the sixteenth century.[2] The dividing wall, thrown up hurriedly at the time, had stood firm for almost five centuries.

Understandably, both groups entered into the dialogue with some trepidation. Mennonites brought to the table the bitter experience of persecution at the hands of state and church, a memory kept alive to this day. Catholics brought the memory of how

---

1. This story, attributed to William Barclay, is found in various versions throughout the Internet.

2. The author of this essay was one of the Mennonite representatives to the dialogue, and served as co-chair together with Bishop Joseph Martino of the United States. The group held six week-long meetings over a span of five years.

the Anabaptists, along with other "radicals," shattered the unity of the Catholic Church. Would it be possible to "move the fence" so as to include rather than exclude each other?

It was agreed at the outset that the dialogue should take place "in the spirit of friendship and reconciliation."[3] The stated purpose was threefold: "to learn to know one another better; to promote better understanding of the positions on Christian faith held by Catholics and Mennonites; and to contribute to the overcoming of prejudices that have long existed between them."[4] Underlying the dialogue was the persistent assumption, on both sides, that Catholics and Mennonites had an obligation to take seriously the prayer of our Lord for his disciples "that they may all be one . . . so that the world may believe that [the Father] has sent [the Son]" (John 17:21).[5] The entire "high priestly prayer" of Jesus was read often at morning or evening prayers over the course of the dialogue.

In what follows, I will consider to what extent the five-year dialogue has served to "move the fence" in favor of inclusiveness. My summary and commentary will proceed according to four major features of the historic division between Catholics and Mennonites: differing interpretations of history; disparate ecclesiologies; disagreement over sacraments; and separate pathways to peace.

Interpretations of History

In the attempt to reconcile differing interpretations of the past, Catholics and Mennonites turned to three periods of history: the sixteenth-century Reformation, the Constantinian period, and the Middle Ages. The sixteenth century holds the story of the rupture in which the Mennonite community was born. Obviously, Catholics and Mennonites have interpreted this era from widely divergent points of view. The same holds for the Constantinian period of the fourth century and for the Middle Ages. Meanwhile, lack of communication between the two churches has only accentuated their disparate viewpoints and deepened their prejudices. Thus it was important for Catholics and Mennonites to return to the roots of their divisive past and to read their versions of the past to each other, *together*.

The aim of this rereading of history has been described as "the purification of memory."[6] This is not the same as finding a common viewpoint. It would be unrealistic to think that the rereading of history could result in a common interpretation of the past. Historical accounts will bear the mark of those engrossed in the recorded events, and of those who inherit these histories. Selectivity and personal perspective will of necessity shape interpretation. Commenting on the Catholic-Mennonite dialogue, Catholic Professor Jos E. Vercruysse has said that "all social memories and the writing of history will necessarily be diverse, because the standpoints of the witnesses and of the story-tellers

---

3. "Called Together," §1; Radano, *Information Service*, 111.

4. "Called Together," §15; Radano, *Information Service*, 113.

5. In recent years both Catholics and Mennonites have referenced John 17:21 when challenging their churches to more concerted ecumenical pursuits. On the Catholic side, see "Decree on Ecumenism," §8, in Trouvé, *Sixteen Documents*, 248–49. On the Mennonite side, see "God Calls Us to Christian Unity," issued by the Executive Committee of Mennonite World Conference.

6. "Called Together," §192–97; Radano, *Information Service*, 144–45.

are necessarily diverse... The outcome can only be a unity in reconciled diversity."[7] Given this reality, it is important, says Professor Vercruysse, that Mennonites and Catholics tell their stories "*to* and not *against*" each other. This allows each tradition to learn from the other and make corrections where necessary.

The Sixteenth Century: Reformation or Disruption?

Mennonites have interpreted the Reformation of the sixteenth century, and in particular their part in it, as a positive and necessary undertaking for the restoration of the New Testament church. Catholics have interpreted the same period as an unfortunate schism, causing a major disruption in the church's sacred unity and in the historic continuity of the church. What happens when Catholics and Mennonites, gathered around the same table, share their versions of the sixteenth-century story in each other's presence? Insights can be grouped under four observations.

First, Catholics and Mennonites came to the realization that the social milieu at the end of the fifteenth century, marked by transitions of radical proportion, affected all social groups of the time and shaped their responses to the changes facing them.[8] The Catholic Church was suffering a loss of authority in the face of the rise of the first modern states. Christendom was losing respect as a unifying force. The Catholic Church found it difficult to adjust to these changes. Population growth and economic redistribution brought uncontrollable social unrest. This was also the era of humanism, characterized by a rapid growth in free thinking. The Anabaptist movement was in large part a product of the widespread spirit of reform and the quest for freedom. In rereading their histories together, Catholics and Mennonites realized that they were, to some extent, common players under the same social forces of the time.

Second, while Mennonites have understood their birth in the sixteenth century as a renewal movement, Catholics also claim the sixteenth century as a time of spiritual renewal.[9] Renewal showed itself in sincere preaching, in a more intentional religious education, and in the spirituality of discipleship. As the report of the dialogue states: "In the sixteenth century, the Protestant Reformation, the Radical Reformation, as well as the Catholic Reform benefited significantly from these yearnings for a higher spirituality."[10]

Third, the sixteenth-century milieu was fraught with considerable confusion, as evidenced, for example, by the Peasant Wars (1524–1525) and the Münster Rebellion (1534–1535).[11] These uprisings raised the specter of anarchy in the minds of both Protestants and Catholics. In this whirlwind, the slightest provocation by Anabaptists (such as re-baptisms) prompted political and ecclesial leaders to consider action against them. In the minds of secular and religious authorities, the very existence of state and church were at stake.

---

7. Vercruysse, "Comment on 'Called Together to be Peacemakers,'" 151.
8. See "Called Together," §30–33; Radano, *Information Service*, 116.
9. See "Called Together," §34–37; Radano, *Information Service*, 116–17.
10. "Called Together," §37; Radano, *Information Service*, 117.
11. For an elaboration of this confusing milieu, see "Called Together," §41-43; Radano, *Information Service*, 118–19.

The fourth point concerns the story of suffering and persecution endured by many who embraced the Anabaptist-Mennonite movement. Those committing themselves to the movement endured extreme and unwarranted suffering at the hands of the "confessional state" and its official church.[12] Catholic representatives in the dialogue conceded that they found no theological justification for these atrocities.[13] The Mennonite delegates welcomed this acknowledgment. When the group was reminded that Catholics, too, faced martyrdom in the postmedieval period, it was suggested that this awareness "could help both Catholics and Mennonites to reach a renewed understanding of the meaning of martyrdom in the painful division of the Christian church in the early modern period."[14]

We can conclude that the open and receptive exchange of viewpoints on the troublesome sixteenth century and the realization that all religious groups were struggling to come to grips with the situation helped significantly to temper prejudice between Catholics and Mennonites and to evoke empathetic understanding of the difficult situation in which opposing factions found themselves.

The Constantinian Era: Shift or Fall?

Interpreters of Mennonite history have pointed to events in the fourth century as a major backdrop to the Radical Reformation of the sixteenth century. In 313 CE, the Emperor Constantine issued the Edict of Milan, which brought great relief to Christians by allowing Christianity to exist without persecution alongside other religions of the Roman Empire. Then in 380 CE, Emperor Theodosius I gave imperial status to the Creed of Nicea (325). With these initiatives, the Christian church gained official recognition by the Roman Empire, and Christians came to be regarded as respectable law-abiding citizens.

Was this a good development, as Catholics have claimed? Or did the "Christianization" of the Roman Empire perpetuate the fall of the church, as some Mennonites have argued?[15] Was it not under Constantine that the church began to compromise its distinctive stand against militarism, its practice of "believers' baptism," and its status as a free church unencumbered by submission to the state?

---

12. See Dyck, "Suffering Church," 5.

13. See "Called Together," §45–48; Radano, *Information Service*, 52. Recent statistics suggest that of the ca. 5,000 people put to death for religious reasons in Europe in the sixteenth century, between 2,000 and 2,500 were Anabaptist men and women. The majority of these were put to death in Catholic territories. For a detailed account of Anabaptist persecution and martyrdom by a Catholic historian, see Gregory, *Salvation at Stake*, chap. 6. See also Stayer, "Numbers in Anabaptist Research." It must be pointed out that there are no recorded instances of physical violence by Anabaptists against Catholics. Catholic delegates noted, and Mennonite participants agreed, that the harsh language used by Menno Simons and others in their indictment of the Catholic Church amounted to a form of violence, albeit by way of "the tongue."

14. "Called Together," §52; Radano, *Information Service*, 120. Joint study of martyr theology and martyr history is already underway: see for example Erb, *Martyrdom in an Ecumenical Perspective*; and within that volume, Harder, "Toward an Ecumenical Memory of Martyrs," and Bergen, "Problem or Promise?" For continuing reflection by Mennonite theologians on Mennonite martyrology, see for example Huebner, *A Precarious Peace*, 133–44.

15. See Yoder, *Royal Priesthood*, 242–61; Yoder, *Priestly Kingdom*, 135–47.

In the course of the dialogue, it became evident that Catholics and Mennonites were not diametrically opposed in their views of the Constantinian era. The Catholic delegation challenged the Mennonites to recognize some good in church-state cooperation, despite its negative aspects. Mennonites admitted that today in many countries, Mennonite churches relate positively to the state. Meanwhile, Catholic delegates conceded that the Catholic Church has undergone significant modification of its views on the relation of the church to the state. While the Second Vatican Council's "Declaration on Religious Freedom" calls upon Catholics to respect the state, the declaration puts considerable distance between church and state and "reflects in many ways the position that was taken by sixteenth-century Anabaptists."[16] The two groups agreed that given the changing times and the variety of governmental systems throughout the world, it was not possible, nor was it warranted, to insist on a rigid theology of the relationship between church and state.[17] Changing times and diverse contexts require flexibility. In any case, the two churches agreed that the church should be free of state control, and that the church should not seek to control the state.

On the one hand, the exchange served to modify traditionally held viewpoints on the Constantinian era. The Catholic delegates positioned themselves against servile church-state relations. Both sides preferred to characterize the fourth century as a "shift" rather than as the "fall" of the church. Yet on the other hand, Mennonite delegates were of the mind that their perspective on the fourth century, with its critique of infant baptism, of the compliance of the church to the state, of the acceptance of militarism by the church, should receive more serious consideration than was forthcoming in the dialogue.[18] It was agreed that issues raised in light of the Constantinian era and its aftermath are still with us in one form or another, and require continuing joint study and discernment.[19]

The Middle Ages: Dark or Enlightened?

Did the Catholic Church thrive spiritually in the Middle Ages? Or did it fail to live up to its calling? Were the Middle Ages a time of enlightened development, or were they a continuation of the "dark ages," necessitating the sixteenth-century Reformation? Catholics have tended to view these centuries as "deeply Christianized," while Mennonites have regarded them as "barbaric and decayed."[20]

In the course of the dialogue, both groups were challenged to modify their views. Catholics acknowledged the church's unfortunate compliance with secular power and the inappropriate use of violence during the Middle Ages. They pointed to the troublesome

---

16. "Called Together," §60; Radano, *Information Service*, 122. See also the papal "Declaration on Religious Freedom," in Trouvé, *Sixteen Documents*, 491–503.

17. "Called Together," §58; Radano, *Information Service*, 122.

18. See Klaassen, "The Anabaptist Critique"; and Kreider, *The Change of Conversion*.

19. See "Called Together," §58–62; Radano, *Information Service*, 122–23. The following issues are identified in the report: the interpretation of the Constantinian era (§58); differing interpretations of the witness of the church in the Middle Ages (§59); clarification and implications of statements in the Catholic Church's "Declaration on Religious Freedom" (§60–61); the historical development and interpretation of baptism, in particular of infant baptism (§62).

20. "Called Together," §63; Radano, *Information Service*, 123.

fourteenth century, when rival popes and rival centers of power detracted from the mission of the church. Yet in their view, the medieval church also played an important role in criticizing secular power and influencing political authorities for good. The Catholics drew attention to "an uninterrupted tradition of ecclesiastical peace movements" throughout the Middle Ages, as well as to "an ongoing tradition of Christian spirituality, of discipleship (*Nachfolge*), and of the imitation of Christ."[21] Recent scholarship, both Catholic and Mennonite, has suggested that the origin of the Anabaptist-Mennonite tradition's theology of discipleship as well as its catechetical roots can be traced in part to the medieval period.[22] It was agreed that the centuries preceding the Reformation offer fruitful ground for future joint research.

Healing Historical Memories

This brief summary of the conversation between Catholics and Mennonites on historical issues shows that significant clarification of past events occurred as the dialogue groups revisited their divisive past together and shared their viewpoints. But the healing of memories depends not only on the purification of memory and the convergence of viewpoints. Healing also requires admission of wrongdoing, expressions of repentance, and overtures of forgiveness.[23]

As the Catholic-Mennonite dialogue drew to a close, the two groups offered to each other their statements of regret for wrongs of the past. The Catholic statement, couched in the words of Walter Cardinal Kasper, President Emeritus of the Pontifical Council for Promoting Christian Unity, was offered on the occasion of the Mennonite delegation's visit to the Vatican (November, 2001). He said, in part: "Especially, in the sixteenth century, the Anabaptists were among those who suffered greatly . . . I surely regret those instances when this took place in Catholic societies."[24] Furthermore, members of the Catholic delegation reminded their Mennonite counterparts that when, on the occasion of the Day of Pardon on the first Sunday of Advent in the Jubilee Year 2000, Pope John Paul II led the church in a confession of sins of the past committed by members of the Catholic Church, his request for forgiveness included wrongdoing against the Mennonites.[25]

---

21. "Called Together," §65; Radano, *Information Service*, 123.

22. See "Called Together," §66–67; Radano, *Information Service*, 123–24. For substantive research on the medieval roots of Anabaptist-Mennonite theology, see Davis, *Anabaptism and Asceticism*; Snyder, "Monastic Origins"; Nissen, "De Moderne Devotie"; and Martin, "Catholic Spirituality and Anabaptist and Mennonite Discipleship."

23. To understand assumptions that Catholics and Mennonites brought to the dialogue concerning repentance, as well as the process in which the representatives of the two communions engaged, see "Called Together," §198–210; Radano, *Information Service*, 145ff.

24. "Called Together," §202; Radano, *Information Service*, 146.

25. See "Called Together," §202; Radano, *Information Service*, 146, which, referring to the "Universal Prayer of Forgiveness" offered by Pope John Paul II (March 12, 2000), stated in part: "Without compromising truth, Catholics in this dialogue can apply this spirit of repentance to the conflicts between Catholics and Mennonites in the sixteenth century and can express a penitential spirit, asking forgiveness for the sins which were committed against Mennonites."

The Mennonite representatives offered their expression of regret as well. They stated, in part: "We regret Anabaptist words and deeds that contributed to fracturing the body of Christ. We confess also that in spite of a commitment to follow Jesus Christ in daily life, we and others in our family of faith have frequently failed to demonstrate love toward Catholics . . . For this, we express our regret and ask forgiveness."[26]

Shared clarifications, conciliatory changes of viewpoint, and heartfelt expressions of regret regarding damaging actions of the past constitute significant fence-moving gestures that open the door to reconciliation and a spirit of unity. While the expressions of regret and repentance voiced during the dialogue did not put all hurtful matters to rest, they represented significant steps in the process of reconciliation.

Comparing Ecclesiologies

Judging by appearances, the theologies and practices of the Catholic Church and of the Mennonite family of churches suggest a study in contrasts. The Catholic Church is global and conciliar; Mennonite churches are local and congregational. The Catholic Church is structured hierarchically; Mennonite churches have a grassroots polity. Catholic worship is liturgical and formal; Mennonite worship is free and informal. Catholics focus on the creeds and on the mass; Mennonites focus on Scripture and preaching. Catholic soteriology has a sacramental orientation; Mennonite soteriology focuses on personal conversion and discipleship. Catholics build ornate cathedrals; Mennonites gather in plain meetinghouses. Where, in the face of this diversity, are the possibilities for convergence?

Elements of Agreement

A close look at ecclesiological foundations of both traditions shows that Catholics and Mennonites occupy significant common ground.[27] Both Catholics and Mennonites give high priority to the concept of the church as the people of God, the body of Christ, and the temple of the Holy Spirit. Both affirm Christ as the foundation upon which the church is built. Both value the ecclesiological significance of baptism and the Eucharist/Lord's Supper as central practices that contribute to the spiritual formation of the church. Both embrace mission and witness as an essential mark of the church. Both eagerly pursue the catholicity of the church, although from different starting points.[28] Both regard the Christian community as an essential element in God's work of salvation. Ministry is understood by both as the responsibility of the whole people of God. For both, discipleship is central to ecclesial holiness. Both churches expect a personal faith commitment to Christ as a condition of membership in the body of Christ. While Catholics and Mennonites may differ significantly at the level of the "experienced church" (the manner in which the church expresses itself), they discover significant common ground at the level of the

---

26. "Called Together," §203–4; Radano, *Information Service*, 146–47.

27. See "Called Together," §93–102; Radano, *Information Service*, 129–30.

28. See "Called Together," §98; Radano, *Information Service*, 130. For views on "catholicity" from a Mennonite point of view, see Yoder, "Catholicity in Search of Location," in *The Royal Priesthood*, 300–20; Koop, "Holiness, Catholicity, and Unity."

"believed church" (what the church believes about the church and the faith upheld by the church).[29]

Divergences

The dialogue group also identified divergences, but these make up a much shorter list.[30] For Catholics, the church's teaching authority is based on Scripture *and* tradition, while Mennonites hold to *sola scriptura* (Scripture alone) as the only "fully reliable and trustworthy standard for Christian faith and life."[31] For Catholics, the membership of the church is constituted by people of all ages, provided the water of baptism has been conferred on them. Mennonites also link church membership with baptism. However, baptism is for those who "are of the age of accountability and who freely request baptism on the basis of their response to Jesus Christ in faith."[32] For Catholics, the visible church consists of congregations united around their bishops, who are in turn united around the successor of Peter. For Mennonites, the visible church consists of local congregations and ever-widening groupings of congregations, united in communion under the Lordship of Christ. Finally, Catholics hold to a hierarchically appointed priesthood, while in Mennonite churches pastors are chosen by local congregations, usually from a list of candidates approved by wider church bodies.

While these differences are important, they need not be church-dividing. Each of these apparent differences merits further joint study. On the matter of Scripture and tradition, Mennonites will concede that tradition plays a role in their discernment of divine authority. Catholics, for their part, need to ponder the significance, for ecumenical dialogue, of the statement in the "Decree on Ecumenism" that "Sacred Scriptures provide for the work of dialogue an instrument of the highest value in the mighty hand of God for the attainment of that unity which the Savior holds out to all."[33] Further attention needs to be given to the Mennonites' claim that apostolic authority is a matter the Mennonite church takes seriously, although in a way different from the historic Catholic view.[34] In matters of

---

29. Fernando Enns offers a helpful distinction between "believed" church (*"geglaubte" Kirche*) and "experienced" church (*"erfahrene" Kirche*). See Enns, *Peace Church*, 1ff. These dimensions, which hold together the necessary tension between "being" (*Sein*) and "existing" (*Existenz*), are particularly useful in identifying common foundations of ecclesiology as distinct from diverse practices.

30. See "Called Together," §103–6; Radano, *Information Service*, 130–31.

31. *Confession of Faith*, 21.

32. Ibid., 47. See also "Called Together," §104; Radano, *Information Service*, 131. Regarding baptism as a prerequisite for church membership, outstanding issues remain, as will be discussed below. Meanwhile, it is of symbolic significance that given the troublesome history of the sixteenth century, the Catholic Church recognizes persons baptized in Mennonite churches as having fulfilled the requirement for Christian baptism. See Trouvé, *Sixteen Documents*, §22–23, 256–57.

33. "Decree on Ecumenism," §21, in Trouvé, *Sixteen Documents*, 256. Does this suggest the relative primacy of the authority of Scripture?

34. On the question of apostolic authority, the Catholic Church claims succession from the New Testament church's apostles by way of a continuous line (a "ground route") of popes beginning with St. Peter. The Mennonite Church claims apostolic continuity by way of a spiritual connection between the teachings and practices of the New Testament church and congregational faithfulness to the teachings of the New Testament in every time and place. For Mennonites, faithfulness to the apostolic tradition means faithfulness

polity, the two churches take their places within a wide range of structural arrangements and leadership systems. In short, there is room for further dialogue and discernment between Mennonites and Catholics on their differing viewpoints on ecclesiology.[35]

As evidenced in the Mennonite-Catholic conversation on ecclesiology, the claim that Catholics and Mennonites share significant common ecclesiological ground relies not primarily on current expressions and structures of church (the "experienced" church), but on the churches' foundational ecclesiology (the "believed" church). In that respect, the initial five-year dialogue bears ample evidence that Catholics and Mennonites have more reason to celebrate their ecclesial unity than to accentuate their separateness.[36]

Revisiting Sacraments

The theology and practice of the sacraments figured prominently in the sixteenth-century rupture. Anabaptist-Mennonite leaders saw in Catholic Church practices the abuses of the sacramental system. In this they agreed with Lutheran and Reformed movements. Catholics replied with a vigorous defense of traditional practices. It is understandable that the Catholic-Mennonite dialogue should revisit the theology of sacraments (the preferred designation among Catholics) and ordinances (the preferred term among Mennonites). In the dialogue, conversation focused in particular on baptism and the Eucharist/Lord's Supper.

Foundational Agreements

The dialogue group discovered fundamental agreement between Catholics and Mennonites on basic confessional points. Regarding the sacraments/ordinances of baptism and the Eucharist/Lord's Supper, both churches affirm that "their origin and point of reference [is] Jesus Christ and the teachings of Scripture."[37] Both regard these sacraments/ordinances as "extraordinary occasions of encounter with God's offer of grace revealed in Jesus Christ."[38] For both, these two rituals are "important moments in the believers' commitment to the body of Christ and to the Christian way of life."[39] Both see the sacraments/ordinances as "acts of the church."

Regarding baptism in particular, Catholics and Mennonites claim significant points of agreement. Baptism signifies "a dying and rising with Christ" as well as "the outpouring of the Holy Spirit and the promised presence of the Holy Spirit in the life of the believer

---

to the apostolic witness of the Scriptures. It should be noted that the history of Mennonite confessions of faith reveals a respectful continuity of belief from the earliest confessions (e.g., the Schleitheim Confession of 1526) until today. See Loewen, *One Lord, One Church*, 23–60.

35. For a sample of study topics, see "Called Together, §107–10; Radano, *Information Service*, 131–32.

36. The Catholic Church continues to make a distinction between the Catholic Church, which embraces the fullness of unity, and those Christian communities not in full communion with the Catholic Church, designated as "separated brethren" and "ecclesial communities." "Decree on Ecumenism," §20–22, in Trouvé, *Sixteen Documents*, 255ff.

37. "Called Together," §128; Radano, *Information Service*, 136.

38. "Called Together," §128; Radano, *Information Service*, 136.

39. "Called Together," §128; Radano, *Information Service*, 136.

and the Church."⁴⁰ Both hold that baptism is a public witness to the church's beliefs, as well as "the occasion for the incorporation of new believers into Christ and the Church."⁴¹ For both, baptism is a one-time act. Both Catholics and Mennonites require a public profession of faith at the time of baptism. Mennonites baptize upon the candidates' *personal* confession of faith, as do Catholics in cases where the candidates are adults. In the case of infant baptisms in the Catholic Church, parents and godparents make the profession of faith *on behalf of* the child. This profession is personalized later in the sacrament of confirmation. In both churches, baptism is carried out by water (effusion or immersion) in the name of the Father, the Son, and the Holy Spirit (Matt 28:19).⁴²

Catholics and Mennonites agree on basic aspects of the Eucharist/Lord's Supper. The celebration is rooted in God's gift of grace available to all people. It is a meal of remembrance of Christ's suffering. The meal provides an occasion for confessing sin and receiving forgiveness. The meal nourishes Christian life and witness and offers a foretaste of the heavenly banquet in the coming kingdom of God. Catholics and Mennonites agree that the risen Christ is present at the celebration of the Eucharist/Lord's Supper. Both churches take care to designate a duly ordained priest or minister to preside over the communion meal. These are significant and foundational points on which Catholics and Mennonites find themselves in accord.

Divergences

The dialogue also brought to light some major issues on which Mennonite and Catholic viewpoints diverge.⁴³ While the two churches hold that baptism is a sign of cleansing from sin, Catholics believe that administering baptism "purifies from all sins . . . [and] makes the neophyte 'a new creature,' an adopted son of God, who has become a 'partaker of the divine nature,' member of Christ and co-heir with him, and a temple of the Holy Spirit."⁴⁴ Further, while the two churches understand the presence of Christ in the Lord's Supper as a spiritual presence, with Christ as Lord of the gathered body of believers, Catholics add a crucial point: Christ is "substantially contained"⁴⁵ in the elements of bread and wine when they are consecrated by a person ordained in the Catholic tradition. Also, while the two churches foster a close connection between the sacraments and the recipient's incorporation into the church, Catholics understand the sacrament of the Eucharist as a "sacrament of unity," with the implication that its effectiveness requires the participant to be in full communion with the Catholic Church. Persons who do not hold to the Catholic Eucharistic doctrine and have not submitted to apostolic authority and lineage as under-

---

40. "Called Together," §129; Radano, *Information Service*, 136.

41. "Called Together," §130; Radano, *Information Service*, 136.

42. "Called Together," §136; Radano, *Information Service*, 137. Catholics accept Mennonite baptism for membership purposes, provided it is done with water and in the name of the Trinity. Mennonite practices vary with regard to recognition of Catholic baptism for purpose of membership in Mennonite churches. No Mennonite churches practice infant baptism.

43. See "Called Together," §135–40; Radano, *Information Service*, 136–37.

44. *Catechism of the Catholic Church*, §1265, 354.

45. Ibid., §1374, 383–84. The expression is drawn from the Council of Trent (1551), DS 1651.

stood by the Catholic Church are not welcome to participate in the Catholic Eucharist. Mennonites take varying views on the issue of inclusion beyond their own church circle. On the one side of the spectrum are those who welcome all who confess Jesus Christ as Lord and Savior, regardless of denominational affiliation. On the other side are those who restrict participation to members of the particular Mennonite church in which communion is being celebrated.

While the Catholic Church's practice of the Eucharist has a policy of exclusiveness, it acknowledges that "when [non-Catholic ecclesial communities] commemorate [the Lord's] death and resurrection in the Lord's Supper, they profess that it signifies life in communion with Christ."[46] This concession leads the Catholic Church to conclude that "the teaching concerning the Lord's Supper, the other sacraments, worship, the ministry of the Church, must be the subject of [inter-church] dialogue."[47] Issues for discussion would include the following: Are the rituals of baptism and the Eucharist/Lord's Supper signs and symbols only, or are they also media (sacraments) of the grace of God? Is the rite of baptism reserved for adult believers only, or is it also applicable to infants?[48] Must apostolicity be understood and validated via historical succession alone, or can apostolicity also be understood and validated via renewed faithfulness to the biblical apostolic revelation? Answers to these questions hinge on an underlying issue: Does authority rest on Scripture alone, or on tradition also?

Pathways to Peace

In recent decades Catholics have given increasing attention to Mennonite perspectives on peace. Mennonites have reciprocated by showing an interest in Catholic peace initiatives.[49] In the context of the dialogue, Catholics and Mennonites presented their respective theologies of peace. Again a remarkable convergence came to light in the two churches' theologies of peace.[50] There were also significant divergences.[51]

Convergences

Catholic and Mennonite peace theologies converge at three major points, relating to Christology, to ecclesiology, and to the intersection of peace and justice. Both Catholics and Mennonites embrace Christology as the foundation of their peace witness. For both, the Gospel of peace engages all of creation. Christ's work of redemption broke the power of original sin and empowered God's new creation to reconcile the world unto God. Both

---

46. "Decree on Ecumenism," §22, in Trouvé, *Sixteen Documents*, 257.

47. Ibid.

48. See Schlabach, *On Baptism*, for a recent discussion between Mennonites and Catholics on baptism issues.

49. The participation of the Executive Secretary of the Mennonite World Conference in the Assisi Day of Prayer for Peace (October 1986) at the invitation of Pope John Paul II is viewed by Catholics and Mennonites as a historic gesture of mutual respect for the peace witness of both churches.

50. "Called Together," §172–85; Radano, *Information Service*, 141ff.

51. "Called Together," §186–88; Radano, *Information Service*, 143–44.

churches hold that the way of peace and the work of reconciliation build on the revealed teachings, life, death, and resurrection of Jesus Christ. Christians identify with the peace of Christ through cross-bearing discipleship, marked by God's nonviolent love for friend and enemy and sustained by prayer and worship.[52]

Catholics and Mennonites hold that ecclesiology and peace are integral to each other.[53] The church is called to be a peace church, a peacemaking church. Mennonites put the accent on the church as a *peace church* by definition and by confession.[54] Catholics prefer to characterize themselves as a *peacemaking church*,[55] with peace as an activity and an aspiration. Both agree that by virtue of their baptism and membership in the church, Christians are called to be peacemakers; that is, to be living signs and effective instruments of the coming peaceable reign of God.

Further, Catholics and Mennonites agree that peace and justice are intertwined.[56] The biblical concept of *shalom* expresses the holistic concept of peace implied by the intersection of peace and justice. *Shalom* is defined as well-being, wholeness, harmony, and right relations. Its agenda includes social justice for the oppressed, health and wholeness for the sick and destitute, security for protective community life, freedom from violence and warfare, and spiritual well-being in accordance with the will of God.

Divergences

While there is good reason for Catholics and Mennonites to celebrate convergences in their stances on peace, a comparison of the two churches' peace theology and practice also reveals significant divergences.[57] Both Catholics and Mennonites regard political rule as part of the God-given moral order. Yet Catholics tend to trust political policies and participate in political programs, while Mennonites shy away from national and international political involvement. Both Catholics and Mennonites are committed to the way of peace. Yet Catholics allow for the use of military force as a last resort in the case of a "just war," while Mennonites position themselves against warfare. Both Catholics and Mennonites support pacifism.[58] Yet Catholics understand the pacifist position as a "counsel of perfection" for those committed to a "higher calling," while Mennonites call all Christians to the pacifist stance. Both churches affirm nonresistance. Yet Catholics allow for exceptions, while Mennonites hold that it is possible, through the power of the Holy Spirit, to be faithful to the nonviolent way taught by Jesus. Both Catholics and Mennonites support conscientious objection to war. Yet Catholics allow conscientious objection as an option, while Mennonites advocate the "CO" position as a standard for all. These differences call

---

52. "Called Together," §180–85; Radano, *Information Service*, 143.
53. "Called Together," §175–76; Radano, *Information Service*, 142.
54. See also "Called Together," §164; Radano, *Information Service*, 140. See also Lange, *Gestalt*.
55. "Called Together," §153; Radano, *Information Service*, 139.
56. See "Called Together," §177–79; Radano, *Information Service*, 142.
57. See "Called Together," §186–88; Radano, *Information Service*, 143–44.
58. For a recent discussion between Mennonites and Catholics on the issue of pacifism, see Kauffman, *Just Policing*.

for continuing dialogue, guided by a common study of the Scriptures, and in a spirit of openness to new insights.[59]

"Called Together to Be Peacemakers"

On the strength of a mutual commitment to peacemaking, the Catholic-Mennonite dialogue group has issued a challenge to its constituent churches. The challenge is contained in the very title of the concluding dialogue report: "Called Together to be Peacemakers." Various initiatives have already been undertaken by the two churches. In the summer of 2003, Catholic and Mennonite leaders in Colombia collaborated with one another in addressing the violence in that country. Jointly sponsored symposia focusing on "Called Together to be Peacemakers" have been held at the University of Notre Dame (July 30, 2007) and at the University of Hamburg (September 21–22, 2007). In preparation for the International Ecumenical Peace Convocation (2011), which will mark the conclusion of the World Council of Churches' initiative on addressing violence, Mennonites and Catholics together have submitted "A Mennonite and Catholic Contribution to the World Council of Churches' Decade to Overcome Violence." In these ways, Catholics and Mennonites are bearing witness to "the unity of the Spirit in the bond of peace" (Eph 4:3).

An Unanticipated Conclusion

The first official interchurch dialogue after the sixteenth-century schism yielded at least two surprising results, both of which hold the promise of a paradigm shift in the way Catholics and Mennonites may relate to one another and to the world in the future. The first was the welcome discovery of significant agreement in basic theological convictions. While a comparison of theological viewpoints on ecclesiology, on sacraments and ordinances, and on peace theology revealed continuing differences, there was enough agreement to suggest that these two communions can claim substantial common ground within the circle of Christian unity that Jesus envisioned when he prayed that his erstwhile disciples and those who would believe through their witness "may be one" (John 17:21a).[60] Overtures of reconciliation from both sides provide a sure foundation for Christian unity.

A greater surprise was the decision of the dialogue partners, during the latter part of the dialogue process, to challenge their respective Catholic and Mennonite churches to spread the Gospel of peace *together in the world*. Why should these two churches unite in public peacemaking? First, Catholics and Mennonites had identified significant common

---

59. See "Called Together," §189; Radano, *Information Service*, 144. John Howard Yoder has persistently called upon ecumenical dialogue to move beyond a comparison of convergences and divergences, and to begin by together seeking common ground through the examination of Scripture and in the spirit of *ecclesia reformata semper reformanda* (the church, even when reformed, always still needs reforming). See for example his "Catholicity in Search of Location," in Yoder, *Royal Priesthood*, 314ff.

60. This assessment is affirmed by Mennonite theologian Fernando Enns, whose analysis of the Catholic–Mennonite dialogue concludes with the statement: "The report gives indication of impressive progress in mutual respect and recognition as churches; the two communions are referred to as 'our respective ecclesial communities' and as 'church communities.' These gestures are a reversal of past attitudes." Enns, *Peace Church*, 225.

elements in their commitment to peace, enough to assure the integrity of a joint peace witness and provide a basis for peace initiatives.[61] Second, their story of an unimaginable reconciliation, against the background of a history of persecution and prejudice, offers the potential for a powerful witness to the authenticity of the Gospel of Jesus Christ, the Prince of Peace, in the world. In reading and rereading Jesus's prayer for his disciples together over the course of five years, the dialogue group heard the Spirit say: "[B]e one . . . so that the world may believe that you [Father] have sent me" (John 17:21c).

---

61. Fernando Enns writes: "It is of great significance that Mennonites and Catholics would recommend a joint venture in Christian mission." Ibid.

Bibliography

Bergen, Jeremy M. "Problem or Promise? Confessional Martyrs and Mennonite–Roman Catholic Relations." In *Martyrdom in an Ecumenical Perspective: A Mennonite-Catholic Conversation*, edited by Peter C. Erb, 175–205. Kitchener, ON: Pandora, 2007.

"Called Together to Be Peacemakers." Report of the International Dialogue between the Catholic Church and Mennonite World Conference, 1998–2003. Available online at http://www.mwc-cmm.org; also published in *Information Service* 113, II/III, edited by John A. Radano, 111–48. Vatican City: Pontifical Council for Promoting Christian Unity, 2003.

Catechism of the Catholic Church. New York: Doubleday, 1995.

Confession of Faith in a Mennonite Perspective. Scottdale, PA: Herald, 1995.

Davis, Kenneth Ronald. *Anabaptism and Asceticism: A Study in Intellectual Origins*. Eugene, OR: Wipf & Stock, 1998.

Dyck, Cornelius J. "The Suffering Church in Anabaptism." *Mennonite Quarterly Review* 59 (1985) 5–23.

Enns, Fernando. *The Peace Church and the Ecumenical Community: Ecclesiology and the Ethics of Nonviolence*. Translated by Helmut Harder. Kitchener, ON: Pandora, 2007. Originally published as *Friedenskirche in der Ökumene: Mennonitische Wurzeln einer Ethik der Gewaltfreiheit*. Göttingen: Vandenhoeck & Ruprecht, 2003.

Erb, Peter C., editor. *Martyrdom in an Ecumenical Perspective: A Mennonite-Catholic Conversation*. Kitchener, ON: Pandora, 2007.

"God Calls Us to Christian Unity." Executive Committee, Mennonite World Conference. Goshen, IN: Mennonite World Conference, 1998. Online: http://www.info@mwc-cmm.org.

Gregory, Brad S. *Salvation at Stake: Christian Martyrdom in Early Modern Europe*. Cambridge, MA: Harvard University Press, 1999.

Harder, Helmut. "Toward an Ecumenical Memory of Martyrs: Report and Reflections on a Consultation Held at the Monastic Community of Bose, Italy, March 12–15, 2004." In *Martyrdom in an Ecumenical Perspective: A Mennonite-Catholic Conversation*, 121–46. Kitchener, ON: Pandora, 2007.

Huebner, Chris K. *A Precarious Peace: Yoderian Explorations on Theology, Knowledge, and Identity*. Waterloo, ON: Herald, 2006.

Kauffman, Ivan J. *Just Policing*. Kitchener, ON: Pandora, 2004.

Klaassen, Walter. "The Anabaptist Critique of Constantinian Christendom." *Mennonite Quarterly Review* 55 (1981) 218–30.

Koop, Karl. "Holiness, Catholicity, and Unity." In *Creed and Conscience: Essays in Honour of A. James Reimer*, edited by Jeremy M. Bergen, Paul G. Doerksen, and Karl Koop, 65–82. Kitchener, ON: Pandora, 2007.

Kreider, Alan. *The Change of Conversion and the Origin of Christendom*. Harrisburg, PA: Trinity, 1999.

Lange, Andrea. *Die Gestalt der Friedenskirche*. Wiesenheim/Berg: Agape, 1988.

Loewen, Howard John. *One Lord, One Church, One Hope, and One God: Mennonite Confessions of Faith*. Elkhart, IN: Institute of Mennonite Studies, 1985.

Martin, Dennis D. "Catholic Spirituality and Anabaptist and Mennonite Discipleship." *Mennonite Quarterly Review* 62 (1988) 5–25.

Nissen, Peter. "De Moderne Devotie en het Nederlands-Westfaalse Doperdom: Op zoek naar Relaties en Invloeden." In *De Doorwerking van de Moderne Devotie: Windesheim 1387–1987*, edited by P. Bange et al., 95–118. Hilversum: Verloren, 1988.

Radano, John A., editor. *Information Service* 113, II/III. Vatican City: Pontifical Council for Promoting Christian Unity, 2003.

Schlabach, Gerald W., editor. *On Baptism: Mennonite-Catholic Theological Colloquium, 2001-2002*. Kitchener, ON: Pandora, 2004.

Snyder, C. Arnold. "The Monastic Origins of Swiss Anabaptist Sectarianism." *Mennonite Quarterly Review* 57 (1983) 5–26.

Stayer, James M. "Numbers in Anabaptist Research." In *Commoners and Community: Essays in Honour of Werner O. Packull*, edited by C. Arnold Snyder, 51–73. Waterloo, ON: Herald, 2002.

Trouvé, Marianne Lorraine, editor. *The Sixteen Documents of Vatican II*. Boston: Pauline, 1999.

Vercruysse, Jos E., S.J. "Comment on 'Called Together to be Peacemakers.'" In *Information Service* 113, II/III, edited by John A. Radano, 149–57. Vatican City: Pontifical Council for Promoting Christian Unity, 2003.

Yoder, John Howard. *The Priestly Kingdom: Social Ethics as Gospel*. Notre Dame, IN: Notre Dame University Press, 1984.

———. *The Royal Priesthood: Essays Ecclesiological and Ecumenical*, edited by Michael G. Cartwright. Scottdale, PA: Herald, 1998.

15

Pentecost

Learning the Languages of Peace[1]

Stanley Hauerwas

Being Particular about Particularity

IN HIS JUSTLY CELEBRATED BOOK, *THE DIGNITY OF DIFFERENCE: HOW TO AVOID THE CLASH of Civilizations*, Jonathan Sacks, the Chief Rabbi of the United Hebrew Congregations of the Commonwealth, argues that the "greatest single antidote to violence is *conversation*, speaking our fears, listening to the fears of others, and in that sharing of vulnerabilities discovering a genesis of hope."[2] Some assume, according to Sacks, that if such conversations are to avoid becoming interminable debates between incommensurable positions, the participants must abandon their particularistic perspectives in favor of a more universal point of view.[3] A more universal perspective is required because it is assumed that if we are to speak truthfully to one another we must do so from a position available to anyone.[4]

Drawing on his own tradition, and in particular on the story of Babel, Sacks argues that it is not true that truth is timeless or the same everywhere for anyone. It was at Babel that people, seduced by the technological breakthrough of learning to make bricks, concluded that they had become godlike because they were now free from the limitations of nature and their particular histories. For Sacks, therefore, Babel represents a turning point in history: it is after Babel that God, who had first made a covenant with all creation, chooses to call out one people that they might be a witness to God's will for all people. The

---

1. This essay is based on a lecture given for Amnesty International at Oxford on February 20, 2008.

2. Sacks, *Dignity of Difference*, 2. As much as I admire Sacks's book, I think he mistakenly underwrites the description "clash of civilizations." Talal Asad rightly argues that "there is no such thing as a clash of civilizations because there are no self-contained societies to which fixed civilizational values correspond." *On Suicide Bombing*, 12.

3. Sacks, *Dignity of Difference*, 83. One of the great virtues of Sacks's book is that he not only commends conversation but also exemplifies what he commends. He writes unapologetically as a Jew, yet in a manner that is accessible to those who do not share his faith. I am not as accomplished as Sacks, and I may even be more unapologetic as a Christian than he is as a Jew, but I hope nonetheless to follow his example in this essay. Of course, given the position I take, I assume that some Christians may find themselves in deeper disagreement with me than those who are not Christian.

4. Ibid., 19.

builders of Babel had tried to impose a man-made unity on a divinely created diversity, but after Babel God "turns to one people and commands it to be different *in order to teach humanity the dignity of difference.*"⁵

Sacks acknowledges that his refusal to abandon the distinctive perspective of Judaism means some will brand him a "tribalist."⁶ Yet he argues that the very universalism that many assume to be the antithesis to the resurgence of tribalism—or worse, terrorism—is an inadequate account of the human situation. A global culture may bring about much good, but from Sacks's perspective such cultures, particularly when they take the form of empires, do much harm because they fail to be capable of acknowledging difference. That Sacks should distrust the universal pretensions of empires is not surprising, for as he observes, Judaism was born as a protest against empire.⁷

I am extremely sympathetic to Sacks's attempt to recover the significance of conversation as an alternative to violence. Enda McDonagh and I have even drafted a "Call for the Abolition of War" in order to try to begin such a conversation.⁸ I confess, however, I doubt such conversations can lead to peace without some specification of what they should be about. It is my presumption that if conversing with the other for the sake of "diversity" becomes an end in itself, we are just as likely to want to kill each other as to make peace.⁹ But I will state again that I am sympathetic to Sacks's attempt to recover "the dignity of difference" by resisting the presumptive universalism associated with liberal regimes that allegedly stand for peace, in contrast to the terrorism exemplified by the attacks of September 11, 2001.¹⁰

Of course, it may seem odd for a Christian to underwrite Sacks's claim that God loves difference. It has, after all, been the Christian conceit that the Jews are particularistic while Christians represent a universalistic faith. For example, in 1923 Ernst Troeltsch gave a

---

5. Ibid., 53. Sacks's account of Babel has striking similarities with that of John Howard Yoder. See Yoder's essay, "Disavowal of Constantine: An Alternative Perspective on Interfaith Dialogue."

6. One of the reasons I am sympathetic to Sacks may be because of the accusation that I am also a "sectarian, fideistic, tribalist." For my response to that charge, see the introduction to my book, *Christian Existence Today*, 1–23.

7. Sacks, *Dignity of Difference*, 60. One of the challenges for positions like Sacks's and my own is how the very descriptions used to critique us are part of the problem. For example, words like *religion* or *pluralism* are, from my perspective, problematic. See for example the chapter "The End of Religious Pluralism: A Tribute to David Burrell, C.S.C." in my book *State of the University*.

8. See my "Reflections on the 'Appeal to Abolish War.'"

9. See, for example, my chapter titled, "The Non-Violent Terrorist: In Defense of Christian Fanaticism," in *Sanctify Them in the Truth*.

10. Drawing on the work of Richard Tuck, Asad argues that there is a kind of violence inherent to liberal states not simply because such states require armies for their defense, but "rather that violence founds the law as it founds political community. Violence is therefore embedded in the very concept of liberty that lies at the heart of liberal doctrine. That concept presupposes that the morally independent individual's right to violent self-defense is yielded to the state and that the state becomes the sole protector of individual liberties, abstracting the right to kill from domestic politics, denying to any agents other than states the right to kill at home and abroad. The right to kill is the right to behave in violent ways toward other people—especially toward citizens of foreign states at war and toward the uncivilized, whose very existence is a threat to civilized order. In certain circumstances, killing others is necessary, so it seems, for the security it provides." Asad, *On Suicide Bombing*, 59–60.

lecture at Oxford titled "The Place of Christianity among the World-Religions." He argued that Christianity is the only "world religion" that can claim absolute and unconditional universality because it alone has produced a philosophy of history that recognizes there is a historical development that promotes unconditional worthwhile goals. The name he gives that development is Europe. In Troeltsch's words,

> It is impossible to deny facts or to resist fate. And it is historical facts that have welded the civilizations of Greece, Rome and Northern Europe. All our thoughts and feelings are impregnated with Christian motives and Christian presuppositions; and, conversely, our whole Christianity is indissolubly bound up with elements of the ancient and modern civilizations of Europe. From being a Jewish sect Christianity has become the religion of all Europe. It stands or falls with European civilization; whilst, on its own part, it has entirely lost its Oriental character and has become hellenised and westernized. Our European conceptions of personality and its eternal, divine right, and of progress towards a kingdom of the spirit and of God, our enormous capacity for expansion and for the interconnection of spiritual and temporal, our whole social order, our science, our art—all these rest, whether we know it or not, upon the basis of this deorientalised Christianity. Its primary claim to validity is thus the fact that only through it have we become what we are, and that only in it can we preserve the religious forces that we need. Apart from it we lapse either into a self-destructive titanic attitude, or into effeminate trifling, or into crude brutality . . . We cannot live without a religion, yet the only religion we can endure is Christianity, for Christianity has grown up with us and has become a part of our very being.[11]

As much as I should like to attribute Troeltsch's views to his commitment to the prejudices of the Enlightenment, it cannot be denied that Troeltsch gives expression to the Christian presumption that Christianity, in contrast to Judaism, represents a universal faith.[12] This presumption is based on a story Christians believe is the answer to Babel—Pentecost. Accordingly, Christians have gone into the world with missionary zeal, convinced that they possess the truth that all people desire but may not have yet realized they do.[13] The political form this presumption takes is called Constantinianism.

---

11. Troeltsch, *Christian Thought*, 24–25. For an insightful analysis of Troeltsch's understanding of Christianity amid the world religions, indeed of the very creation of the idea of "world religions," see Masuzawa, *Invention of World Religions*, 309–23. Troeltsch reflects Kant's judgment that Judaism is not really a religion at all "but merely a union of a number of people who, since they belonged to a particular stock, formed themselves into a commonwealth under purely political laws and not into a church." Kant, *Religion within the Limits of Reason Alone*, 116. By church Kant meant the invisible church of reason, not the one "grounded on dogmas" and organized by men (140).

12. Which of course raises the question of the extent to which the Enlightenment is the result of Christian presuppositions. It is my own view that the Enlightenment is a secularized form of Christianity and, in particular, of Constantinian Christianity—which, from my point of view, makes it all the more dangerous.

13. Troeltsch observes that the "heathen races are being morally and spiritually disintegrated by the contact with European civilization; hence they demand a substitute from the higher religion and culture. We have a missionary duty towards these races, and our enterprise is likely to meet with success amongst them, although Christianity, be it remembered, is by no means the only religion taking part in this missionary campaign. Islam and Buddhism are also missionary religions. But in relation to the great world-religions we need to recognize that they are expressions of the religious consciousness corresponding to certain definite types of culture, and that it is their duty to increase in depth and purity by means of their own interior impulses, a

Constantinianism has taken many different forms, but Troeltsch's claim for the inseparability of Christianity and Europe is as good an example as one could want for one of its most recent incarnations.[14]

It is, of course, hard to know which came first; that is, the presumption that the Christian faith represents universal knowledge that only needs to be explained to those who are not yet Christian, or the politics of empire. Either way it is now clear that Christian presumption of universality either as knowledge *qua* knowledge or as a politics is—or at least should be—over.[15] This does not mean I believe the Christian faith is not true, but what it means for it to be true cannot be secured by a theory of truth more determinative than the faith itself.

Interestingly enough, Christians now confronted by philosophical and political alternatives that claim universality as a necessary position to address the challenges of living in a global environment find themselves in the awkward position Jews have long occupied. From a cosmopolitan perspective, Christianity represents a parochial tradition that cannot pass muster as knowledge or as an ethics or politics. Thus the presumption that the language of rights and a faith based on revelation are in fundamental tension.

One strategy for Christians confronted by the challenge of showing their faith to be compatible with more secular and universal alternatives is to criticize the arrogance

---

task in which the contact with Christianity may prove helpful, to them as to us, in such processes of development from within. The great religions might indeed be described as crystallizations of thought of great races, as these races are themselves crystallizations of various biological and anthropological forms. There can be no conversion or transformation of one into the other, but only a measure of agreement and of mutual understanding." "Christianity among the World-Religions," in Troeltsch, *Christian Thought*, 29–30. One could not wish for a more determinative expression of the racist presumptions that formed the thought world of the Enlightenment. My colleague, Jay Carter, has written a book that I believe will force us to recognize the racialized character of recent theology. See Carter, *Race: A Theological Account*.

14. Popes and theological liberals are seldom thought to share common assumptions, but Benedict XVI's famous lecture, "Faith, Reason, and the University," delivered at Regensburg on September 12, 2006, sounded themes quite similar to those of Troeltsch. For example, Benedict described the rapprochement between biblical faith and Greek philosophical inquiry as one of "intrinsic necessity." He elaborated this claim, noting that the rapprochement "was an event of decisive importance not only from the standpoint of the history of religions, but also from that of world history—it is an event which concerns us even today. Given this convergence, it is not surprising that Christianity, despite its origins and some significant developments in the East, finally took on its historically decisive character in Europe. We can also express this the other way around: this convergence, with the subsequent addition of the Roman heritage, created Europe and remains the foundation of what can rightly be called Europe." One cannot help wondering what Benedict might mean by the phrase, "despite its origins," as well as his suggestion that it was only with Europe that Christianity took on its historically decisive character. Given Benedict's Augustinianism, one might think he would find the presumption that Christianity has assumed a final decisive character problematic.

15. In *A Secular Age*, Charles Taylor provides the most compelling account we have that Christendom, that is, the attempt to imbue a civilization and society with the Christian faith, is over. He does not deny that the societies of the West will remain historically informed by Christianity, but he suggests "that it will be less and less common for people to be drawn into or kept within a faith by some strong political or group identity, or by the sense that they are sustaining a socially essential ethic" (p. 314). I think Taylor is right for no other reason than that the Christianity so often represented by those who seek to maintain a Christian social order is little more than a parody of the Gospel. From my perspective I regard this development as a positive good, because I assume that Christians made a decisive mistake when they thought they could use the power of the state or its equivalent to make the church secure.

of that presumption. It should not be surprising that Christians, long experienced in the exercise of such arrogance, are able to spot the same in others. Put more philosophically, I think there are deep questions that bedevil attempts to develop a cosmopolitan perspective that is free of particularistic convictions.[16] Advocates of cosmopolitan perspectives too often fail to be as candid as Troeltsch was in his identification of Christianity with Europe. After all, who wants to acknowledge that the universalism they represent is that of the new Europe; that is, America?[17]

I think it is equally unlikely that a coherent account of natural rights has been given.[18] I have no difficulty with rights claims that express social and legal duties, but claims of human rights *qua* human rights involve philosophical difficulties that cannot be resolved. In particular, questions of what kind of human being we need to be to have rights are very troubling in relation to those with mental disabilities. Moreover, once rights language is legitimated in the abstract, rights seem to multiply faster than rabbits.

My deepest worry about rights, however, is how the language of rights can eviscerate more determinative moral descriptions. For example, during the civil rights campaign in the American South, the killing of a civil rights worker was described as a violation of his rights. If "rights" are considered more basic than the description "murder," you have an indication that language has gone on a holiday.

But rather than going over the well-worn ground surrounding questions of rights, I want to use this occasion to explore the agony I take to be at the heart of the humanism that informs the cosmopolitan defense of rights. For the humanism that motivates many to try to create a better world in the name of global responsibility is too often caught between trying to do too much or too little.[19] For example, Sacks notes that our increasing

---

16. Kwame Anthony Appiah has provided, at least as far as I know, the best account of cosmopolitanism that negotiates this tension. According to Appiah, cosmopolitans hold in tension two ideas: (1) that we have obligations to others that reach beyond those that give us the resources for identity; and (2) that the other is valued not just as human life, but as a particular human life. Appiah does not deny that these ideas are often in tension, which indicates that cosmopolitanism is not the name of a solution, or even a "position," but a challenge. See his *Cosmopolitanism*, xv. Appiah provides a more developed philosophical defense of his understanding of what he calls "rooted cosmopolitanism" in *The Ethics of Identity*, 213–72. There he draws primarily on John Stuart Mill to sustain his defense of autonomy that allegedly does not undermine the "local." I remain unconvinced.

17. Oliver O'Donovan observes that publicity mediates universalism just to the extent that its aspiration is to overcome differences in order to unify communications within a single world communication sphere. According to O'Donovan, modernity, which began its career with three centuries of conquest, produced colonialism, which on being exhausted found its new home in communications. The potential of globally transmitted images became the spearhead of an expansive movement that seemed to bypass obstacles posed by differences of language and national politics. O'Donovan notes it is hardly surprising, therefore, that these anarchistic aspirations, easily underestimated by Western observers, were identified in other parts of the globe with colonial intent. Accordingly, it is not difficult to see the revival of radical Islamism as a protest against the universal ambitions of Western communications. He concludes, "In this universalizing thrust we may observe how Western society has forgotten how to be secular. Secularity is a stance of patience in the face of plurality, made sense of by eschatological hope; forgetfulness of it is part and parcel with the forgetfulness of Christian suppositions about history." *Common Objects of Love*, 68–69. I am indebted to Adam Hollowell for drawing my attention to O'Donovan's argument.

18. For an attempt to provide a theological defense of "natural rights," see Esther Reed, *The Ethics of Human Rights*.

19. Charles Taylor characterizes this form of humanism as "exclusive" in order to indicate that such a

awareness of our global interrelation tends to undermine our sense of moral responsibility. No longer able to identify who does what to whom, we are tempted to assume we bear no responsibility except for our immediate actions.[20] With his customary insight, Zygmunt Bauman observes that as we become ever more knowledgeable about our plights and those of others, we are overwhelmed and become less able to respond with ethically inspired action. Paradoxically, according to Bauman, "our shared capacity to do harm seems infinitely greater than our shared capacity to do good."[21]

Joseph Amato, in his unfortunately little-known *Victims and Values: A History and a Theory of Suffering*, suggests that this transformation in our consciousness—that is, that we know ourselves in relation to the suffering of the distant other—is inseparable from the "replacement of the traditional individual, who was attached by life and imagination to a single locality, by the modern individual, who by thought, opinion, and empathy is joined to a changing world."[22] The problem with such a consciousness, according to Amato, is that not only are there more victims at our door than our front steps can hold, but that the attempt to sympathize with those who suffer occurs at the same time as "people in ever greater numbers discard the notion that suffering is an inevitable part of human experience."[23] As a result, those who refuse to be liberated from the particularity of their religious convictions, who suffer from traditions in which suffering is not assumed to be antithetical to being human, or who refuse to cease suffering, can only be ignored or eliminated.[24]

---

humanism, which may have come from a religious tradition, is now offered as the only alternative to religion. In short, Taylor suggests that what it means to call our age "secular" is that now we live in a time in which "the eclipse of all goals beyond human flourishing" is conceivable. *Secular Age*, 18–19. Taylor's story of the development of this kind of humanism is complex, to say the least, but crucial, I believe, is his insight that as a correlative of the development of deism came a sense of invulnerability necessary to sustain a sense of self-possession (300–301). He then, in a manner like Foucault, suggests that the measures to ensure safety can make us insensitive to whatever lies beyond this human world. In particular, suffering becomes a threat to such a world, reminding us as it does that we are not invulnerable. Ironically, the altruism that such a humanism produces can result in some humans being more "civilized" than others.

20. Sacks, *Dignity of Difference*, 14.

21. Bauman, "The Liquid Modern Adventures of the 'Sovereign Expressions of Life,'" 133.

22. Amato, *Victims and Values*, xxi. Amato thinks the development of sympathy for the distant other originates in Christianity and humanism, but more recently in Enlightenment and Romantic sensitivities.

23. Ibid., xxii. Talal Asad notes that the modern sufferer's sense of pain no longer has any moral significance, which may make it easier to bear. In contrast, modern poverty is experienced as more unjust, making it less tolerable. By calling attention to these developments Asad denies he is suggesting that the distribution of pain engendered by modern power is worse than that of premodern societies. Rather, he is only trying to suggest that they are different. Nor is he claiming that it is an undeniable social fact that there has been an amelioration of illness and improvements in public health. He calls attention to these differences to stress "that more is at stake in secularism than compassion for other human beings in plural democratic societies. And nothing is less plausible than the claim that secularism is an essential means of avoiding destructive conflict and establishing peace in the modern world. Secular societies—France among them—have always been capable of seeking solidarity at home while engaging in national wars and imperial conquests." "Trying to Understand French Secularism," in *Political Theologies*, 24.

24. I think this stance toward suffering that is so defining of modern humanism helps explain the violence often characteristic of as well as justified by appeals to our common humanity. Thus Asad argues "that the cult of sacrifice, blood, and death that secular liberals find so repellent in pre-liberal Christianity is a part of the

I hope to show that the Christian experience of Pentecost and what it means to learn to speak as well as understand another's language is a continuing resource God has given the church to sustain our ability to suffer as well as to respond to those who suffer for the long haul. Our ability to communicate means we do not have to be isolated from one another by what we endure. There is, therefore, a crucial relationship between being human, suffering, and the gift of speech. In order to pursue this claim, I want to direct our attention to an understanding of communication as the paradigm of ethics, as developed by Herbert McCabe, O.P. I do so because McCabe's stress on the bodily character of communication challenges the presumption that communication can take place without people actually being present to one another.

Moreover, by focusing on McCabe's account of language, I hope to show how, at least for Christians, the assumption that we must choose between membership in a particularistic community or some version of a more inclusive humanism is a false alternative. For the very presumption that we must so choose is an assumption that such a choice makes sense in the abstract. But we are never people in the abstract; we are people who are embedded in the narratives of particular linguistic communities. Our humanity depends on our ability to speak to one another, but that very ability is also the source of our differences. We are united by what divides us. Any attempt to overcome the reality of our linguistic constitution, and in particular any attempt to suggest that we suffer from that which constitutes our very being, threatens to hide from us a cruelty we perpetrate on one another in the name of a common humanity.

The "Humanism" of Herbert McCabe, O.P.

In 1957, in response to the question, "Does Oxford Moral Philosophy Corrupt Youth?" Elizabeth Anscombe answered that of course Oxford moral philosophy does not corrupt the youth. From Anscombe's perspective the problem is much deeper. Oxford moral philosophers do not corrupt the youth because their philosophy reflects as well as reproduces the corrupt moral presumptions of the spirit of the time. Such philosophy might be called, in Anscombe's words, "the philosophy of the flattery of that spirit."[25]

I have no stake in taking sides as to whether Anscombe's evaluation of Oxford moral philosophy was fair or unfair. I only call attention to her assessment to suggest that at the same time she was so judging Oxford philosophers there was someone in Oxford developing an account of ethics that was anything but a "flattery of the spirit of the time." His name was Herbert McCabe, O.P. McCabe was perhaps more theologian than philosopher, but as will become apparent he was well acquainted with the philosophical alternatives of the day.

---

genealogy of modern liberalism itself, in which violence and tenderness go together . . . There is the imperative to use any means necessary (including homicide and suicide) to defend the nation-state that constitutes one's worldly identity and defends one's health and security and, on the other hand, the obligation to revere all human life, to offer life in place of death to universal humanity; the first presupposes a capacity for ruthlessness, the second for kindness." *On Suicide Bombing*, 88. For the significance of the phrase, "the refusal to cease suffering," see Bell, *Liberation Theology after the End of History*.

25. Anscombe, "Does Oxford Moral Philosophy Corrupt Youth?" 167.

In 1968 McCabe published *Law, Love and Language*, a book I believe should have changed the way we think about ethics.[26] Unfortunately, that was not to be, but it is never too late to make use of a good thing. Indeed, we may now be in a better place to appreciate McCabe's position because he argues, as Sacks's emphasis on conversation implies, that our ability to communicate, to be in conversation, makes us human. To be human, to share a common nature, according to McCabe, is to share a biological and linguistic nature. Humans are animals that talk (37).

McCabe avoids, therefore, any account of the human that might tempt us to forget our bodily nature. To be sure, to be a human being requires that at least in principle we are able to communicate with other human beings by using conventional signs. But if we came across any form of life that seemed to share our nature in only one of these ways—bodily or communicative—we would not be sure whether it could be called human. A creature from Mars, for example, might be able to communicate with us, but if we could not breed with it we should not call our guest human (38).

Our language, therefore, is the culmination of organic life (68).[27] "It is because I have this sort of body, a human body with a human life, that my communication can be linguistic. The human body is a source of communication" (90). McCabe puts it this way: "Instead of saying that I have a private mind and a public body, a mind for having concepts in and body for saying and hearing words, I say that I have a body that is able to be with other bodies not merely by physical contact but by linguistic communication. Having a soul is just being able to communicate; having a mind is being able to communicate linguistically" (86).[28]

Our shared bodily nature is not sufficient to sustain a common humanity, because as linguistic animals we can to some extent create responses to our world that constitute

---

26. McCabe, *Law, Love and Language*. Page references will appear in the text. I wrote a foreword for the new edition of *Law, Love and Language*, which the publisher forgot to include but which has been published in *New Blackfriars*; see Hauerwas, "Unpublished Foreword."

27. McCabe was a great Aquinas scholar, and his emphasis on the body reflects not only what he learned from Wittgenstein but also Aquinas's emphasis on our bodily nature. For example, Aquinas asks if the body of man was given an apt disposition, that is, was it appropriate that humans have an upright stature? He answers it was appropriate for us to have an upright stature for four reasons: (1) our senses were given not only for procuring the necessities of life, but for knowledge, which means in contrast to animals humans alone take pleasure in the beauty of sensible objects; (2) for greater freedom of the acts of the interior powers; (3) if humans were prone to the ground they would need to use their hands as forefeet and thus lose their utility for other purposes; and (4) "because if man's stature were prone to the ground, and he used his hands as fore-feet, he would be obliged to take hold of his food with his mouth. Thus he would have a protruding mouth, with thick and hard lips, and also a hard tongue, so as to keep it from being hurt by exterior things; as we see in other animals. Moreover, such an attitude would quite hinder speech, which is reason's proper operation." Aquinas, *Summa Theologica*, I.91.3.3.

28. McCabe's emphasis on the body obviously reflects the profound influence of Wittgenstein. I fear that too often Wittgenstein is interpreted as assuming all language is purely conventional, if not arbitrary. John Bowlin, however, rightly argues that Wittgenstein thought that some of the moral and ontological commitments that constitute the foundation of our linguistic practices are set in place by custom or convention shared by those who inhabit a linguistic community that is not shared by all, but that not all of our commitments are so constituted. Some are constituted by "nature," what Wittgenstein calls in *On Certainty* (no. 505) "nature's grace," by which we know anything at all. See Bowlin, "Nature's Grace."

quite distinct worlds.[29] Our language not only distinguishes us from other animals, but it also distinguishes our animality from that of other animals as well as us from each other (68). Therefore, "there is no such thing on earth as a purely linguistic community" (46). Communication requires sharing a common life that is intensified through language. We only become language users through the training provided by a particular language community in which we learn the ever-changing, thus provisional, character of the language that speaks us.

The challenge facing linguistic animals, therefore, is to learn to live in a world in which the linguistic community is never coextensive with the genetic community. We are not able to communicate with one another by virtue of our shared humanity, but rather our ability to communicate depends on being a member of a particular community.[30] Accordingly, the more intense work our language does, the more we become isolated from one another. As a result, the story of human life is not and cannot be a single story. Indeed, attempts to create a stable human community, to ensure that we can communicate, have ended in failure (111).

You may begin to wonder what all this has to do with ethics. Ethics, for McCabe, is the study of human behavior as communication, because what we are able to accomplish or what we fail to accomplish is determined by what we can and cannot say (94). Just as literary criticism enables us to enjoy a poem or a novel more deeply, so the purpose of ethics is to enable us to enjoy life more fully "by entering into the significance of human action" (95). So ethics, like literary criticism, is never finished seeking, as it must, the deeper meaning of an action within the terms of a specific system of communication (98). Determining what we want—that is, discovering what it means to be free—is the great challenge that confronts us because we so seldom know what it is we desire (61).

To be sure, the dual character of human existence—that is, that we are at once a natural and a linguistic community—means that there is sufficient basis for what can be described as natural law. We do have a law in the depth of ourselves, and to act contrary to this law is to violate our nature (45). Yet that law is known primarily through what McCabe calls the "county council" understanding of natural law. For it is through the deliberation of county councils that decisions are made that create laws of expectation through which it is made possible for life to flourish. But natural law so understood cannot be identified with the "highest common factor of the moral codes of different societies" (59).[31]

---

29. Appiah seems quite close to McCabe in this respect, arguing as McCabe does that we share a biology, "but that does not give us, in the relevant sense, a shared ethical nature." Appiah, *Ethics of Identity*, 252. Indeed, in *Cosmopolitanism*, 98, he remarks, "Humanity isn't, in the relevant sense, an identity at all."

30. Sacks says something quite similar by observing, "There is no universal language. There is no way we can speak, communicate or even think without placing ourselves within the constraints of a particular language whose contours were shaped by hundreds of generations of speakers, storytellers, artists and visionaries who came before us, whose legacy we inherit and of whose story we become a part. Within each language we can say something new. No language is fixed, unalterable, complete. What we cannot do is place ourselves outside the particularities of language to arrive at a truth, a way of understanding and responding to the world that applies to everyone at all times. That is not the essence of humanity but an attempt to escape from humanity." *Dignity of Difference*, 54–55.

31. McCabe observes that Aquinas's account of natural law presumes such an understanding of the "county council" because he thought God, as "the inventor of mankind, the one who made the decisions about what

This means McCabe's account of ethics as communication cannot ensure anything like a common morality. Just as we have no basis for guaranteeing our ability in principle to communicate, neither do we have the ability to view the history of humankind as a dramatic unity. Of course some have tried to write such a history by utilizing the idea of progress or some analogue of that story, but such views inevitably come to grief when confronted by concentration camps and nuclear weapons.

Instead, McCabe argues that the biblical view is that though we cannot now write a history of humanity, we must live in the hope that in the end such a history can be written (112–13). However fragmented the human race may be, a people have been called into the world to sustain the hope for a common destiny (113).[32] The Bible, at least after the first eleven chapters of Genesis, does not try to be a history of humankind, but rather tells the story of a people whose history is a sacrament of the history of the human race.[33] The law, particularly the Decalogue, was given to these chosen people so they might learn to avoid the idolatrous temptation to assume, because they have been chosen, that they are the end of history.

Christians believe they have been grafted into the history of Israel by Jesus, who we believe is the very word of Yahweh. Thus in the Gospel of John the coming of Jesus is compared with the coming of a new language. McCabe writes, "Jesus is the word, the language of God which comes to be a language for man" (129). Accordingly, McCabe makes the extraordinary claim that Jesus, not Adam, is "the first human being, the first member of the human race in whom humanity came to fulfillment, the first human being for whom to live was simply to love—for this is what human beings are for."[34] The witness of Jesus's

---

sort of institutions mankind should be, had as a matter of fact issued the basic laws of mankind." Aquinas thought the Decalogue was God telling us the natural law, but McCabe suggests the matter is better put that God does not reveal to us the Ten Commandments, but the Ten Commandments reveal God to us. They do so because the Decalogue, particularly the prohibition against work on the Sabbath, is given to stop us from presuming that we are our own creation. *Law, Love and Language*, 57.

32. Sacks makes a similar point, suggesting that "the central insight of monotheism—that if God is the parent of humanity, then we are all members of a single extended family—has become more real in its implications than ever before. The Enlightenment gave us the concept of universal rights, but this remains a 'thin' morality, stronger in abstract ideas than in its grip on the moral imagination. Far more powerful is the biblical idea that those in need are more brothers and sisters and that poverty is something we feel in our bones." *Dignity of Difference*, 112.

33. Oliver O'Donovan suggests that Israel's being so called means we "must allow that divine providence is ready to protect other national traditions besides the sacred one." Which implies, according to O'Donovan, "something about the limits of collective identities. To be a human being at all is to participate in one or more collective identities. But there is no collective identity so overarching and all-encompassing that no human beings are left outside it. In that sense it is true that to speak of 'humanity' is to speak of an abstraction. Only in that sense, for in fact 'humanity' has a perfectly conceivable referent, and we should not hesitate to say that 'humanity' is real. But it is not a reality that we can command politically. We do not meet it in any community, however great, of which we could assume leadership. We meet it only in the face of Christ, who presents himself as our leader and commander. The titanic temptation which besets collectives needs the check of a perpetual plurality at the universal level. There are always 'others,' those not of our fold whom we must respect and encounter." O'Donovan, *Desire of the Nations*, 73. I am obviously sympathetic with O'Donovan's suggestion, but I worry that his use of the language of "national traditions" may reproduce romantic understandings of politics.

34. McCabe, *God Matters*, 93.

love does not provide a utopian plan for a new society. Rather, Jesus offers himself as the source that makes possible the creation of a community of communication in which the miracle of our common humanity occurs.

The crucifixion of Jesus displays our determination to be less than human. Yet Jesus is risen. That his love conquered death, that he was able to achieve his mission through failure, means that whatever people may mean by ethics has been transformed into the problem of sin and holiness.

Pentecost marks the birth of a people through the restoration of communication between people of different languages and stories (111). At Pentecost we experience God's future, which, according to McCabe, means "the business of the church is to 'remember' the future. Not merely to remember that there is to be a future, but mysteriously to make the future present" (141). Such a remembering is possible because Christ can be present through the work of the Spirit, offering the world an alternative mode of communication. It is in this sense that the church is the

> "sacrament of the unity of mankind," a continuing creative interpretation of human life; revealing and realizing in her proclamation of the gospel the presence of the risen Christ to the world; revealing therefore and realizing the revolutionary future of the world. The sacramental life as a whole, centering on the eucharist, is an articulation both of human life now in its real but only dimly discernible revolutionary depth and of the world to come. It is only by the utter openness implied in faith that the revelation of this depth and this future can be received. (145)[35]

Such a people cannot help but be revolutionary, calling into question as they must all revolutionary movements.[36] As a result the Christian moral position will always seem unreasonable, based as it is on the virtue of hope. Christian hope reaches out beyond this world toward a future world of freedom in which real communication is possible. Such freedom should not be confused with the autonomy promised by capitalist societies, that is, the freedom associated with the bourgeois secular city in which we suffer nothing other than having to endure our own desires. Rather, the Christian seeks to transform the media of domination into the media of communication in which people are free to love one another without fear (158).

The Church as God's New Language[37]

The strong Christological claims at the center of McCabe's work may seem to be exactly the kinds of claims many assume should be avoided if Christians are to be responsible

---

35. By "sacrament," McCabe understands those actions that mark "the intersection of the world to come with this present world; or, as we say, the presence of the risen Christ." *Law, Love and Language*, 150.

36. In a recent interview, Rowan Williams made the point this way: Jesus was "so revolutionary that he puts all revolutions into question. The change is so different that it is not so much a change from one system to another, but a change from one world to another. A new creation where our relations to each other are no longer mutually suspicious or exclusive or competitive, but entirely shaped by giving and receiving—building one another up by a community of transformed persons, not just by a new legal system. That's revolutionary." Joseph, "Table Talk with the Archbishop of Canterbury," 36.

37. For those interested, this is the title of a chapter in my book, *Christian Existence Today*, 47–66. (The book was originally published in 1988). I call attention to this chapter, which was originally written to honor

actors in a world of difference.[38] Yet McCabe's account of what makes us human is the exemplification of the Christian conviction, in the words of Karl Barth, of the humanity of God.[39] It is in Christ that we see our common humanity—a humanity that cannot avoid suffering if we are to be of service to one another.[40]

As Christians we will do little good for ourselves or our neighbors by trying to convince those who do not share our story that we also can be liberal cosmopolitans. Rather, we must be what we are—the church of Jesus Christ. For if that church is not the anticipation of the peace God wills for all people, then we are without hope.[41] To sustain that peace, to care for the stranger when all strangers cannot be cared for, to know how to go on in the face of our suffering, the suffering of those we love and the suffering of those we do not know, is possible because we believe that God abandons no one. Our belief in God's persistence takes the form of a story that receives us as strangers and destines us to be friends.

The Christian word for universality is "catholic." That way of putting the matter can be misleading because it gives the impression that "catholic" is but another way to say "universal." But "catholic" is not the name of a logical category or a philosophical position. It is the name of a people sent into the world to discover places and people whose difference is a necessary condition for self-recognition.[42] Indeed, the very presumption

---

Hans Frei, because when I reread it for this essay I was surprised I had made no reference to McCabe. Yet I am sure I could not have written the essay without having learned from McCabe what it means for the church to be a "language."

38. At the beginning of his book *Stillborn God*, Mark Lilla gives voice to what I take to be the sentiment of many: "We are disturbed and confused. We find it incomprehensible that theological ideas still inflame the minds of men, stirring up messianic passions that leave societies in ruin. We assumed that this was no longer possible, that human beings had learned to separate religious questions from political ones, that fanaticism was dead. We were wrong" (3). I am more than happy to be identified with the "fanatics," because by being so identified I may at least be able to avoid the arrogance of Lilla's "we."

39. Barth, *Humanity of God*. Though many might doubt that McCabe and Barth could be made theologically compatible, I find in their work a common spirit. Theology in their hands is done with joy, which means all things human can be celebrated.

40. In a quite moving passage, Charles Taylor observes that the self-giving of Christ can be seen as how God repairs the breach between God and humans. Such a view begins with the fact of human resistance to God, which we call sin, but it is God's initiative to enter, in full vulnerability, the heart of the resistance by offering humans participation in the divine life. "But the nature of the resistance is that this offer arouses even more violent opposition, not a divine violence, more a counter-divine one. Now Christ's reaction to the resistance was to offer no counter-resistance, but to continue loving and offering. This love can go to the very heart of things, and open a road for the resisters. This is the second mystery. Through this loving submission, violence is turned around, and instead of breeding counter-violence in an endless spiral, can be transformed. A path is opened of non-power, limitless self-giving, full action, and infinite openness. On the basis of this initiative, the incomprehensible healing power of this suffering, it becomes possible for human suffering, even of the most meaningless type, to become associated with Christ's act, and to become a locus of renewed contact with God, an act which heals the world." *Secular Age*, 654.

41. Miroslav Volf puts the matter just right in an article in the *Christian Century*. Volf writes, "If we strip Christian convictions of their original and historic cognitive and moral content, and reduce faith to a cultural resource endowed with a diffuse aura of the sacred, we are likely to get religiously legitimized and inspired violence in situations of conflict. If, on the other hand, we nurture people in historic Christian convictions that are touted in sacred texts, we will likely get militants for peace." "Guns and Crosses," 39.

42. Oliver O'Donovan puts it this way: "No community should ever be allowed to think of itself as universal. It is essential to our humanity that there should always be foreigners, human beings from another

that there is something called "the world" that can be identified depends on a people who have been separated from the world to be of service to the world. What the people called "catholic" have to offer is the patience and humility learned through the story called "Gospel," which teaches us how to live at peace when we are not able to write the history of humankind.

If the church is rightly understood to be God's new language, it is crucial that it not displace our particular languages. At Pentecost we are told that the followers of Jesus came together in one place and a violent wind filled the house in which they were sitting. Divided tongues, as of fire, rested on each of them, and "all of them were filled with the Holy Spirit and began to speak in other languages, as the Spirit gave them the ability." We are then told that devout Jews from every nation—Parthians, Medes, Elamites, residents of Mesopotamia, Judea, Cappadocia, Pontus, Asia, Egypt, visitors from Rome, Cretans, and Arabs—who were living in Jerusalem, heard the followers speaking in their native language. "Amazed and astonished, they asked, 'Are not all these who are speaking Galileans? And how is it that we hear, each of us, in our own native language?'" (Acts 2:7–8). What they heard from these diverse speakers, moreover, was about God's deeds of power.

What I take to be remarkable about this account of Pentecost in the second chapter of Acts is that the Spirit does not replace the different language each person speaks.[43] They begin to speak in other languages, but by the gift of the Spirit they are able to understand one another. This means that the language the church must be is not that which forces uniformity, but rather that which is shaped by the practices, as McCabe suggests, of love and vulnerability that are necessary for the required patience that enables us to tell our different stories.[44] Pentecost has restored Babel not by mitigating the diversity granted by Babel but by creating a people who have learned how to be patient, how to be at peace, how to listen in a world of impatient violence.

---

community who have an alternative way of organizing the task and privilege of being human, so that our imaginations are refreshed and our sense of cultural possibilities renewed. The imperialist argument, that until foreigners are brought into relations of affinity within one's cultural home they are enemies, is simply a creation of xenophobia. The act of recognition and welcome, which leaps across the divide between communities and finds on the other side another community which offers the distinctive friendship of hospitality, is a fundamental form of human relating. Xenophilia is commanded us: the neighbor whom we are to love is the foreigner whom we encounter on the road." *Desire of the Nations*, 268.

43. Surely one of the most startling effects of Pentecost is the presumption that Christian Scriptures could be translated. The very language that Jesus spoke is not the language in which the New Testament was written. Accordingly, Christians have assumed that the Scriptures can be translated into other languages.

44. I am deeply sympathetic with Appiah's suggestion that what makes cosmopolitanism possible is not necessarily a shared "culture," not even universal principles or values or a shared human understanding. Rather, it is "stories—epic poems as well as modern forms like novels and films, for example—it is the capacity to follow a narrative and conjure a world: and, it turns out, there are people everywhere more than willing to do this. This is the moral epistemology that makes cosmopolitanism possible . . . If there is a critique of the Enlightenment to be made, it is not that the *philosophes* believe in human nature, or the universality of reason: it is rather that they were so dismally unimaginative about the range of what we have in common." *Ethics of Identity*, 258. One might then ask, how is the position I have taken in this paper different than Appiah's cosmopolitanism? I have no reason to emphasize the differences, but there is a difference—Pentecost. Put differently, it is not clear who is the agent of Appiah's cosmopolitanism. I hope it is clear that I believe an agent exists that makes it imperative, at least for Christians, to listen to the stranger. We call that agent the Holy Spirit.

But the gift of Pentecost entails slow, hard work. We must not only learn to suffer one another as Christians; we must learn how to suffer others whose stories might make us vulnerable. Indeed, the gift of Pentecost is but the beginning of hard and painful lessons in failure. Yet even failure turns out to be a gift, if through failure the church is reminded that others are included in God's promise. At its best, the church learns to receive the stories of different linguistic communities and in the process discovers that its own speech requires constant revision.

Toward the end of his book, Sacks observes that retaliation is the instinctual response to perceived wrong. There seems, moreover, to be no end to the wrongs we have perpetrated on one another. The only alternative, according to Sacks, is a willingness to be forgiven and to forgive if there is to be an end to our endless violence. In a painful yet beautiful passage, Sacks writes:

> Forgiveness is the ability to let go, and without it we kill what we love. Every act of forgiveness mends something broken in this fractured world. It is a step, however small, in the long, hard journey of redemption. I am a Jew. As a Jew I carry with me the tears and sufferings of my grandparents and theirs through the generations. The story of my people is a narrative of centuries of exiles and expulsions, persecutions and pogroms, beginning with the First Crusade and culminating in the murder of two-thirds of Europe's Jews, among them more than a million children. For centuries, Jews knew that they or their children risked being murdered simply because they were Jews. Those tears are written into the very fabric of Jewish memory, which is to say, Jewish identity. How can I let go of that pain when it is written into my very soul? And yet I must. For the sake of my children and theirs, not yet born.[45]

But learning the languages of peace cannot, in the name of universality, require that Sacks forfeit the particularity of his tradition's memory. If forgiveness is the way to peace, then we cannot be asked to forget what has been forgiven; for it is impossible to remain forgiven if the memory of suffering no longer exists. Redemption requires memory.

Where does this leave us, then? How can we begin the conversations Sacks talks about if there is no universal language with which to speak? I would like to make a modest proposal: let us begin by learning to speak the language of peace within our own traditions. Perhaps the violence we perpetrate on those whose language is different than ours is the result of our losing our own language of peace. The greatest gift I believe Christians can give the world is to refuse to kill other human beings *because* we are Christians. Until Christians understand that loving Christ means refusing to kill those whom he died for, until we recover our own language of peace, there is little hope that we will be able to engage others in conversation without perpetuating a shallow discourse that leaves us all speechless.[46]

---

45. Sacks, *Dignity of Difference*, 190.

46. I am thankful to Sam Wells, Greg Jones, Adam Hollowell, and Carole Baker for reading and revising portions of this paper.

Bibliography

Amato, Joseph. *Victims and Values: A History and a Theory of Suffering*. New York: Praeger, 1990.

Anscombe, Elizabeth. "Does Oxford Moral Philosophy Corrupt Youth?" In *Human Life, Action, and Ethics: Essays by G .E. M. Anscombe*, edited by Mary Geach and Luke Gormelly, 161–68. Exeter: Imprint Academic, 2005.

Appiah, Kwame Anthony. *Cosmopolitanism: Ethics in a World of Strangers*. New York: Norton, 2006.

———. *The Ethics of Identity*. Princeton: Princeton University Press, 2005.

Aquinas, Thomas. *Summa Theologica*. Translated by the Fathers of the English Dominican Province. Westminster, MD: Christian Classics, 1947.

Asad, Talal. *On Suicide Bombing*. New York: Columbia University Press, 2007.

———. "Trying to Understand French Secularism." In *Political Theologies*, edited by Henri de Vries, 494–526. New York: Fordham University Press, 2006.

Barth, Karl. *The Humanity of God*. Richmond, VA: John Knox, 1963.

Bauman, Zygmunt. "The Liquid Modern Adventures of the 'Sovereign Expressions of Life.'" In *Concern for the Other: Perspectives on the Ethics of K. E. Logstrup*, 113–38. Notre Dame, IN: University of Notre Dame, 2007.

Bell, Daniel. *Liberation Theology after the End of History: The Refusal to Cease Suffering*. London: Routledge, 2001.

Benedict XVI, Pope. "Faith, Reason, and the University." Lecture delivered on September 12, 2006, Regensberg.

Bowlin, John. "Nature's Grace: Aquinas and Wittgenstein on Natural Law and Moral Knowledge." In *Grammar and Grace: Reformulations of Aquinas and Wittgenstein*, edited by Jeffrey Stout and Robert MacSwain, 154–74. London: SCM Press, 2004.

Carter, Jay. *Race: A Theological Account*. Oxford: Oxford University Press, 2008.

Hauerwas, Stanley. *Christian Existence Today: Essays on Church, World, and Living In Between*. Grand Rapid: Brazos, 2001.

———. "The End of Religious Pluralism: A Tribute to David Burrell, C.S.C." In *The State of the University: Academic Knowledges and the Knowledge of God*, 58–75. Oxford: Blackwell, 2007.

———. "The Non-Violent Terrorist: In Defense of Christian Fanaticism." In *Sanctify Them in the Truth: Holiness Exemplified*, 177–90. Edinburgh: T & T Clark, 1998.

———. "Reflections on the 'Appeal to Abolish War.'" In *Between Poetry and Politics: Essays in Honor of Enda McDonagh*, edited by Linda Hogan and Barbara Fitzgerald, 135–47. Dublin: Columba Press, 2003.

———. "An Unpublished Foreword." *New Blackfriars* 86 (2005) 291–95.

Joseph, Sarah. "Table Talk with the Archbishop of Canterbury." *Emel Magazine* 39 (2007) 32–36.

Kant, Immanuel. *Religion within the Limits of Reason Alone*. Translated by Theodore Greene and Hoyt Hudson. New York: Harper & Row, 1960.

Lilla, Mark. *The Stillborn God: Religion, Politics, and the Modern West*. New York: Knopf, 2007.

Masuzawa, Tomoko. *The Invention of World Religions*. Chicago: University of Chicago Press, 2005.

McCabe, Herbert, O.P. *God Matters*. Springfield, IL: Templegate, 1987.

———. *Law, Love and Language*. London: Continuum, 2003.

O'Donovan, Oliver. *Common Objects of Love: Moral Reflection and the Shaping of Community*. Grand Rapids: Eerdmans, 2002.

———. *The Desire of the Nations: Rediscovering the Roots of Political Theology*. Cambridge: Cambridge University Press, 1996.

Reed, Esther. *The Ethics of Human Rights: Contested Doctrinal and Moral Issues*. Waco, TX: Baylor University Press, 2007.

Sacks, Jonathan. *The Dignity of Difference: How to Avoid the Clash of Civilizations*. London: Continuum, 2002.

Taylor, Charles. *A Secular Age*. Cambridge, MA: Harvard University Press, 2007.

Troeltsch, Ernst. *Christian Thought*. Edited and translated by Baron von Hugel. London: University of London Press, 1923.

Volf, Miroslav. "Guns and Crosses." *Christian Century*, May 17, 2003, 39.

Wittgenstein, Ludwig. *On Certainty*. Edited by G. E. M. Anscombe and G. H. Wright. Translated by Denis Paul and G. E. M. Anscombe. New York: Harper, 1972.

Yoder, John Howard. "The Disavowal of Constantine: An Alternative Perspective on Interfaith Dialogue." In *The Royal Priesthood: Essays Ecclesiological and Ecumenical*, edited by Michael G. Cartwright, 242–61. Grand Rapids: Eerdmans, 1994.

www.ingramcontent.com/pod-product-compliance
Lightning Source LLC
Chambersburg PA
CBHW080432230426
43662CB00015B/2253